Theory and Concepts in Qualitative Research

Perspectives from the Field

Theory and Concepts in Qualitative Research

Perspectives from the Field

Edited by
David J. Flinders and Geoffrey E. Mills

Foreword by Elliot W. Eisner

Teachers College, Columbia University
New York and London

Published by Teachers College Press, 1234 Amsterdam Avenue
New York, NY 10027

Library of Congress Cataloging-in-Publication Data

Theory and concepts in qualitative research : perspectives from the
    field / edited by David J. Flinders and Geoffrey E. Mills ; foreword
    by Elliot W. Eisner.
        p.   cm.
    Includes bibliographical references and index.
    ISBN 0-8077-3290-7 (cloth). — ISBN 0-8077-3289-3 (pbk)
    1. Social sciences — Methodology.   2. Social sciences — Field work.
    I. Flinders, David J.   II. Mills, Geoffrey E.
    H61.T4648   1993
    300′.72 — dc20   93-21507

ISBN 0-8077-3290-7
ISBN 0-8077-3289-3 (pbk.)

Printed on acid-free paper
Manufactured in the United States of America
98 97 96 95 94 93   7 6 5 4 3 2 1

Contents

Foreword

Interest in the meaning and function of theory in the conduct of qualitative research represents, in many ways, an advance in the methodological conversation. Theory has not been the long suit of ethnography, the field most closely associated with qualitative research in education, or qualitative methods that emphasize narrative and other artistically grounded approaches to research. Ethnographers have, in the main, been concerned with descriptive matters, and although it is true that knowing what counts in a social situation, indeed knowing how to frame the situation itself, requires "theory," the ethnographic enterprise has been focused mainly on matters of particularity; grand theory is hard to find.

As for those working within narrative and other artistically based approaches, theory too has been less than central. Those addressing the qualitative details of local circumstances have tried to make those circumstances vivid to the reader and have paid less attention to forms of explanation that are deduced from scientific theory. The fact that this volume explores the role of theory in qualitative research methodology reflects a growing sophistication among qualitative researchers: new terrain and new problems are being explored.

Theory in its most typical scientific sense represents an effort to account for what has been given an account of. Theory attempts to satisfy the human need for scientific rationality by providing explanations that will meet that need. The adequacy of such explanations is tested not only by their appeal, their cogency, and their aesthetic quality, but by the extent to which they can be used to help us anticipate, if not control, the future. In this sense, theory is a very desirable commodity. Those who can foretell the future or who can bring it under control have power. If qualitative research yields only vivid descriptions of past events, one can only wonder why it would be pursued, apart from the aesthetic satisfaction that its encounter might provide. Put another way, if there is no instrumental utility to qualitative studies, why invest time and energy in doing them?

Theory is supposed to be the conceptual vehicle that assigns pattern to individuality. Theory is intended to make coherent what otherwise appears as disparate and disconnected individual events. Theory is the means through which we learn lessons that can apply to situations we have yet to encounter. In this sense, theory is a fundamental and indispensable guide. Yet, the benefits of theory are not without their costs.

Theory, we have also learned in the past two decades, not only reveals, it conceals. The theoretical constructs with which we work define in large measure the features of the universe we are likely to see. The visions that we secure from the theoretical portholes through which we peer also obscure those aspects of the territory they foreclose. And foreclose they do. Thus the dilemma. Without categories and patterns we have little utility. With categories and patterns we secure utility but risk obscuring what is individual, unique, specific. How do we reach such apparently irreconcilable aspirations? How can we savor the uniqueness of the situation and at the same time recognize it as an instance of a larger class?

I want to suggest that this apparent dilemma is not at all unique to theory in qualitative research or, for that matter, in conventional research of a more quantitative kind. Socialization itself requires the child to recognize not only that the face before him is his mother, but that his mother is also a woman. The oscillation between the particular and the general is a part of what it means to become a social human being functioning within a set of cultural constraints. The problem is not, as I see it, that there are irreconcilable tensions between the theoretically general and the particular or, as Dilthy put it, between the ideographic and the nomothetic; the problem is learning how to have it both ways. Fresh perception borne of contact with qualitative circumstances can yield theoretical categories and insights that can be used by others to push perception even further.

I do not believe that theory once and for all defines what we can see. If it did, progress in observation and interpretation would be enormously diminished. Rationality borne solely of speculation has its limits. Contact with the world is one way to expand rationality. At the same time, the theoretical ideas that good qualitative research fosters can enable us not only to anticipate the future, but to know what to look for when we arrive. Concepts such as formative and summative evaluation, turn-taking, with-it-ness, and other such notions are reminders of what to look for in the school situations we encounter. In all likelihood, they were generated through observation and have contributed significantly to the enhancement of both our theoretical life and our perception.

There is another relationship between theory and qualitative research that I wish to identify. In one sense, it is an atheoretical conception of the ways in which qualitative research, particularly that kind which is artistically rendered, contributes to our comprehension of events beyond the events studied. I speak of the fact that when qualitative research is portrayed in vividly artistic terms, the events take on a significance that is larger than life. In this sense, the rendering of the events help us formulate canonical images that serve as prototypes for thinking about events like them. Who can forget the images of great teachers that we have known or those moments of insight that serve as epiphanies in our life. When portrayed by artistic hands, these products carry a meaning and have an impact that truly shape our way of seeing. Although not theoretical in the customary sense, it is my contention that these canonical images perform functions very close to those performed by theories of a scientific character. If we recognize that theory itself can be redefined or redescribed, as Schwandt points out, then the "theoretical" contributions of artistically rendered qualitative research emerge not in the mathematical or propositional explanations of causal events, but through canonical images that guide our thoughts and perceptions. The examination of such contributions to our understanding will require a reinterpretation of what constitutes knowledge and, in turn, the kinds of methods that can be employed in its construction. If this reinterpretation occurs, qualitative research will contribute to a significantly expanded conception of mind and to a fuller appreciation for the ways in which human understanding is enlarged. This volume pushes the conversation in a direction that I believe may help us do this. It invites us to reflect again about the meaning of theory — or should I say the meanings of theory — so that qualitative research can secure the kind of conceptual foundation it needs to withstand the scrutiny that it deserves. In doing so, this book makes an important contribution both to the construction of that foundation and to the ways we think about how we come to understand the complex social world we inhabit.

Elliot W. Eisner
Stanford University

Introduction

Theory and *qualitative research* — we could not have chosen two more elusive and thorny topics around which to organize the chapters in this book. While both topics suffer from uncertainty and equivocation, they are by no means trivial. An increasing number of educational researchers either practice or are being trained in the use of qualitative methods. Previously unrecognized applications of qualitative research continue to surface, and renewed interest in qualitative work continues to grow. Many researchers are also taking steps to actively promote qualitative thought — organizing conferences, establishing journals, publishing books, and forming professional associations.

In tandem with these developments, qualitative researchers have experienced what might be called a loss of theoretical innocence. Few of us now claim to enter the field *tabula rasa*, unencumbered by preconceived notions of the phenomena we seek to understand. Our faith in "immaculate perception" is on the wane. Seeing the world as it really is, objectively, without distortion or bias or partisanship — such aspirations seem neither as reachable nor as realistic as they once did. Today we are more circumspect, having begun to turn a critical eye toward our own conceptual frames of reference.

The rising popularity of qualitative methods and our newfound theoretical self-consciousness are trends that make the focus of this book timely. Yet as important as these topics have become to our ongoing professional discourse, theory and qualitative research remain complicated — perhaps obscured — by fundamental ambiguities. On the side of qualitative research, we find neither definite nor conclusive answers to the question of what makes a qualitative study qualitative. Like a friend's face in a crowd, we recognize a qualitative study when we see one; its features seem unmistakable, but few of us can explain why. That familiar face, the melody of a song, or the aroma of food are among the many aspects of everyday life that we learn to recognize from repeated, firsthand experience. Our knowledge is largely tacit, and so, it would seem, is our knowledge of qualitative research.

The scope of this tacit knowledge is a key factor in the debate over whether qualitative methods can be taught formally as part of a graduate student's coursework. Often cited in this debate is a story involving the anthropologist Alfred Kroeber (1876–1960). One of Kroeber's students was preparing to leave the university and begin fieldwork. On the eve of his departure, the student went to his mentor and asked for advice. Reflecting on the matter, Kroeber could offer only two suggestions: take a frying pan, and lend it to no one. Courses in qualitative methods are now more common than they were in Kroeber's day. Nevertheless, what qualitative researchers have to teach about doing inquiry is still far less than what students have to learn. Harry Wolcott (1992) candidly sums up the situation:

> Qualitative research is not a field of study, and there is no clearly specified set of activities or identifiable group of specialists who practice them. To claim competence in qualitative research is, at most, to claim general famil-iarity with what is currently being done, coupled perhaps with experience in one or two particular facets (e.g., to "be good at" collecting and interpreting life histories, or to "be" a symbolic interactionist). Claims to familiarity often amount to little more than a sympathetic attitude toward descriptive or interpretive work, accompanied by a far more deeply expressed antagonism for that "other kind" of research for which we have begun attaching the neg-ative label "positivist." (p. 4)

So much for qualitative research. But what about theory? Is this topic any less difficult to pin down? Theory, after all, is such a sturdy and time-honored companion to all forms of disciplined inquiry. Do we have a clear sense of what theory is and how it works? Consider the following issues.

First, as the chapters in this book repeatedly illustrate, precise defini-tions of theory are hard to come by. In everyday settings, for example, people refer to "theory" in at least two ways. *Theory* can signify a set of formal propositions or axioms that explain how some part of the world operates. These theories are explicit, and often associated with an individ-ual's name (e.g., Kohlberg's theory of moral development, Herzberg's mo-tivation hygiene theory, or Festinger's theory of cognitive dissonance). At the same time, people also use *theory* to refer to any general set of ideas that guide action. This usage encompasses beliefs ranging from one's per-sonal philosophy and intuitive hunches to implicit assumptions, guesses, and suspicions about the everyday world in which we live. As William James is reported to have said: "You can't pick up rocks in a field without a theory" (Agar, 1980, p. 23).

As editors we chose the words in our title, "theory *and* concepts," to accommodate researchers who are uncertain as to whether their hunches and ideas qualify as formal "theory." The term *concepts* allows them to be more modest than does the term *theory* when making claims about whatever knowledge they bring to or gain in the course of their work. Yet, the point we wish to stress is that not all researchers agree on exactly what theory is. It can be defined in both narrow and broad terms, as formal explanatory propositions, explicitly stated, or as tentative musings.

A second issue on which we find little agreement concerns the relative status of theory. Is theory a vice or a virtue? Is it good or bad? On the one hand, theory can be thought of as one of the cultural icons of science and learning. In this respect, theory lends a certain legitimacy and prestige to what qualitative researchers do; it is heady stuff, and researchers are eager to prove themselves on grounds that are well respected within the academies at which many of them work. To status-conscious ears, "My theory is . . . " sounds better than "My guess is. . . ." Researchers look up to theory and would be unhappy if colleagues were to describe their research as "conceptually thin."

On the other hand, researchers seem to believe that theory can be as much a bane as it is a blessing. They want to be neither wedded to their theories nor blinded by them. In speaking of educational theory, Elliot Eisner (1985) rightly cautions that "when you provide a window for looking at something, you also, if I can use the analogy, provide something in the way of a wall" (pp. 64–65). Empirical researchers across the board take a certain pride in allowing observations to directly inform their thinking. They are wary of theoretical imposition. They talk of emergent theory and are quick to note the simplemindedness of theory in the face of an uncertain and complex world. Some researchers rationalize that other folks — perhaps the foundation types or the philosophers of education — will take care of the big questions, while they find enough status and nobility in their modest efforts to make sense of Ms. Carter's classroom or the Southtown School's first-grade reading program.

A third complication arises from the multiple yet distinct levels at which theory operates. There are those theories and concepts that researchers use in particular situations in order to understand a given topic — turn-taking patterns or student motivation, for example. These theories can be further subdivided into what Robert Merton (1957) called grand theories, theories of the middle range, and minor working hypotheses. Then there are epistemological theories that apply not only to what researchers observe but also to how they go about making observations. These are methodological theories, what Thomas Schwandt refers to as "theories of the instrument" (see Chapter 1). And finally, lurking somewhere in the background of research, are metatheories that implicitly tell researchers about the role of theory itself. This level of theory includes a broad range of critical assumptions about the relationships among theory, practice, knowledge, and the aims of inquiry.

When researchers speak of theory, they naturally take for granted that they will be understood at the level they intend to be understood. Yet, because these various levels of meaning are simultaneously at play, what researchers take for granted may not be shared by others. They sometimes find themselves talking about theory at one level, while their colleagues are thinking about it at quite another level. At best, this leads to muddled communication. At worst, researchers are left wondering how otherwise intelligent people could be so obtuse as to misunderstand what they mean.

Taking these complications into account—the ambiguities of theory and its multiple levels of meaning—many researchers may prefer not to discuss the matter at all. They might argue that talking about theory is too much of a black hole, a sink or swamp out of which nothing truly instructive can come. We disagree. Theoretical issues are not only unavoidable, but of significant consequences to research. If anything, ongoing confusions and anxieties make it all the more important to openly address these issues, look closely at what researchers do, and subject their uses of theory to review by others. Readers should not expect to take away definite answers or prescriptive rules as a result, but rather an improved understanding of both how others use theory and what they have learned in the process of doing so.

These aspirations can be put another way. The primary aim of this volume is not to probe the fundamental essence of theory, recount philosophical debates, or analyze the logic and merits of competing definitions. Highly abstract questions do surface time and again in all of the chapters that follow, but these questions are less valued for their own sake than they might have been had the book been written with a decidedly philosophical bent. As editors, we set out to approach theory and research from another angle. We turned to the practitioners of research, individuals for whom theory is pragmatically bound up with the activities of planning a study, gaining entry into the field, recording observations, conducting interviews, sifting through documents, and writing up the research. Theory looked at in this context is what we call "perspectives from the field."

These perspectives serve as the book's center of gravity, and we have organized the volume to reflect this. The beginning and ending chapters address the relevance of theory and provide an overview of related issues. Their purpose is to frame the rest of the book, a series of chapters focusing on "theory at work." Here we invited researchers to speak frankly about their own uses and misuses of theory. They do exactly that, openly admitting blunders and owning up to lapses of conceptual naivete, but also pointing out useful ways of thinking about theory and judicious ways of acting on its guidance. Their chapters offer a series of narratives drawn from firsthand experience, accounts that situate theory in the practical affairs of intelligently getting on with one's work.

It is fitting that narratives should figure so prominently in this book. The narrative format adopted by so many of the contributing authors allows them to take up the familiar task of making sense and turn it back on the research process itself. They are, in other words, enlisting qualitative skills to better understand qualitative research. This approach is not without its challenges, for the narratives at hand express personal as well as professional points of view. Individual voices come through loud and clear, but our purposes are more broadly conceived. In the best traditions of storytelling, we seek to share experiences, reflections, and lessons from which others can benefit.

This brings us to our final point. Common concerns are reinforced rather than undercut by the particularities of each separate story. Where chapters differ, and they do considerably, they do not contradict the recurrent struggle with questions of theory and its role in research. In focusing on theory, we seem to have hit a central and sensitive issue, giving us further reason to believe that this type of forum is long overdue.

REFERENCES

Agar, M. H. (1980). *The professional stranger: An informal introduction to ethnography*. New York: Academic Press.

Eisner, E. W. (1985). *The art of educational evaluation: A personal view*. Philadelphia: Falmer Press.

Merton, R. K. (1957). *Social theory and social structure*. Glencoe, IL: The Free Press.

Wolcott, H. F. (1992). Posturing in qualitative research. In M. D. LeCompte, W. L. Millroy, & J. Preissle (Eds.), *The handbook of qualitative research in education* (pp. 3–52). New York: Academic Press.

Theory and Concepts in Qualitative Research

Perspectives from the Field

DEFINING THE ISSUES

The chapters in Part I provide some of the reasons researchers would want to attend to theory in the first place. Most researchers and theorists would probably agree that the importance of theory is "obvious." However, we want to be explicit about this obviousness, not so much to convince skeptics, but to help identify relevant issues and thus bring the book's topic into clear focus. The following chapters, both in this and subsequent parts of the book, suggest that there are special reasons to revisit questions of theory at this particular time in the development of qualitative research and evaluation. In short, we do not want to neglect conversations already taking place.

A central aim of Chapter 1 is to clear the ground for understanding "that debates about theory are proxies for debates about the nature and purpose of social scientific inquiry." Thomas Schwandt begins this task with a brief yet cogent summary of why all observations presuppose theory, why atheoretical research is impossible, and why theory often takes on multiple meanings. He goes on to suggest that the rehabilitation of theory is now centered less on questions of whether theoretical commitments significantly shape our observations of people and society, and more on questions of how.

The second issue Schwandt takes up stems from an equally fundamental question: Is scientific theorizing, as defined in a logical empiricist framework, an adequate purpose for interpretive inquiry? Suggesting an alternative to theory (at least as we know it), Schwandt looks to Aristotle's notion of *phronesis*, or practical wisdom. This conception of knowledge takes its lead from the narrative forms and pragmatic traditions of ethical reasoning. In part, *phronesis* involves a shift from epistemology, with its emphasis on discovering the way things really are, to hermeneutics, with its emphasis on contextuality and interpretation. The crux of this distinction might be described as the difference between knowledge *of* the world and knowledge *in* the world. None of this repudiates the value of explanatory theory, but it does stress the significance of theory in relation to the quality of social life and the welfare of others. Schwandt readily concedes that these considerations do not as yet "form a coherent, systematic perspective." They do, nevertheless, point the way to an informed position from which to reconsider the roles of theory in qualitative research.

Chapter 2 stands midway between Schwandt's broadly conceived approach to theory and the more focused accounts of research that will follow in Part II. In this bridging chapter, Jennifer Greene looks at theory in the context of qualitative program evaluation. Her arguments echo Schwandt's emphasis on two critical points. The first is that theory's role in research depends at least implicitly on basic questions of purpose. The second point is that conventional views of theory are not well suited to the overall concerns of qualitative evaluation, and these views will lead qualitative evaluators in the wrong direction unless careful attention is paid to redefining the relationship between theory and qualitative methods.

Greene finds renewed acceptance of conventional thinking in the recent theory-driven evaluation movement. This trend has sought to re-establish the science of evaluation along the traditional lines of theory-verification, but it provides little guidance for program evaluators whose work is not primarily quantitative in nature. As an alternative, one more in tune with the practices of qualitative inquiry, Greene suggests theory-oriented evaluation. This approach seeks to include theory as part of the context and emergent focus of evaluation efforts, explicating theory in order to enhance an evaluation's responsiveness and authority. Greene also makes four specific recommendations and illustrates how each might be used in the context of program evaluation to promote a theory-oriented approach.

What these first two chapters offer is a compelling rationale for believing that theory makes a difference in how we practice qualitative inquiry. But more than this, Schwandt and Greene signal a certain uneasiness with conventional understandings of theory and their appropriateness to the aims of qualitative studies in education. Both Schwandt's distinction between theory and *phronesis*, and Greene's distinction between theory-driven and theory-oriented evaluation, reflect an effort to redefine the roles of theory in ways specifically relevant to qualitative work. Both authors recognize that rejecting con-

ventional views of theory will certainly not allow qualitative researchers to opt out of attending to theory. Admitting that conventional
views are not the ticket for qualitative research simply poses the challenge of finding a better fit. Schwandt and Greene's insights are valuable for just this reason.

Theory for the Moral Sciences

Crisis of Identity and Purpose

THOMAS A. SCHWANDT

Current discourse on social science methodology reveals conceptual confusion and misunderstanding surrounding what theory is, and how it is and should be manifest in qualitative or, more broadly, interpretive studies.[1] Listening to students and colleagues talk about theory brings to mind a story about St. Augustine. When he was asked, "What is time?" he said: "If no one asks me, I know what it is. If I wish to explain it to him who asks me, I do not know." The situation surrounding our understanding of theory may not be quite so enigmatic, but it is worrisome; not so much because we cannot get on with our work as inquirers without a clear understanding of theory, but because we would like a shared working vocabulary of key notions that shape the nature and purpose of our practice as interpretive social inquirers. Our confusion about theory is characteristic of the spirit of our times that is marked by a variety of epistemological, political, and moral critiques of the methods and aims of the natural sciences that have long served as the model for the rationalization of the social sciences. Within this broad critique of the naturalistic interpretation of the social sciences, epistemological concepts like knowledge, truth, and theory that lie at the very heart of this model are being scrutinized and redescribed.

In this chapter, I sort through some of the intellectual activity surrounding our efforts to define the nature and meaning of the concept called "theory." My purpose is to clear the ground in such a way that we can grasp what I believe fundamentally is at issue in arguments about the role of theory in interpretive studies. This discussion begins with a review of several relatively uncontested claims as well as some misunderstandings about theory, partially to make it clear what the current controversy surrounding theory is *not* about. I then take up an examination of the thesis that debates about theory are proxies for debates about the nature and purpose of social scientific inquiry. Theory is a standard-bearer in the dispute over the definition of what it means to inquire into human meaning and activity.

ON MISUNDERSTANDINGS AND
RELATIVELY UNCONTESTED TERRAIN

Given the current tendency to thoroughly deconstruct just about any claim to know, I realize I am inviting criticism by claiming that there are some *relatively* uncontested senses of the term *theory* and some common misunderstandings as well. Nonetheless, I will take that risk in order to try to clear away the underbrush, so to speak, so that we might get to the theory thicket that is the source of our discomfort. I make no subsequent claim to relieve that discomfort; my objective here is only to identify its locus. A broad examination of writing about theory in philosophy of science and social science would reveal that there is general agreement among theorists, methodologists, philosophers, researchers, and the like on the meaning of several senses of the term *theory*. To be sure, there are debates that swirl around these ideas and particularly their implications, but for the most part these debates do not seem to be at the heart of the matter for our understanding of theory in interpretive studies. With this caveat in mind, I offer the following as generally accepted understandings about theory:

1. Observation statements presuppose theory.
2. Atheoretical research is impossible.
3. Theory in the social sciences and the humanities is currently being rehabilitated in this era of postpositivism and the interpretive turn.
4. Theory in the social sciences is multivalent, that is, it has various meanings and there are different ways of theorizing about human affairs.
5. Theory plays a role in both fieldwork and deskwork in social science investigations.

Observation Statements Presuppose Theory

The claim that observation statements presuppose theory has been so thoroughly discussed in the philosophy of science literature (e.g., Garrison, 1986; Hesse, 1980; Phillips, 1985; Suppe, 1977) that it requires little further elaboration here. Only the most naive inductivist still clings to the notions that scientific investigations start with observations and that observation statements form the unimpeachable bedrock of scientific theory.

A. F. Chalmers (1982) provides us with a neat little illustration of how observation statements of all kinds must be made in the language of some theory.

> Consider the simple sentence in commonsense language, "Look out, the wind is blowing the baby's pram over the cliff edge!" Much low-level theory is presupposed here. It is implied that there is such a thing as wind, which has the property of being able to cause the motion of objects such as prams, which stand in its path. The sense of urgency conveyed by the "Look out" indicates the expectation that the pram, complete with baby, will fall over the cliff and perhaps be dashed on the rocks beneath, and it is further assumed that this will be deleterious for the baby. Again, when an early riser in urgent need of coffee complains, "The gas won't light," it is assumed that there are substances in the world that can be grouped under the concept "gas," and that some of them, at least, ignite. . . . When we move towards statements of the kind occurring in science, the theoretical presuppositions become less commonplace and more obvious. That there is considerable theory presupposed by the assertion, "the electron beam was repelled by the North Pole of the magnet," or by a psychiatrist's talk of the withdrawal symptoms of a patient, [or by a teacher's talk of a student's inability to read, for that matter], should not need much arguing. (pp. 28–29)

Of course, the collapse of a strict empiricism or of an absolute theory–observation distinction does not mean that observation no longer plays an important role in scientific investigations. Just exactly what role it does play and how we should interpret the theory-dependence of observations and the consequent undetermination of theories by facts or evidence are still debated. For example, there is controversy over whether separating the context of discovery from the context of verification solves the problem of theory-dependence of observation; over whether falsificationism can be sustained in light of the fallibility of observation statements, and over whether it is reasonable to accept some observation statements as true. But these matters need not concern us here, for the primary consequence of our understanding that observations are theory dependent – namely, the abandonment of a strict foundationalist epistemology (the idea that theory can and must be absolutely justified by an appeal to facts, observations, or experience) – is generally acknowledged, regardless of one's particular nonpositivist epistemological or metaphysical preference.

Atheoretical Research Is Impossible

Likewise, it is generally accepted as both a consequence and an extension of the dissolution of the absolute theory–fact distinction that atheoretical investigation is impossible. A simplistic Baconian view (something like, first gather the facts through what we see, hear, touch, etc., and then form knowledge claims by induction) simply does not adequately describe the activity of scientific inquiry. We know that inquiry does not start with pure observation because some kind of theory precedes the collection of observations. (We also know that observations do not provide a secure foundation for theory because all observations are fallible.) In a paper exploring this claim, James Garrison (1988) uses the *Meno* paradox to illustrate the point here: The paradox says that all inquiry is impossible because either we know what we seek, in which case why search for it, or we have no idea what we seek, in which case how would we recognize it? The way out of this paradox is to recognize that we have partial fore-knowledge of the phenomena we inquire into. Prior conceptual structure (theory and method) provides the foreknowledge necessary to initiate and guide the observations we make as inquirers. Garrison further argues that those who claim to do atheoretical inquiry actually do one or more of the following:

> 1) They hold their theories tacitly, in which case they need to reflect upon them and state them explicitly; 2) They hold them explicitly but deliberately withhold them from public view; 3) They pack structural concepts that properly belong to theory into their methodology where they are hidden from their view as well as ours. (p. 24)[2]

Two misunderstandings are evident in the discourse on interpretive inquiry when these generally accepted ideas about theory are ignored. The first, naive naturalism, is a variant on naive inductivism. Naturalism is based on the presupposition of fidelity to phenomenon. That is, it as-sumes that the inquirer must remain faithful to the object under study (the social world must be understood as it is in its "natural" state) by not imposing some prior commitment to scientific method. As Martyn Hammersley and Paul Atkinson (1983) have pointed out, this doctrine has served as a much-welcomed antidote to the central features of logical positivism; however, it can be wrongly taken to mean something very much like observation and description of the way things really are, free of any prior conceptual scheme or theory. A little reflection reveals why this is not possible: The doctrine of naturalism (as manifest in symbolic interactionism, phenomenology, ethnomethodology, naturalistic inquiry, and the like) is itself a cognitive theoretical frame that orients the inquiry. Further, it is impossible to observe and describe what goes on in "natural" settings without some theory of what is relevant to observe, how what is observed is to be named, and so on. This is readily evident when we compare, say, the efforts of materialists and idealists to understand and portray the same "culture." Furthermore, even seemingly simple or mundane typological schemes for organizing and classifying data, for example, as advocated by Robert Bogdan and Sari Biklen (1982), are theoretically informed.

A second similar misunderstanding surrounds the practice of grounded theory. Again, the fallacy seems to be that the inquirer enters the inquiry *tabula rasa* and collects data, and then theory actually emerges inductively from the data. In fact, grounded theory is a complex process of both induction and deduction, guided by prior theoretical commitments and conceptual schemes. In this means of analysis, as well as in any other attempt to move from fieldnotes to concepts and interpretations, the task is far from purely inductive and inferential (Van Maanen, 1988; Woods, 1985). To be sure, the grounded theory approach emphasizes fidelity to the phenomenon under study by arguing against grand or speculative theories; however, grounded theory is not simply a methodological scheme for initiating and guiding inquiry; it requires prior theoretical understandings as well, something very much like what Northrop Frye (1963) called an "educated imagination." Consider, for example, Anselm Strauss's (1987) emphasis on the importance of a "coding paradigm" in grounded theory. This paradigm helps the inquirer to go beyond simple naming (itself requiring a theory) to construct conceptually dense codes that identify the conditions, interactions among actors, strategies and tactics, and consequences associated with what is named. To engage in such coding activity the inquirer must have what Strauss calls "theoretical sensitivity" that facilitates the identification and interrelation of these conditions. Or consider the central notion of theoretical sampling in grounded theory: One decides what to sample on the basis of its contribution to the evolving analytical scheme. This scheme arises from prior knowledge of potentially relevant concepts, ideas, and other schemes continually tested for adequacy against the data at hand.

Substantive Theory Is Being Rehabilitated

Empiricists and logical positivists argued that if we sharply distinguished specific, concrete, empirical observations from general, abstract statements, then we could successfully purge metaphysical elements from science and get on with the business of describing and explaining the way things really are.[3] They assigned epistemological priority to observation statements, leaving theoretical statements (concepts) entirely dependent for their meaning on the particular observation statements into which they could be unpacked. This is represented in Herbert Feigl's (1970) visual image of theoretical concepts growing out of the "soil" of observation: Theory is meaningful *precisely because* of "an 'upward seepage' of meaning from the observation terms to the theoretical concepts" (p. 7). In effect, these thinkers elevated the importance of fact or empirical evidence in our construction, judgment, and accumulation of knowledge claims over the relevance of theoretical concerns. Certainly, general theoretical commitments of the philosophical or metaphysical kind were regarded as unimportant in the development of scientific knowledge.

The criticisms of this strict empiricist or logical positivist stance made by Kuhn, Polanyi, Feyerabend, Lakatos, and others in effect challenged this relative priority of observation statements over theoretical statements. Their efforts can be interpreted as attempts to restore theoretical considerations to an equal footing with observation statements in our picture of the development of scientific knowledge. Much of postpositivistic philosophy of science is concerned with defining and explicating the role that theoretical commitments, conceptual schemes, beliefs, assumptions, and the like play in our conduct and understanding of scientific inquiry.

There is now general agreement that the formation, testing, and success of scientific theories is not solely an empirical matter. Of course, what kind of role such alleged extra-scientific considerations do and should play is debated, but the central question is not *whether* there is a place for these concerns but *how* they operate. In this sense, we can say that postpositivism is concerned with rehabilitating the theoretical by examining how substantive or, more accurately, interpretive theoretical commitments (i.e., behaviorism, symbolic interactionism, materialism, critical theory, feminist theory, structuralism, poststructuralism, etc.) and values shape, organize, and give meaning to our observations about people and society (see, for example, Alexander, 1987; Gouldner, 1970; Hesse, 1980).

This restoration of a focus on theoretical commitments is misunderstood if it is taken to refer to ongoing efforts in the social sciences to improve, refine, and criticize *methodological* theories or theories of the instrument that help us acquire or analyze data (e.g., generalizability theory, item response theory, grounded theory, narrative interview theory, aspects of fieldwork concerned with theories of trust or social relations). Despite contemporary fascination with the recovery of interest in fieldwork methodologies and the philosophy of *verstehen*, the hallmark of social science today is *not* debates over methodological approaches. Debates over theories of method are endemic to the social scientific disciplines and date at least from the writings of Vico and Herder in the eighteenth century (see Berlin, 1976). What sets contemporary debates in social science apart are not methods debates but debates about the very substance of social science—large-scale disagreements about the nature, meaning, and purpose of human activity, including the activity of human inquiry. I will have more to say about this claim in the second section of this chapter.

Theory Is Multivalent

It is generally recognized that there are different approaches to building theory and different theories, all of which are in some way useful in making sense of social phenomena. Of course, there is debate over which approaches are more useful, but little debate over multivalency as a general condition. Space does not permit a full explication of this claim here, but it can be sketched. For example, Jeffrey Alexander (1987) argues that there are good cognitive and evaluative reasons why the social sciences will always be characterized by multiple theoretical orientations and will never achieve the degree of consensus about empirical referents or explanatory schemes characteristic of the natural sciences.[4] He notes that social science has a distinctive evaluative nature and invites us to consider, for example, how ideological implications accrue to the very descriptions of these social objects: calling a society "capitalist" or "industrial," claiming that there has been "individuation" or "atomization." Alexander cites Mannheim on this point: "Every definition depends necessarily on one's perspective, i.e., it contains within itself the whole system of thought representing the position of the thinker in question especially the political evaluations which lie behind this system of thought" (p. 21).

Alexander claims that given the difficulty of establishing consensus on even the most basic of empirical referents, consensus on more abstract concepts forming the bases of substantive social theory is even less likely. The lack of agreement on empirical referents and concepts means that "the full range of non-empirical inputs to empirical perception become objects of debate" (p. 21). Because there is such endemic disagreement, moreover, social science will "invariably be differentiated by traditions and schools" that become the "bases upon which scientific disagreements are promoted and sustained" (p. 21).

Theory Plays a Role in Fieldwork and Deskwork

Theory plays a role both in orienting the field-based inquirer to the object of study and in writing about what one has researched. A moment's reflection on, for example, the existentialist posture of fieldworkers like Peter and Patricia Adler or Jack Douglas, the commitment of Paul Rabinow to phenomenology, or Shirley Brice Heath's sociolinguistic conceptual scheme reveals that one enters the field with a theoretical language and attitude. That substantive theory is essential for making meaning out of or interpreting the data one has gathered needs little further explanation. There are, of course, disagreements, as John Van Maanen (1988) points out, on whether theory is best employed and emphasized in fieldwork or deskwork. He notes that confessionalist ethnographers unlike, say, realist ethnographers seem to find theory most relevant during the writing phase: "Theory doesn't determine the fieldwork experience, but it may provide the dictionary with which it is read" (pp. 97–98). Yet, these kinds of disagreements do not obviate the claim that theory plays some kind of role in both aspects of interpretive work.

We could spend our time wrestling with the nuances and implications of the general understandings or claims about theory that have been sketched above. We could also spend our time examining the difference between a theory and a model; exploring whether a minimalist view of theory—one that does not emphasize nomological networks and systems of postulates—qualifies as theory; investigating whether theory development or testing is more important in interpretive work, and so forth. But I do not believe that such exertion will necessarily pay off in a greater awareness of what is fundamentally astir in the controversy surrounding theory in interpretive work. The claims presented above are really not much more than background to a more profound issue, namely, is scientific theorizing, as typically defined in empiricist social science, an adequate purpose and frame of reference for human inquiry? The remainder of this chapter is a long answer to this question. I begin with an explanation of the activity of scientific theorizing as a total intellectual orientation shaping our received view of the goal and practice of social inquiry. That view is then contrasted with a different intellectual orientation. The chapter then concludes with a discussion of the implications of this new orientation for our thinking about theory.

THEORY AS A TOTAL INTELLECTUAL ORIENTATION AND AN ALTERNATIVE

When, for example, the ethnographer Martyn Hammersley (1990) argues that "sociologists have a collective duty to attempt the production of well-established theory" (p. 109) (understood as a set of conditionally universal causal claims stated in deductive form), what is at stake? Hammersley admits that not all social research should be preoccupied with this goal, but he believes that striving for this kind of theory "gives us the best hope of producing effective explanations for social phenomena and thereby a sound basis for policy" (p. 108) and is essential to the cumulative development of knowledge. On one reading, we might say that Hammersley is seeking to get beyond the internecine quarrels over whether ethnography can properly include cultural description and theory development only by making a case for including theory verification and testing. This may be true enough, but I suggest that more is at issue. In linking the "collective duty" of social inquirers to the activity of developing theory and in claiming that this activity offers the "best hope" for generating useful explanations of social phenomena, Hammersley points to theory as the most appropriate intellectual orientation for the practice of social inquiry, and thereby introduces us to the issue that lies at the heart of our current discomfort over theory in interpretive inquiry.

In this view, the development of causal, explanatory theory is not simply some critical element in the armamentarium of the social science methodologist or researcher; it is the *raison d'etre* for the practice of social inquiry. In other words, to talk of the importance of empirical theory is not to talk simply of some feature of scientific investigations, but to talk of a pervasive and dominant intellectual orientation, purpose, or goal of social and political inquiry. Richard J. Bernstein (1976) explains this thesis as follows:

> At the core of the naturalistic understanding of social and political inquiry is the demand for empirical explanatory theories of human behavior. When this idea of empirical theory is fully articulated, it requires that we discover basic invariants, structures, or laws that can serve as a foundation for theoretical explanations—explanations that will take a deductive form, and from which we can derive counterfactual claims about the relationships between independent and dependent variables. It has been projected that the social sciences, as they mature, will discover well-tested bodies of empirical theory which will eventually coalesce in ever more adequate and comprehensive theories. (p. 227)

The defense of this view extends from Comte through Merton to Homans and Turner in the social sciences and from Feigl and Hempel to Popper and Newton-Smith in philosophy of science. Its lineage and development need not be recounted here. What is important for present purposes is to recognize two points. First, by this definition the development of social science theory requires a disinterested scientist; hence, theory clearly excludes any normative considerations, that is, it is empirical and descriptive, not prescriptive (Bernstein, 1976). Second, an essentialist argument is implicit in this insistence on a unified model of the sciences, with a formal, deductive paradigm for developing and testing theory at its core. In other words, the inherent nature of the practice of social inquiry—its very essence, meaning, and rationale—is thought to reside in the naturalistic interpretation. To engage in social inquiry *is* to pursue this kind of empirical theory. Likewise, the essence of social scientific knowledge *is* empirical explanations. The activity of constructing and testing empirical theory is the very heart of the social scientific enterprise.

Because the notion of a solely empirical explanatory theory signals the essence of what it means to engage in social inquiry, we can view theory as the standard-bearer in debates about the purpose of social inquiry. Thus, for example, when we question the importance of developing and testing empirical theory, we are questioning not only the rationality of the social sciences, but their very essence. We are questioning whether it is our "collective duty" to organize our social practice of inquiry so as to achieve the goal of formulating empirical theory, and we are questioning whether empirical theory offers us the "best hope" of progress toward the realization of ideals and social goals.[5] Hence, our discontent with theory is an identity crisis of sorts, a struggle with what it means to be a social scientist and to engage in social investigation.

The pursuit of empirical theory by a disinterested inquirer is what marks the practice of the social scientist from that of the humanist. Merton, for example, claimed that although social scientists are pressured to straddle scientific and humanistic orientations, they should resist such pressures and act "wholly the scientific role," for failure to do so denies the empirical, systematic, and cumulative nature of scientific theorizing (quoted in Alexander, 1987, p. 13). That image of the collective duty of social inquirers to act as scientists is what is currently being redescribed. Paul Rabinow and William Sullivan (1987) observe, for example, that

> The time seems ripe, even overdue, to announce that there is not going to be an age of paradigm in the social sciences. We contend that the failure to achieve paradigm takeoff is not merely the result of methodological immaturity, but reflects something fundamental about the human world. *If we are correct, the crisis of social science concerns the nature of social investigation itself.* The conception of the social sciences as somehow necessarily destined to follow the path of the modern investigation of nature is at the root of the crisis. (p. 5; emphasis added)

At the risk of being redundant, "the nature of social investigation itself" *is* the idea of discovering and testing empirical explanatory theory by adopting a disinterested scientific attitude toward the world. It is this nature, this essence of social inquiry that gives rise to our discomfort with theory. And it is this defining feature or essence that is currently being re-examined. Clifford Geertz (1980), for example, referred to this refiguration of the nature of social inquiry as the blurring of genres, a radical alteration in the sociological imagination evidenced by a turning away from dreams of social physics to the imagery, method, theory, and style of the humanities. What we are wrestling with then is defining the boundaries of a different intellectual orientation for our practice as social inquirers.

This new intellectual orientation is emerging and not yet clearly understood. Its outlines are less apparent in quarrels over methodological paradigms and more evident in discussions of the inquirer's role; the inquirer's obligations to self, to society, and to the people he or she studies; and the status or place of social inquiry among other efforts to understand ourselves. The call of Robert Bellah and colleagues (1985) for social science as public philosophy; Norman Birnbaum's (1988) plea that social science develop *sagesse* — a kind of wisdom stemming from reflectiveness that is inseparable from purposive moral action; and Richard Rorty's (1989) argument that solidarity not objectivity should serve as the regulative ideal for our activity as inquirers all point to new ways of conceiving of the meaning and goal of social inquiry. The remainder of this chapter explores some themes that characterize the effort to redefine the intellectual orientation of social inquiry.

A Focus on an Ethical Model of Reasoning

Scientific reasoning requires bringing particulars under universal rules. Scientists deductively demonstrate necessary truths from premises that themselves are necessarily true. The familiar form of explanation is

1. Laws and theories	Explanans
2. Initial conditions	
———————————	
3. Event to be predicted or explained	Explanandum

Aristotle distinguished scientific reasoning from ethical reasoning. He maintained that because of the complexity of human behavior there are no first principles (laws and theories) on which to construct a science of ethics. Hence, ethical reasoning requires deliberation — sizing up a situation and weighing information — and making decisions on a case-by-case basis.

What guides our ethical deliberation is the virtue of practical wisdom and a kind of knowledge that Aristotle called *phronesis* that can be acquired only through experience. This kind of knowledge is always context-bound or situated and guided by qualitative analogies rather than abstract principles. It emphasizes interpretation over logical analysis. This model of an ethical deliberator — one who must actively participate in the life he or she seeks to interpret — or, more accurately, the model of ethical reasoning — is emerging as a way of characterizing the activity and purpose of the social inquirer. G. B. Madison (1988), for example, contrasts an abstract, formal sense of scientific method characteristic of empiricist social science with a normative sense of method more compatible with a hermeneutical understanding of human inquiry. He argues that the former is a form of demonstrative reasoning; that it seeks to eliminate personal, subjective judgment; and that "the only criterion in applying the method is correctness of application . . . one's guide is the method itself, not the subject matter to which it is applied" (p. 28). On the contrary, method in a normative sense — modeled after ethical reasoning — is a matter of persuasive or practical reasoning and is "meant as an aid to good judgement" (p. 28).

The Shift from Epistemology to Hermeneutics

The renewed interest in an ethical (as opposed to a scientific) model of reasoning is facilitated by a shift from epistemology to hermeneutics. If the tradition of epistemology can be characterized as the separation of the inquiring subject from the object of inquiry, by the search for the foundations of knowledge, by the quest to discover the way things really are, by a bid to find a final vocabulary for explaining human action untainted by the vicissitudes of time, place, and human intention, then the hermeneutic tradition amounts to saying farewell to all that (Rorty, 1979, 1989). It is a tradition emphasizing situatedness, contextuality, and contingency of all knowledge and action. Hermeneutics is not a method that the inquirer employs to generate a kind of objective knowledge of human lives, just as scientific method properly employed yields objective knowledge of the natural world. Rather, it is a condition of our being-in-the-world; it emphasizes that the social world is itself a multivocal interpretation.

> Our capacity to understand is rooted in our own self-definitions, hence in what we are. We are fundamentally self-interpreting and self-defining, living always in a cultural environment, inside [what Charles Taylor called] a "web of signification we ourselves have spun." There is no outside, detached standpoint from which we gather and present brute data. When we try to understand the cultural world, we are dealing with interpretations and interpretations of interpretations. (Rabinow & Sullivan, 1987, p. 7)

The Emphasis on a Narrative Paradigm
for Human Understanding

The analytical logic and method of demonstration characteristic of the scientist's role are part of a larger frame of reference for understanding the world, namely, the rational-world paradigm. The growing interest in narrative and story is a concern for not simply a different textual form but a different paradigm of understanding (Brodkey, 1987; Bruner, 1986, 1990; MacIntyre, 1981; Marcus & Cushman, 1982). This notion can be outlined here by reference to Walter Fisher's (1987) work discussing narration as the condition for understanding human communication. I have chosen to quote him at length because he summarizes several key issues discussed in a number of other sources. Fisher claims that the rational-world paradigm presupposes that

> (1) Humans are essentially rational beings; (2) the paradigmatic mode of human decision making and communications is argument—discourse that features clear-cut inferential or implicative structures; (3) the conduct of argument is ruled by the dictates of situations—legal, scientific, legislative, public, and so on; (4) rationality is determined by subject-matter knowledge, argumentative ability, and skill in employing the rules of advocacy in given fields; and (5) the world is a set of logical puzzles that can be solved through appropriate analysis and applications of reason conceived as an argumentative construct. (p. 59)

For Fisher, the key notion here is *argument*, which in the rational-world paradigm is "*the* means of being human, the agency of all that humans can know and realize in achieving their *telos*" (p. 60; emphasis in original). Epistemology is the philosophical ground of this rational-world paradigm, a notion consistent with the views of Richard Rorty and Jerome Bruner. In contrast, Fisher summarizes the presuppositions of the narrative paradigm as follows:

> (1) Humans are essentially storytellers. (2) The paradigmatic mode of human decision making and communication is "good reasons," which vary in form among situations, genres, and media of communication. (3) The production and practice of good reasons are ruled by matters of history, biography, culture, and character. . . . (4) Rationality is determined by the nature of persons as narrative beings—their inherent awareness of *narrative probability*, what constitutes a coherent story, and their constant habit of testing *narrative fidelity*, whether or not the stories they experience ring true with the stories they know to be true in their lives. . . . (5) The world as we know it is a set of stories that must be chosen among in order for us to live life in a process of continual re-creation. In short, good reasons are the stuff of stories,

the means by which humans realize their nature as reasoning-valuing animals. (p. 31)

Fisher's emphasis here on reasoning with an audience through a text or an utterance rather than arguing places this thinking about narrative squarely within the Aristotelian tradition of practical wisdom. The stress here is on ontology, not epistemology, and thus the focus on narrative also takes up the interest in hermeneutics. Following Rorty and Bernstein, Fisher subscribes to the notion that it is in the context of dialogue and conversation (not in the context of the search for essences or foundations) that knowledge is to be understood.

A Recovery of an Interest in Pragmatism

Pragmatism is its own thicket, of course, but it is possible to sketch the influence of current apologists for pragmatism, most notably Rorty and Bernstein, on the redescription of the nature of social inquiry. The interest in pragmatism should not be taken to mean a naive or vulgar pragmatism of the "if it works, it's true" variety.[6] Rather, pragmatism refers to an anti-essentialist approach to knowledge, science, and the like. The tradition of epistemology is the search for principles that constitute the essence of knowledge, and the search for procedures or methods that will unquestionably lead us to those principles.

The epistemologist is thus preoccupied with the question, "Did I get it right?" In contrast, the pragmatist thinks it nonsensical to search for an ahistorical, noncontingent, and necessary reality, truth, or morality that somehow lies behind appearances and reveals the way things really are. There is nothing more fundamental than contingent languages and practices that have been worked out in the course of human history. Thus, when confronted with a knowledge claim, the pragmatist is less concerned with whether it is right and asks instead, "What would it be like to believe that?" "What would happen if I did?" "What would I be committing myself to?" (Rorty, 1982, p. 163). This shifts the focus of social inquiry from verification and the appeal to method, to practice and an appeal to deliberation and conversation.

REPRISE

The debate over methodological paradigms that continues to be waged in some quarters of academe is but symptomatic of a more profound redefinition of the identity and purpose of the social inquirer. This sketch of themes suggesting new intellectual orientations for the practice of social inquiry is intended to show that something quite different from the pursuit of empirical, explanatory theory is emerging as a way of shaping our sense of what it means to engage in social inquiry. However, the themes that have been outlined do not form a coherent, systematic perspective; in fact they are partially at odds with one another. Aristotelian ethical reasoning is not anti-essentialist; deconstructionists seek to weaken (not enhance) the explanatory power or role of narratives (particularly metanarratives); one cannot simultaneously claim with Fisher that "humans are essentially storytellers" and hold to a pragmatic rejection of essentialist thinking. Hence, it will not be a simple matter to fashion a sensible, coherent intellectual orientation for social inquiry from a combination of these new directions. At present, it seems best to regard them as sources of ideas for reconceiving the meaning of social inquiry and our sense of purpose as social inquirers.

Alasdair MacIntyre (1981) has argued that *characters* are "an object of regard by the members of the culture" and "furnish them with a cultural and moral ideal" (p. 29). Characters embody our culture's definition of the intellectual virtues and "morally legitimate a mode of social existence" (p. 31). At present, in our culture at large and within what we might call the narrower culture of social science inquiry, the character of the disinterested natural scientist bent on the pursuit of empirical theory no longer serves as an adequate embodiment of the identity and purpose of the social inquirer.

No fully formed new character has yet emerged; however, some outlines are visible: This new character does not repudiate the value of empirical explanatory theories, but she no longer sees their pursuit as the sole purpose for engaging in human inquiry. Her aim is not to produce knowledge of the social world as an entity but to engage in knowledge making as a human activity. This is fundamentally a normative undertaking. It requires that we come to terms with a sense of moral purpose and responsibility in human inquiry. She does not dispute that the search for regularities in social and political life are important, but seeks to understand the significance of such findings for our social practices. Her view is that there can be no neat separation of empirical theory about human nature from the "critical evaluation of the quality, direction, and fate of public life" (Bernstein, 1976, p. 234).

This new character sees the practice of social inquiry as a set of research discourses shaped, as Cleo Cherryholmes (1988) has noted, by beliefs and commitments, explicit ideologies, tacit worldviews, linguistic and cultural systems, politics and economics, and power arrangements. Disputes within and among discourses are not solved by appeal to the ways and means of scientific reasoning, that is, the appeal to method and the search for nomothetic explanations to encompass empirical instances. Rather, discourses take on meaning in the context of conversation and deliberation. We seek to persuade one another of the value or goodness of a way of thinking. Alexander (1987) emphasizes that the persuasiveness of discourses "is based on such qualities as logical coherence, expansiveness of scope, interpretive insight, value relevance, rhetorical force, beauty, and texture of argument" (p. 22).

In this reconception of the practice of social inquiry, theory no longer functions solely in the modern sense of explaining how things work so that we might be better social engineers. Rather, theoretical knowledge operates in the classic sense as providing a sense of grasping a *telos*, a sense of our ends and place in the world. Theory as incontestable *episteme* or as a kind of *techne*, a productive or technical application, is not part of this recovery of a classical explanation of what it means to know in human affairs. To live well in the world, to inquire into, understand, and direct moral, political, and social life requires a different kind of knowledge, *phronesis* — practical wisdom.[7] Further, the practice of inquiry itself, that is, the bid to understand the social and political world, as Hunter McEwan (1991) explains, is not some atheoretical object — something theories are about; rather it is inherently theoretical, reflecting a contingent theory of what it means to engage in rational, purposeful human action. This contingent theory, most often expressed as narratives (stories of being in the world) is not only about the practice of inquiry but is part of the practice it shapes.

What we are engaged in is casting about for a new understanding of what it means to do social inquiry. Our method, as Rorty claims, is one of redescription. We redescribe ourselves, our situation, our past as social inquirers, our key concepts like theory, knowledge, and so forth in ways that we hope will be more useful for understanding what we are about as inquirers. Ultimately, we hope, by this continual redescription, "to make the best selves for ourselves that we can" (Rorty, 1989, p. 80). If we lose sight of this purpose, then our struggles with theory in interpretive inquiry become nothing more than methodological quarrels, interesting perhaps, but not, ultimately, very useful.

NOTES

Acknowledgments. My thanks to Barry Bull and Peter Magolda for their comments on an earlier draft of this chapter.

1. Although widely used, the term *qualitative* is troublesome because it denotes a type of measure or data and may (wrongly) imply that quantitative mea-

sures or data have no place in the kinds of studies we call "qualitative." "Naturalistic" is also a troublesome label because of potential confusion with the naturalistic interpretation of the social sciences (a position quite the opposite of that endorsed by naturalistic inquirers). Following the lead of Rabinow and Sullivan (1987), I prefer the term *interpretive*. It is a more (though not necessarily the most) satisfying term because it connotes an affiliation with an intellectual tradition (*verstehen*) that underlies most of the current expressions of this kind of inquiry in the humanities, the social sciences, and education (e.g., naturalistic inquiry, case study, ethnography, life history, participant observation, educational connoisseurship and criticism, and so forth).

2. Lincoln and Guba (1985) have been particularly keen on emphasizing the importance of Garrison's first condition, i.e., the need to make one's substantive and methodological presuppositions, theory, or conceptual framework explicit.

3. This famous statement from Hume's *Enquiry Concerning Human Understanding* served as a motto of sorts for the hardline positivists of the Vienna Circle who argued that only analytical and synthetic statements had any purchase in forming testable knowledge claims: "When we run over libraries, persuaded of these principles, what havoc must we make? If we take in our hand any volume of divinity or school metaphysics, for instance, let us ask: Does it contain any abstract reasoning concerning quantity or number? No. Does it contain any experimental reasoning concerning matter of fact and existence? No. Commit it then to the flames, for it can contain nothing but sophistry and illusion." Quoted in A. J. Ayer (1959, p. 10).

4. See, for example, Shapiro (1981). The lack of this kind of consensus also supports arguments that the social sciences cannot develop the kind of exemplars described by Kuhn in the natural sciences; see, for example, Eckberg and Hill (1980).

5. Ross (1991) provides an important historical examination of the origins of the regulative ideal of social scientific progress.

6. See Cherryholmes (1988) for a critique of this version of pragmatism. This naive pragmatist view is evident in a recent argument for ending discussion about research methodologies; see Howe (1988).

7. For an understanding of the recovery of these notions in moral and political life, see Sullivan (1986). The distinction between the practical and the technical is also discussed in Habermas (1973).

REFERENCES

Alexander, J. C. (1987). The centrality of the classics. In A. Giddens & J. Turner (Eds.), *Social theory today* (pp. 11–57). Stanford, CA: Stanford University Press.

Ayer, A. J. (1959). *Logical positivism*. New York: Free Press.

Bellah, R., Madsen, R., Sullivan, W., Swidler, A., & Tipton, S. (1985). *Habits of the heart*. Berkeley: University of California Press.

Berlin, I. (1976). *Vico and Herder: Two studies in the history of ideas*. New York: Random House.

Bernstein, R. J. (1976). *The restructuring of social and political theory*. Philadelphia: University of Pennsylvania Press.

Birnbaum, N. (1988). *The radical renewal*. New York: Pantheon Books.

Bogdan, R., & Biklen, S. (1982). *Qualitative research for education*. Boston: Allyn & Bacon.

Brodkey, L. (1987). Writing ethnographic narratives. *Written Communication, 4*, 25–50.

Bruner, J. (1986). *Actual minds, possible worlds*. Cambridge, MA: Harvard University Press.

Bruner, J. (1990). *Acts of meaning*. Cambridge, MA: Harvard University Press.

Chalmers, A. F. (1982). *What is this thing called science?* (2nd ed.). St. Lucia: University of Queensland Press.

Cherryholmes, C. H. (1988). *Power and criticism: Post-structural investigations in education*. New York: Teachers College Press.

Eckberg, D. L., & Hill, L., Jr. (1980). The paradigm concept in sociology: A critical review. In G. Gutting (Ed.), *Paradigms and revolutions* (pp. 117–136). Notre Dame, IN: University of Notre Dame Press.

Feigl, H. (1970). The "orthodox" view of theories. In M. Radner & S. Winoker (Eds.), *Minnesota studies in the philosophy of science, IV* (pp. 3–16). Minneapolis: University of Minnesota Press.

Fisher, W. (1987). *Human communications as narration: Toward a philosophy of reason, value, and action*. Columbia: University of South Carolina Press.

Frye, N. (1963). *The educated imagination*. Toronto: CBC Publications.

Garrison, J. (1988). The impossibility of atheoretical science. *Journal of Educational Thought, 22*, 21–26.

Garrison, J. W. (1986). Some principles of postpositivistic philosophy of science. *Educational Researcher, 15*, 12–18.

Geertz, C. (1980, Spring). Blurred genres: The refiguration of social thought. *American Scholar, 49*, 169–179.

Gouldner, A. (1970). *The coming crisis of Western sociology*. New York: Basic Books.

Habermas, J. (1973). *Theory and practice* (John Viertel, Trans.). Boston: Beacon Press.

Hammersley, M. (1990). From ethnography to theory: A programme and paradigm in the sociology of education. In M. Hammersley (Ed.), *Classroom ethnography* (pp. 101–113). Milton Keynes, UK: Open University Press.

Hammersley, M., & Atkinson, P. (1983). *Ethnography: Principles in practice*. London: Tavistock.

Hesse, M. (1980). *Revolutions and reconstructions in the philosophy of science*. Bloomington: Indiana University Press.

Howe, K. R. (1988). Against the quantitative–qualitative incompatibility thesis, or: Dogmas die hard. *Educational Researcher, 17*(8), 10–16.

Lincoln, Y. S., & Guba, E. G. (1985). *Naturalistic inquiry*. Newbury Park: Sage.

MacIntyre, A. (1981). *After virtue*. Notre Dame, IN: University of Notre Dame Press.

Madison, G. B. (1988). *The hermeneutics of postmodernity*. Bloomington: Indiana University Press.

Marcus, G. E., & Cushman, D. (1982). Ethnographies as texts. *Annual Review of Anthropology, 11*, 25–69.

McEwan, H. (1991, April). *Narrative understanding in the study of teaching*. Paper presented at the annual meeting of the American Educational Research Association, Chicago.

Phillips, D. C. (1985). What scientists know and how they know it. In E. Eisner (Ed.), *Learning and teaching the ways of knowing* (pp. 37–59). Eighty-fourth Yearbook of the National Society for the Study of Education, Part 2. Chicago: University of Chicago Press.

Rabinow, P., & Sullivan, W. M. (Eds.). (1987). *Interpretive social science: A second look* (2nd ed.). Berkeley: University of California Press.

Rorty, R. (1979). *Philosophy and the mirror of nature*. Princeton, NJ: Princeton University Press.

Rorty, R. (1982). *Consequences of pragmatism*. Minneapolis: University of Minnesota Press.

Rorty, R. (1989). *Contingency, irony, and solidarity*. Cambridge: Cambridge University Press.

Ross, D. (1991). *The origins of American social science*. Cambridge: Cambridge University Press.

Shapiro, M. J. (1981). *Language and political understanding*. New Haven, CT: Yale University Press.

Strauss, A. (1987). *Qualitative analysis for social scientists*. Cambridge: Cambridge University Press.

Sullivan, W. (1986). *Reconstructing public philosophy*. Berkeley: University of California Press.

Suppe, F. (1977). *The structure of scientific theories* (2nd ed.). Urbana: University of Illinois Press.

Van Maanen, J. (1988). *Tales of the field*. Chicago: University of Chicago Press.

Woods, P. (1985). Ethnography and theory construction in educational research. In R. G. Burgess (Ed.), *Field methods in the study of education* (pp. 51–78). London: Falmer Press.

2

The Role of Theory in Qualitative Program Evaluation

JENNIFER C. GREENE

THEORY IN SCIENCE

The business of science is commonly understood as the development of theory—the formulation of causal explanations of phenomena that account for empirical observations of the phenomena and enable their future prediction and control. In this view, scientific theories represent sets of formal propositions intended to universally explain how a certain part of the world operates. The Big Bang theory explains the origins of the universe and predicts its future evolution. Darwinian theory similarly explains the origins and evolution of species of natural life. Piagetian theory explains the development of cognitive functioning in humans. Western supply-side economic theory explains the movement of interest rates. And contemporary feminist theory explains the absence of women in most U.S. health research to date. The contributors to these theories have functioned in accordance with the common understanding that the principal work of the scientist is to develop theory.

THEORY IN PROGRAM EVALUATION

Yet, there is a group of contemporary scientists—of the social, applied sort—whose work is not principally oriented around the development of explanatory theory. These are social and educational program evaluators, whose work is framed around the interests and concerns of selected members of the setting being evaluated. The work of program evaluators is inherently political because it involves issues of resource allocation and policy priorities. So, in all evaluation contexts, there are multiple, often competing potential audiences—groups and individuals who have a vested interest in the program being evaluated, called *stakeholders* in evaluation jargon—ranging from policy makers and funders to program staff, intended beneficiaries, and the citizenry at large. And so, unlike many other scientists who assume an audience of peers, evaluators must negotiate whose questions will be addressed and whose interests will be served by their work.

These negotiations can, but need not, result in a focus on theory development. In practice, stakeholder interests and concerns are characteristically more immediate, practical, and context-specific. Policy makers, for example, often want to know how well a program works, but not why. Program staff and administrators often express interest in augmenting their program's outreach or improving its efficiency, but only rarely in understanding the interrelationships of program processes and outcomes. And, from their experiential base of program participation, beneficiaries are characteristically concerned about issues of program access, relevance, and respect, but again not about theoretical explications of the participation experience.

Negotiations about the specific purpose of a given evaluation study also importantly reflect the beliefs of individual evaluators regarding the social role of program evaluation, including whose interests *should* be served by evaluation and in what ways. Since the catalyzing era of the 1960s, an array of evaluation models or approaches has been developed, representing varied stances on the social role of evaluation and, relatedly, on appropriate methodologies for evaluation practice (Stufflebeam & Shinkfeld, 1985; Worthen & Sanders, 1987). These alternative evaluation approaches were developed largely in response to the failure of initial attempts to apply the conventional experimental model of science to the politicized settings of evaluation, in tandem with increasingly prominent critiques of this model by philosophers of science and theorists of methodology (Greene & McClintock, 1991). The explosive development of qualitative approaches to program evaluation over the last two decades well exemplifies this evolution of evaluation theory and practice. At present, there are 10 or so alternative models of program evaluation, distinguished most visibly by their methodologies and, relatedly but more implicitly, by whose interests are given voice in the evaluation's forum.

Yet, in spite of—or perhaps precisely because of—this evolutionary proliferation of alternative evaluation models, the evaluation field has been repeatedly criticized for being atheoretical and method-driven (Lipsey, Crosse, Dunkle, & Pollard, 1985), and evaluators are now often challenged to adopt roles other than that of technical expert (Cronbach et al., 1980; Guba & Lincoln, 1989). One recent response to these criticisms is a movement toward *theory-driven* evaluation being championed

primarily by proponents of the systems/experimental approach to evaluation (Bickman, 1987a, 1990; Chen, 1989, 1990b; Chen & Rossi, 1983,
1987, 1989). This approach retains a grounding in conventional quantitative methodology, but is tempered by recent postpositivist criticisms of its
underlying philosophical premises.[1] Evaluators within the systems/experi-
mental tradition typically orient their work around the program effectiveness concerns of high-level policy makers.

Qualitative evaluators, in contrast, typically orient their work around
the salient concerns and issues of *multiple* groups of stakeholders, thereby
giving voice to normally silenced groups, notably, direct service staff and
program participants. Qualitative approaches thus represent a sharp break
from tradition in both the form and function of evaluation.[2] Yet, contemporary discussions of qualitative approaches to evaluation are filled with
clamorous dialogue about methodological theory and practice, but only
whispers of concern about the nature and role of substantive or program
theory in qualitative evaluation. There is no call to embrace theory among
qualitative evaluators comparable to the theory-driven movement within
systems/experimental circles. The questions addressed in this chapter are,
Why not? And in what ways, if any, should qualitative evaluators attend
to substantive theory in their work?

While all levels and forms of theory are potentially relevant to program evaluation, one—substantive or program theory—is of central emphasis in the present discussion. Evaluators work with human service programs, which represent planful sets of activities intended to ameliorate an
identified human need for a given group or population. Substantive or
program theories in evaluation hence encompass issues related to the identification of this need, the activities planned to address it, the resources
required for the activities, contextual facilitators and constraints related
to implementation of the activities, and participants' experiences of the
activities, including any changes or outcomes experienced. Substantive
theory in evaluation can address these issues both as planned and as actually experienced.

The argument made in the present discussion is that the systems/
experimental view of substantive theory in evaluation emphasizes causal
interconnections among program resources, activities, and outcomes (or
inputs, processes, and outputs). And with their theory-driven movement,
systems/experimental evaluators appear to be endeavoring to reclaim their
heritage as scientists whose main job it is to develop formal, propositional
theory. Rejecting this view of theory, qualitative evaluators have opted
out of the theory development enterprise and, given the tentative acceptance of their methods among many in the evaluation community, thereby
doubly jeopardized their status as scientists. Yet, explicit attention to alter-

native conceptions of substantive theory could enhance the meaningfulness, value, and authority of qualitative evaluation practice.

This argument is developed by offering a historical note, reviewing the recent movement toward theory-driven evaluation, and then analyzing this movement from a qualitative perspective. A brief critical commentary on both perspectives, which extends concerns about theory into normative spheres, concludes the discussion.

THE ORIGINS OF PROGRAM EVALUATION AS ATHEORETICAL, METHOD-DRIVEN INQUIRY

The current movement toward theory-driven evaluation is based on a recognized need

> to move program evaluation from the black box evaluation, which is concerned primarily with the relationship between input and output of a program, to the theory-oriented evaluation, which emphasizes an understanding of the transformational relations between treatment and outcomes, as well as contextual factors under which the transformation processes occur. (Chen & Rossi, 1989, p. 300)

The black box evaluation approach dominated the early years of program evaluation in the 1960s. Derived from conventional experimental science, this approach systematically assessed program inputs (e.g., participant characteristics, treatment design) and outputs (e.g., treatment-versus-control group comparisons of knowledge, attitude, or behavior change), but left opaque any understanding of actual program implementation or experience.

Program evaluators of this era did not forsake their scientific responsibility to contribute to theory. Quite the contrary. They viewed their work as representing important field tests of established social scientific theories in such areas as child development, education, and consumer or family economics. These pioneer program evaluators understood social programs to be derived from these kinds of theories. They further assumed that programs were implemented as designed, or that the intended treatment was that actually experienced by all program participants in all sites. An assessment of changes in people who participated in a program, compared with similar people who did not and controlling for other possible confounding factors, thus constituted an important field test of theoretical predictions. As important, such an evaluation also efficiently addressed policy makers' needs for information about program effectiveness as input to decisions about future program support. An experimental evaluation of a token economy program for troubled adolescents, for example, would provide a test of the behavioral learning principles upon which the program was based and thereby contribute to general scientific understanding and refinement of behaviorism. It would also help policy makers decide whether or not to continue support for this program. Campbell's (1984) vision of the *experimenting society* eloquently captures this perspective on the nature and role of social program evaluation.

The shortcomings of this approach to evaluation are legendary in the evaluation field (see, for example, Weiss, 1972). They include recognition of the highly politicized (versus data-based) nature of policy making and the lack of fit between the requirements of the experimental model and the exigencies of applied social program settings. For example, serious questions were raised about the ethics of denying a purportedly beneficial program to some people in order to fulfill the randomization requirement of experimental design. More germane to the present discussion were the realizations that program designs were only sometimes or only partially grounded in social scientific theory and, more dramatically, that program treatments were virtually never implemented as designed, but rather evinced substantial variability both across sites and over time. A pre–post (input–output) model makes no sense when what happens between the pre- and posttests is different for different people *and* keeps changing.

Thus, program evaluation failed to contribute meaningfully to the innovation and enthusiasm of the Great Society era, and evaluators began a search for methods that would make their work more meaningful and useful, particularly in the policy arena. Over the course of this search, many evaluation theorists and practitioners shifted their allegiance from the community of scientists and its collective commitment to explanatory theory, to the community of policy and program developers and its collective commitment to improving the quality of social life. Concerns about theory became at best peripheral to adherents of *decision-making, responsive*, and *consumerist* approaches to evaluation, all of which fundamentally seek to address the specific concerns of designated audiences in the setting being evaluated. Evaluators became associated, even enamored, with their methods and thus vulnerable to charges of being driven by them and of renouncing their membership in the theory-oriented community of science.

These charges have been actively dismissed by strong proponents of decision-oriented evaluation (e.g., Patton, 1986) who view evaluation as an important form of social inquiry, legitimized by its contributions to decisions that help strengthen and improve a given program, independent of more general theoretical understanding. These charges have been largely ignored by qualitative evaluators, perhaps because there is little common understanding about the nature and role of theory in applied interpretive inquiry more generally (as discussed in the Introduction). Yet, evaluators whose roots remain in the experimental tradition have apparently been needled by these charges, with the resultant new movement to reclaim theory as the central focus of their work.

THEORY-DRIVEN EVALUATION

Rationale

The theory-driven perspective seeks primarily to redress the failure of the input–output model of evaluation by not only opening its black box, but also making the systematic assessment of formerly ignored program processes, dynamics, and contextual influences the central framework for evaluation. In theory-driven evaluation, "research methods are regarded as one of the integral parts of an evaluation rather than as the central activity" (Chen, 1990a, p. 16). In place of the development and proper application of increasingly sophisticated methods, proponents of this approach reclaim theory development as their central mission. A theory-driven framework, they argue, "will facilitate the accumulation and development of a systematic and comprehensive body of knowledge on how to improve our society" (p. 17) and thereby contribute in important ways to social scientific knowledge (Bickman, 1987b; Riggin, 1990). Just how inputs lead to outputs, the nature and role of important intervening variables, and the possibility of interaction effects, deriving from contextual factors or participant individual differences, are examples of desired findings from theory-driven evaluation.

The theory-driven perspective also aims practically and politically to enhance the usefulness of evaluation findings for policy makers and program decision makers (Bickman, 1987b; Chen, 1990a; Finney & Moos, 1989; McClintock, 1987). The provision of detailed descriptive and explanatory information about not only *if* but also *why* a program is effective enables policy and decision makers, for example, to discern between program failure and theory failure, to make better judgments about the program's applicability to other settings, and to understand its unintended as well as its intended effects (Bickman, 1987b).

The Development and Use of Theory-Driven Evaluation

Within the literature on theory-driven evaluation are some thoughtful discussions of continuing issues and challenges by its leading proponents (Bickman, 1989; Chen & Rossi, 1989). The issues most germane to the present discussion concern sources of program theory and overall applicability.

Sources of program theory. An acknowledged debate within the theory-driven literature is the relative value of general social science theories versus practitioners' local program theories or theories-in-use (Argyris, Putnam, & Smith, 1985) as conceptual guides for evaluation. General social science theories represent formal propositional explanations of human phenomena and thus reflect established bodies of social scientific knowledge. Examples are theories that explain participation rates in democratic societies, incentives to save in capitalistic economies, and key antecedents of drug abuse or risk of HIV infection. Practitioners' local program theories represent the specific program decisions of individuals directly involved in program design and implementation and thus reflect individually unique blends of accumulated knowledge, experience, and wisdom. For example, a League of Women Voters' program developer could decide to use public access television as the medium for a program intended to enhance public participation in environmental policy decisions. And she could base this decision not on the prescriptions of a given educational or communications theory, but rather on her own familiarity with multiple media theories and accumulated field experience. An explication of her rationale for this decision would constitute local program theory.

Most recently, an integrative approach to theory construction in evaluation, which synthesizes both social science theory and stakeholders' theories-in-use, has been advocated (Chen, 1990a; Riggin, 1990). Riggin retrospectively invoked several general theories to reflect on the adequacy of the local program theory used to guide her evaluation of a state-level workfare program. This reflection revealed gaps in both forms of theory, such that each was able to inform and enhance the other.

Applicability. Considerable discussion within the literature on theory-driven evaluation has centered around its applicability. Proponents present it as a comprehensive framework, applicable to formative (McClintock, 1987) as well as summative evaluation, inclusive of implementation (Scheirer, 1987) as well as outcome evaluation, attendant to all forms of validity (Chen & Rossi, 1987) and to important contextual factors. McClintock (1987), for example, suggests that "the process of explicating theory . . . is itself a useful type of formative evaluation" (p. 45).

Cautionary notes about the applicability of theory-driven evaluation have been sounded by proponents and critics alike. Chen and Rossi (1989) themselves do not expect their approach to "replace the leading paradigms or perspectives on the actual conduct of evaluations in either the near or distant future," but rather hope that *"evaluators will attempt to use its key features as guidelines"* (p. 299; emphasis in original). Cordray (1989) and Shapiro (1989) discuss the "contextual press on validity attainment" (Shapiro, 1989, p. 371), and hence theory testing, created by the political pluralism, ethical demands, and limited time frames of evaluation contexts. Bickman (1989) notes the higher costs in both time and money of theory-driven evaluation. He also wonders "who cares?" and surmises that "theory-driven evaluation [may] be of interest only to academically based evaluators" (p. 389). Relatedly, Patton (1989) argues that the theory-driven approach is applicable only to a narrow subset of evaluation practice. And Palumbo and Oliverio (1989) question the appropriateness of validity-oriented causal theory for either describing past program implementation or prescribing its future implementation elsewhere. Particularly for the latter, they argue, criteria based on social justice rather than validity are needed.

Reprise

Theory-driven evaluation hence, in the main, constitutes an effort to re-establish program evaluation as a legitimate scientific enterprise. The unique challenges and demands of evaluation contexts acknowledge continuing concerns about the applicability of this approach and about the kind of theory that should drive its implementation. From the perspective of qualitative evaluation, a host of additional concerns about the theory-driven approach can be raised, leading to a ready dismissal of much of its intended form and function. At the same time, such a critique invokes a self-reflective examination of what theory means to qualitative evaluators, how they might attend more intentionally to theory in their work, and what would be gained by such attention. The discussion now turns to these issues.

THEORY IN QUALITATIVE PROGRAM EVALUATION

A Qualitative Critique of the Theory-Driven Perspective

Qualitative evaluation is rooted in evaluation's responsive tradition (Guba & Lincoln, 1981; Stake, 1975) and grounded in an interpretivist philosophical inquiry framework. In both of these domains — evaluation's role and philosophical base — there are fundamental incompatibilities between qualitative and theory-driven evaluation.

With respect to role, as previously noted, the split within the evaluation community is between advocates of a macro, policy- and theory-relevant role for evaluation and those who promote a more locally responsive, utilization-oriented, or program-relevant evaluation role. Qualitative evaluators typically count themselves among the latter, while theory-driven evaluators have become leading advocates of the former.

Qualitative evaluators seek to explain the meaning and significance of a given program in a particular context as a means to increased program understanding and possible improvement. Guided by the philosophical tenets of interpretivism, qualitative evaluators expect a plurality of program experiences and hence diversity in the meanings constructed from these experiences. The nature and form of this diversity can be neither known in advance nor meaningfully explained by perspectives external to the context, but rather emerge from the evaluator's engagement with those who experience the program firsthand. Hence, the a priori adoption of a conceptual framework that prescribes the substantive direction of an evaluation, as suggested by the theory-driven approach, is antithetical to qualitative evaluation. This is especially so for general, "off-the-shelf" social science theories, because such theories are unlikely to have contextual relevance or meaning.

As an emergent, contextually grounded construct, local program theory is potentially more consonant with qualitative evaluation. Such theory would not appropriately be used as a uniform framework shaping the substantive direction and design of a qualitative evaluation, again as suggested by the theory-driven approach. But, it may well constructively take other forms in qualitative evaluation, as I will explore in the remainder of this discussion.

Qualitative Program Theory

Nature and form. Program theory in evaluation addresses identified social needs, and program resources, activities, contextual influences, and effects. Program theory in qualitative evaluation represents not formal propositions about interrelationships among these program facets, but rather context-specific, multiplistic understanding of the meaning of a given program experience, in which the various facets of a program theory are joined holistically. To illustrate, consider an evaluation I conducted with associates on a community-based group homes program for youngsters, part of which addressed staffing questions of training and prior experience, program role, professional development, and support (Greene, Brod, & Associates, 1991). Findings on these questions represented not isolated enumerations of staff characteristics (education, experience, training, and so forth) nor an assessment of which were most effective in promoting certain youngster outcomes. Rather, the staffing findings in this study portrayed diverse interplays among staff characteristics, representing the experiences of different staff members, and further connected these staff perspectives to contextual issues of resources and to program design issues like the changing needs of the program's clientele. The emergent construction of such program portrayals is what qualitative evaluators are concerned with. They endeavor to understand the meaning of a program experience from the multiple perspectives of diverse stakeholders, and then provide a contextualized explanation of interconnections and patterns of meaning thus understood.

Yet, qualitative evaluators do not characteristically cast their work as theory construction or intentionally attend to facets of program theory. In the group homes evaluation, theory emerged as important to the evaluation questions about program environment, but was not even invoked at the outset of the study as a concern or possible orienting framework. The telling of the program story, including educating stakeholders about the program and each other's perspectives on it and facilitating conceptual use of evaluation findings (Leviton & Hughes, 1981), well characterizes qualitative evaluators' responsive aims, not the development of theory. But with theory reconstrued as contextualized, multiplistic accounts of program experiences, again in which the various facets of program theory are joined holistically, qualitative evaluators might well embrace theory construction as one orienting focus for their work.

Rationale. Importantly, such an orientation could contribute enhanced responsiveness and increased political authority for the work of qualitative evaluators. It could expand the import and impact of qualitative evaluation beyond the "telling of stories." And it could thereby contribute to a revision of the heritage of what it means to do science. Theory-driven evaluation seeks to reclaim the old heritage. A more explicitly theory-oriented qualitative evaluation could help rewrite the heritage toward an expanded view of the nature of knowledge about human phenomena. Complementing or in counterpoint to formal propositional logic, or program theory a la systems/experimental evaluation, would be contextualized accounts of interplays among experience, meaning, and values, or program theory a la qualitative evaluation. And supplementing qualitative evaluations that tell stories of intended relevance to just one context would be an intentionally widened and more authoritative role for qualitative evaluative inquiry.

The social problems of human societies grow only more urgent. As a community of scholar-practitioners committed to improving the quality of social life, qualitative evaluators should not be content with promoting enhanced understanding of these problems, one at a time, town by town. Rather, they should proactively view their work as part of a broader collective effort to understand and find meaningful, expectedly multiplistic solutions to these problems (Cronbach et al., 1980). The legacies of evaluation's responsive tradition, in tandem with the context-oriented tenets of interpretivism, have served to shield qualitative evaluators from scientific responsibility for theoretical understanding. With a more proactive and broadened societal view of responsiveness, interpretivism can become a powerful lever by which qualitative evaluators can reclaim this responsibility in rewritten form.

Incorporating Program Theory into Qualitative Evaluation

Kolb (1991) has proposed and piloted an interpretivist *theory-focused* approach to program evaluation. In this approach, as in all responsive evaluation, stakeholder concerns and questions constitute the evaluation's substantive foci. However, in theory-focused evaluation, the elicitation of stakeholder concerns and questions is directed to and bounded by the domain of program theory. The evaluation then focuses on understanding multiple perspectives on the identified program theory issues, including practitioners' portrayals of the program-as-intended and participants' accounts of the program-as-experienced.[3] In Kolb's own evaluation of an adventure-based professional development program (akin to Outward Bound for corporate executives), the theoretical foci included the role of physical adversity and of metaphorical learning, or transfer of learning from the wilderness to the office, in the design and implementation of the program. By contextually understanding and comparing multiple perspectives on these (and other) program issues, Kolb argued that his findings were enriched with analytical depth, more locally useful, and potentially of greater value to the larger community of experiential educators. The theory-focused approach, in other words, augmented the responsiveness and enhanced the authority of this qualitative evaluation.

Short of explicitly focusing an evaluation around theoretical issues, how else might qualitative evaluators attend to program theory in their work? Although the construal of program theory offered herein is broad, the very idea of a theoretical umbrella may be inappropriate in many evaluation contexts. And in others, the mere introduction of the term *theory* may be intimidating or offputting to stakeholders whose participation in the evaluation is highly desired, if not essential.

In this light, four interrelated suggestions for incorporating program *theory* into qualitative evaluation are offered.

1. Explicate up front the evaluator's own theoretical predispositions
2. Describe local program theories as part of context
3. Attend to theory-relevant issues as an explicit emergent focus of inquiry
4. Integrate program theory into evaluation conclusions and recommendations

These suggestions do not constitute a radical departure from existing qualitative evaluation practice. Thoughtful qualitative evaluators, for example, routinely share their own views on the substantive questions being addressed and review program documentation as one perspective on the social needs addressed, and the planned contextual influences, resources, activities, and effects of the program being evaluated. What is distinctive about these suggestions is the call to frame these practices as contributions to program theory and, thereby, to proactively assert for qualitative evaluation not only legitimacy as science, but, more important, a stronger voice in policy debates. The suggestion here is not to use existing theory to guide the evaluation, or to use the evaluation to inform existing theory—for that is theory-driven evaluation. Rather, the challenge rendered is to incorporate theory-related issues into qualitative evaluation, to inform these issues via local, contextualized perspectives and understandings, and thereby to contribute an interpretive program theory to science and infuse an interpretive voice in the broader policy domain.

In the remainder of this section, these four suggestions for incorporating theory into qualitative evaluation are elaborated and illustrated.

Explicating the evaluator's theoretical predispositions. The interpretivist inquiry framework acknowledges and legitimizes the presence of self in inquiry; all interpretivist studies are colored by the substantive, political, and value predispositions of the inquirer. Qualitative evaluators are urged to make such predispositions explicit, both to help themselves self-reflectively monitor these potential sources of interpretive distortion and, as important, to enable evaluation users to judge for themselves the nature and extent of evaluator bias in the inquiry process and results (Lincoln & Guba, 1985).

Beyond these ends, to help assert greater authority and voice for qualitative evaluation, these explications of evaluator predispositions should include issues framed by program theory. Such advance explications could promote inclusion of some of these issues in the evaluation's foci and provide an additional, perhaps divergent framework within which to interpret and utilize evaluation findings. Given the broad construal of program theory offered herein, there is a wide range of possible theory-relevant issues. These include issues related to the roots of the social problem the program is designed to address, to competing theoretical perspectives relevant to the program area, and to understandings of what would constitute significant program outcomes for participants. To promote inclusion of these kinds of issues in qualitative evaluation, the evaluator should explicate his or her beliefs and hunches, prior experiences, and knowledge on such issues *and* link them to a program theory framework.

Take, for example, Galvin and Bruce's (1987) qualitative evaluation of the technological quality of and enhanced learning opportunities offered by four long-distance telecommunications learning classes cooperatively operated by several rural school districts. This study concentrated on documenting the rationale for and experience of the program from the multiple perspectives of school administrators, teachers, and students. The evaluation recommendations attended in some detail to cross-district administrative challenges that needed resolution for successful continuation and expansion of this *Tele-Learning* program, and the study was quite useful to local administrators (P. F. Galvin, personal communication, 1988).

Local responsiveness and usefulness are important evaluation outcomes. Yet, there are numerous theoretical issues of potential relevance to this setting, for example, in theories of the economies-of-scale gained by school district cooperatives, in theories of learning and instruction (e.g., didactic vs. cooperative theories), and in theories related to educational opportunity and access. If Galvin and Bruce's evaluation had incorporated some of these issues — as specific evaluation foci or as one interpretive frame — this might have not only enhanced the local value of the study but also given it a greater voice in larger policy debates. Galvin and Bruce's administrative management recommendations, that is, might have been more locally meaningful and politically powerful if they had been more explicitly linked to theories concerning, for example, economies-of-scale in school district cooperatives. And one way these evaluators could have proactively promoted the incorporation of such a theoretical perspective in their study would have been to explicate up front their own theoretical predispositions.

Describing local program theories. Another way qualitative evaluators can incorporate program theory into their work is to intentionally include accounts of the local program theory-as-intended as part of their description of context. As interpretivist understandings, such accounts would represent multiple perspectives on how the program is supposed to work and why; for instance, rationales for program resources, activities, and their intended interplay as understood by program developers, administrators, and service deliverers. As well, these accounts would multiplistically reflect the diverse sets of values and beliefs underlying different stakeholders' theories-in-use.

Qualitative evaluators routinely attend to contextual description and multiplistic value perspectives in their work. Rich descriptions of context are needed to situate meaning, to understand key contextual influences on evaluation findings, and to provide a basis for others' judgments about the applicability of the findings to their own contexts (Lincoln & Guba, 1985). And understanding values is the cornerstone of qualitative evaluation, what makes it meaningful (Smith, 1983). Yet, qualitative evaluators do not as routinely include local program theory, or multiplistic accounts of different stakeholders' theories-in-use, as part of their descriptions of context and values. This omission represents missed opportunities for

1. Uncovering implicit program-related assumptions and beliefs and stakeholder differences therein
2. Distinguishing between contextual factors that are and are not integral to the program's conceptualization and implementation, as well as identifying influential causal contextual factors (Finney & Moos, 1989; Stake, 1986)
3. Using the contextually grounded framework of local program theory as one interpretive frame for inquiry findings

Recovering such opportunities via planful attention to local program theory is another way qualitative evaluators can broaden the responsiveness and authority of their work.

Hemwall's (1984) qualitative evaluation of a mainstreaming program for hearing-impaired high school students illustrates some of these missed opportunities. Her ethnographic approach included extended observation of seven selected students in both their hearing-impaired and mainstream classes, and interviews with the students, their teachers and parents, and school administrators. Hemwall framed her results and conclusions around two emergent dimensions of "meaningful integration": (1) the nature and extent of the barriers to interaction between hearing and hearing-impaired students, and (2) the important role of the hearing-impaired students' self-confidence and personal responsibility for learning in the mainstreaming program.

Via explication of stakeholders' mainstreaming theories-in-use, these and other important dimensions of meaningful integration might have surfaced earlier in the study, thus helping to guide data collection and to provide a locally meaningful theoretical perspective on data interpretation. Discrepancies between the theories-in-use of hearing-impaired and regular teachers, for example, might have revealed different assumptions about the capabilities and needs of hearing-impaired students and provided an in-depth understanding of the regular teachers' observed preferential treatment of these students. And an understanding of the intended role of the extensive in-class support services provided for the hearing-impaired students (including interpreters and tutors) might have lent support to Hemwall's emphasis on these services in her recommendations. If these services were viewed as an integral part of the program, then Hemwall's recommendations were probably, as she suggested, highly useful. If, however, support services were viewed as short-term assistance to be phased out as hearing-impaired students adapted to their hearing environments, Hemwall's recommendations for improving these services might have missed the mark. Or, if different stakeholders had different beliefs about the theoretical role and importance of these support services, Hemwall might have directed some of her data collection toward understanding their experienced role and importance.

In short, with focused attention to local program theory, this study's meaningfulness and value in the study site could have been enhanced. Moreover, study findings would have also constituted a stronger assertion of interpretivist social theory, in this case as related to educational mainstreaming, and this qualitative evaluation would have offered more than the telling of a story.

Attending to emergent program theory issues. A hallmark feature of qualitative evaluation is its emergent nature, such that the boundaries, direction, and even major questions of the study can change during the course of inquiry. This feature of qualitative evaluation rests on the interpretivist assumption that all meaning—including the findings of evaluative inquiry—is socially constructed and hence inherently emergent or continually created anew.

Within the practical constraints of evaluation settings, qualitative evaluators honor this interpretivist principle and endeavor to remain open and sensitive to emerging issues of importance to stakeholders. Yet, this openness is often diffuse and ill-focused, like an antenna waving around in search of some signal. Emergent sensitivity could be strengthened if evaluators' antennae were explicitly, though not exclusively, attuned to program theory-related issues. The benefits here are similar to those discussed above as important opportunities gained by explicit descriptions of local program theories. In fact, drafting such descriptions may automatically attune evaluators' emergent antennae to program theory-related issues.

An interesting example of this is offered by Conner's (1988) cross-cultural assessment of health promotion/disease prevention programs. The study was intended to help U.S. practitioners develop more effective programs. Conner presents as part of the background for the study a theoretical contrast between the biomedical model, which focuses only on illness and disease and considers health simply the absence of illness, and other models that incorporate social and psychological factors in addition to biological factors, viewing health as a complex, multiplistically determined relative condition. That is, Conner began his study with a multiplistic theoretical orientation, derived from general social science theory, and intended to include in his data collection descriptions of the local program theories in each site visited.

Given this attentiveness to program theory-related issues, Conner was able to recognize problems in the early stages of his study.

> I began to understand that the approach I had planned was unintentionally and needlessly limited by a Western- and U.S.-based epistemological bias. (p. 181)

> I assumed that the basic health promotion principles would be similar [across sites] and that the most interesting differences would be in the implementation, operation and outcomes of the different programs. While there certainly were illuminating differences of this sort, it quickly became apparent that these differences often arose from variations in underlying concepts about health, wellness, illness, and their interrelationships and about the ways individual society members best changed health attitudes and practices. (p. 180)

Conner's theory-sensitive antenna facilitated this emergent reorientation of his study. He modified his data collection activities accordingly, developed as a result a rich account of cultural contrasts in health promotion program philosophies and practices, and thereby offered a strong, assertive instance of interpretivist theoretical understanding.

Integrating program theory into evaluation conclusions and recommendations. Patton (1980) argues that theory construction in qualitative evaluation is "inductive, pragmatic, and highly concrete" (p. 276) and that all "theoretical statements [should] be clearly emergent from and grounded in the phenomena studied. The theory emerges from the data; it is not imposed on the data" (p. 278). The suggestions made thus far about incorporating program theory into qualitative evaluation have departed from this stance by urging a more proactive, theory-sensitive role for evaluators, toward a stronger, more assertive, and more persuasive role for interpretivist social science.

The final suggestion extends this departure by encouraging qualitative evaluators, in interpreting and presenting their evaluation findings, to incorporate whatever program theories they judge to be meaningfully relevant, clearly identifying the source of each theory. This should include stakeholders' local program theories and their congruence with the program as experienced. This could also include more general social science theories about the human phenomenon of focal interest (e.g., learning, poverty, criminal rehabilitation, health promotion), about organizations and management, about program implementation (Palumbo & Oliverio, 1989; Pressman & Wildavsky, 1973), or about politics, ethics, and values.

A return to my evaluation of a group homes program for youngsters provides a useful illustration of this suggestion. In this study, two expert panels were asked to review the evaluation findings and offer their own interpretations. Panel I comprised program stakeholders and other youth professionals in the community and thus represented local program theory expertise. Panel II comprised academic specialists in family studies and adolescence and thus represented more general program theory expertise. Among the rich insights gained from these reviews were Panel II's perspectives on alternative family-oriented versus therapeutic models for youth residential programs and their varied views on which model was a better match to the group homes program evaluated. This *external, nonemergent* perspective provided a valuable theoretical interpretive frame for the findings from this evaluation. It also broadened the contexts—in domains of both theory and practice—to which the findings could have relevance. An earlier encounter with this perspective might have further enriched and extended this evaluation's potential power.

SUMMARY

Qualitative program evaluation has often been likened to storytelling. The stories told can be richly textured, enlightening accounts of the meaning and significance of a given program as experienced and understood by various stakeholders. Such stories can broaden and deepen stakeholders' conceptual perspectives on the program and suggest valuable directions for program improvement. These are important contributions to social program endeavors. And they are congruent with qualitative evaluation's roots in evaluation's responsive tradition and in interpretivism's philosophical framework. Yet, these same roots have provided qualitative evaluators with powerful disincentives to assert responsibility for more than their story. The applicability of the story to other contexts is a judgment left to others. And the potential contributions of the story to more general social scientific understanding are muted by qualitative evaluators' rejection of formal, propositional explanations for social phenomena. Concomitantly, qualitative evaluators' voice in the policy arena has also been muted, and the stories they tell are only locally powerful.

The argument I have advanced is premised on the stance that qualitative evaluations warrant greater power and influence. It is also based on acceptance of the commonplace idea that doing science means, at least in part, contributing to the collective understanding of human phenomena. As scientists, program evaluators should acknowledge and resume this responsibility. In this sense, the theory-driven folks are right. For qualitative evaluators, however, assuming some responsibility for theory requires neither accepting conventional, dominant views of theory nor forgoing a commitment to local responsiveness. Instead, qualitative evaluators are challenged to make interpretivist forms of social theory heard by proactively incorporating theory-related issues in their work. By accepting such a challenge, qualitative evaluators' stories can gain broadened responsiveness and enhanced authority.

EPILOGUE

From a position outside both the theory-driven and qualitative approaches to evaluation come the questions, *Broadened responsiveness to whom?* and *Enhanced authority for what purpose?* From this critical perspective, the purpose of science, especially social science, is viewed as more than the development of collective understandings of human phenomena. Such understandings are not the end of science, but rather the means to achieving a more equitable, just, and moral society. The need for such a normative basis for program evaluation has been recently argued, in varied forms, by Brunner and Guzman (1989), Guba and Lincoln (1989), Schwandt (1989), and Sirotnik (1990).

Qualitative evaluation is value-relative; it does not have a normative base. Different qualitative evaluators will respond to the questions of audience and purpose with different blends of responsiveness, action, and advocacy. So, in an important sense, encouraging qualitative evaluators to embrace theory as a route to greater authority begs the question of purpose. Scientists do have a responsibility for theory, and, as members of the community of scientists, evaluators — including qualitative evaluators — must share in this responsibility. But theory in the absence of purpose is akin to decontextualized knowledge, empty of meaningful lived experience (van Manen, 1990), without direction or vision. Absent a common normative purpose, qualitative evaluation's authority—even when reaching its fullest height—may simply be not enough.

NOTES

Acknowledgments. An earlier version of this paper was presented as part of a symposium at the annual meeting of the American Educational Research Association, April 1990, Boston. My thanks to symposium critics Elliot Eisner and Harry Wolcott and to Egon Guba, Charles McClintock, and especially Thomas Schwandt for their encouraging and constructive comments on the paper.

1. See Phillips (1987) and Smith (1989) for readable discussions of postpositivist philosophical thought, and Cook (1985) for an excellent illustration of postpositivist methodology, labeled therein "postpositivist critical multiplism."

2. While there are varied qualitative approaches to evaluation, the label is used herein to refer to interpretivist or constructivist qualitative evaluation, most comprehensively promoted by Guba and Lincoln (1981, 1989; Lincoln & Guba, 1985). Major tenets of this approach include a relativist view of reality and a view that all knowledge is socially constructed, value-laden, and context-bound.

3. Consonant with its interpretivist base, theory-focused evaluation also attends to emergent issues of importance.

REFERENCES

Argyris, C., Putnam, R., & Smith, D. M. (1985). *Action science.* San Francisco: Jossey-Bass.

Bickman, L. (Ed.). (1987a). *Using program theory in evaluation. New Directions for Program Evaluation 33.* San Francisco: Jossey-Bass.

Bickman, L. (1987b). The functions of program theory. In L. Bickman (Ed.), *Using program theory in evaluation. New Directions for Program Evaluation 33* (pp. 5–18). San Francisco: Jossey-Bass.

Bickman, L. (1989). Barriers to the use of program theory. *Evaluation and Program Planning, 12,* 387–390.

Bickman, L. (Ed.). (1990). *Advances in program theory. New Directions for Program Evaluation 47.* San Francisco: Jossey-Bass.

Brunner, I., & Guzman, A. (1989). Participatory evaluation: A tool to assess projects and empower people. In R. F. Conner & M. Hendricks (Eds.), *International innovations in evaluation methodology. New Directions for Program Evaluation 42* (pp. 9–18). San Francisco: Jossey-Bass.

Campbell, D. T. (1984). *Can an open society be an experimenting society?* Paper presented at the International Symposium on the Philosophy of Karl Popper, Madrid.

Chen, H. T. (Ed.). (1989). The theory-driven perspective [Special issue]. *Evaluation and Program Planning, 12.*

Chen, H. T. (1990a). Issues in constructing program theory. In L. Bickman (Ed.), *Advances in program theory. New Directions for Program Evaluation 47* (pp. 7–18). San Francisco: Jossey-Bass.

Chen, H. T. (1990b). *Theory-driven evaluations.* Newbury Park, CA: Sage.

Chen, H. T., & Rossi, P. H. (1983). Evaluating with sense: The theory-driven approach. *Evaluation Review, 7,* 283–302.

Chen, H. T., & Rossi, P. H. (1987). The theory-driven approach to validity. *Evaluation and Program Planning, 10,* 95–103.

Chen, H. T., & Rossi, P. H. (1989). Issues in the theory-driven perspective. *Evaluation and Program Planning, 12,* 299–306.

Conner, R. F. (1988). A cross-cultural assessment of health promotion/disease prevention programs. *Evaluation and Program Planning, 11,* 179–187.

Cook, T. D. (1985). Postpositivist critical multiplism. In R. L. Shotland & M. M. Mark (Eds.), *Social science and social policy* (pp. 21–62). Beverly Hills, CA: Sage.

Cordray, D. S. (1989). Optimizing validity in program research: An elaboration of Chen and Rossi's theory-driven approach. *Evaluation and Program Planning, 12,* 379–385.

Cronbach, L. J., Ambron, S. R., Dornbusch, S. M., Hess, R. D., Hornik, R. C., Phillips, D. C., Walker, D. F., & Weiner, S. S. (1980). *Toward reform of program evaluation.* San Francisco: Jossey-Bass.

Finney, J. W., & Moos, R. H. (1989). Theory and method in treatment evaluation. *Evaluation and Program Planning, 12,* 307–316.

Galvin, P. F., & Bruce, R. (1987). *Technology and rural education: The case of audio-graphic telecommunications* (Evaluation Report). Ithaca, NY: Cornell University.

Greene, J. C., Brod, C., & Associates. (1991). *Group homes evaluation technical report.* Ithaca, NY: Cornell University, Department of Human Service Studies.

Greene, J. C., & McClintock, C. (1991). The evolution of evaluation methodology. *Theory into Practice, 30*(1), 12–21.

Guba, E. G., & Lincoln, Y. S. (1981). *Effective evaluation.* San Francisco: Jossey-Bass.

Guba, E. G., & Lincoln, Y. S. (1989). *Fourth-generation evaluation.* Newbury Park, CA: Sage.

Hemwall, M. K. (1984). Ethnography as evaluation: Hearing-impaired students in the mainstream. In D. M. Fetterman (Ed.), *Ethnography in educational evaluation* (pp. 133–152). Beverly Hills, CA: Sage.

Kolb, D. G. (1991). *Understanding adventure-based professional development: The role of theory in evaluation.* Unpublished doctoral dissertation, Cornell University, Ithaca, NY.

Leviton, L. C., & Hughes, E. F. (1981). Research on the utilization of evaluation: A review and synthesis. *Evaluation Review, 5,* 525–548.

Lincoln, Y. S., & Guba, E. G. (1985). *Naturalistic inquiry.* Beverly Hills, CA: Sage.

Lipsey, M. W., Crosse, S., Dunkle, J., & Pollard, J. (1985). Evaluation: The state of the art and the sorry state of the science. In D. S. Cordray (Ed.), *Utilizing prior research in evaluation planning. New Directions for Program Evaluation 27* (pp. 7–28). San Francisco: Jossey-Bass.

McClintock, C. (1987). Conceptual and action heuristics: Tools for the evaluator. In L. Bickman (Ed.), *Using program theory in evaluation. New Directions for Program Evaluation 33* (pp. 43–57). San Francisco: Jossey-Bass.

Palumbo, D. J., & Oliverio, A. (1989). Implementation theory and the theory-driven approach to validity. *Evaluation and Program Planning, 12,* 337–344.

Patton, M. Q. (1980). *Qualitative evaluation methods.* Beverly Hills, CA: Sage.

Patton, M. Q. (1986). *Utilization-focused evaluation* (2nd ed.). Beverly Hills, CA: Sage.

Patton, M. Q. (1989). A context and boundaries for a theory-driven approach to validity. *Evaluation and Program Planning, 12,* 375–377.

Phillips, D. C. (1987). *Philosophy, science, and social inquiry: Contemporary methodological controversies in social science.* Oxford: Pergamon Press.

Pressman, J. L., & Wildavsky, A. B. (1973). *Implementation.* Berkeley: University of California Press.

Riggin, L. J. C. (1990). Linking program theory and social science theory. In L. Bickman (Ed.), *Advances in program theory. New Directions for Program Evaluation 47* (pp. 109–120). San Francisco: Jossey-Bass.

Scheirer, M. A. (1987). Program theory and implementation theory: Implications for evaluators. In L. Bickman (Ed.), *Using program theory in evaluation. New Directions for Program Evaluation 33* (pp. 59–76). San Francisco: Jossey-Bass.

Schwandt, T. A. (1989). Recapturing moral discourse in evaluation. *Educational Researcher, 18*(8), 11–16, 34.

Shapiro, J. Z. (1989). Contextual limits on validity attainment: An artificial science perspective on program evaluation. *Evaluation and Program Planning, 12,* 367–374.

Sirotnik, K. A. (Ed.). (1990). *Evaluation and social justice. New Directions for Program Evaluation 45.* San Francisco: Jossey-Bass.

Smith, J. K. (1983). Quantitative vs. interpretive: The problem of conducting social inquiry. In E. R. House (Ed.), *Philosophy of evaluation. New Directions for Program Evaluation 19* (pp. 27–51). San Francisco: Jossey-Bass.

Smith, J. K. (1989). *The nature of social and educational inquiry: Empiricism versus interpretation.* Norwood, NJ: Ablex.

Stake, R. E. (1975). *Evaluating the arts in education: A responsive approach.* Columbus, OH: Merrill.

Stake, R. E. (1986). *Situational context as influence on evaluation and use.* Paper presented at the annual meeting of the American Educational Research Association, San Francisco.

Stufflebeam, D. L., & Shinkfeld, A. J. (1985). *Systematic evaluation.* Boston: Kluwer-Nijhoff.

van Manen, M. (1990). *Researching lived experience: Human science for an action sensitive pedagogy.* Albany: State University of New York Press.

Weiss, C. H. (Ed.). (1972). *Evaluating action programs: Readings in social action and education*. Boston: Allyn & Bacon.

Wholey, J. S. (1987). Evaluability assessment: Developing program theory. In L. Bickman (Ed.), *Using program theory in evaluation. New Directions for Program Evaluation 33* (pp. 77–92). San Francisco: Jossey-Bass.

Worthen, B. R., & Sanders, J. R. (1987). *Educational evaluation: Alternative approaches and practical guidelines*. New York: Longman.

THEORY AT WORK

We now turn to examine theory relative to what researchers do as they plan, conduct, and report their work. The chapters in Part II take us behind the scenes of research, a context in which theory holds its most immediate implications. Here practical lessons are drawn from experience in the field, and these lessons concern not just the contributions of theory but its pitfalls as well. In each chapter, issues surface that are shaped by the particular circumstances in which the functions and applications of theory are played out.

While differences between chapters also reflect diverse perspectives, this diversity did not emerge entirely of its own accord. It is at least partly the result of two strategies. First, we sought in this part of the book to recognize the growing family of different qualitative forms of inquiry. Included are representatives of case study and ethnographic participant observation, educational criticism, life history research, biography, and various types of "action research." Second, we chose to include a range of experience among the contributing authors. Chapters were written by novice as well as veteran educational researchers. The veterans, of course, have experience on their side, lending sophistication to their insights, but also reminding us that theoretical challenges by no means end with successfully completing one's first study. The stories told by novice researchers are equally informative, but for another reason. Being relatively new to the task, these authors are often acutely aware of norms, expectations, and tensions that their more seasoned colleagues would otherwise take for granted.

In the first chapter of Part II, Sandra Mathison recounts her ongoing work to develop a program of case study and interview research on the sociology of standardized testing. She draws on this research to demonstrate how theory plays multiple roles at various stages in the description, analysis, and interpretation of qualitative data. Mathison's interests in standardized testing stem from a continuing puzzlement over why this form of assessment is as widespread and persistent as it is in American schools. A significant part of her empirical work has examined the lay theories of her research participants, revealing that positive attitudes toward standardized testing are associated with a negative view of teachers, and vice versa. Such lay theories, representing an emic perspective, are often the primary focus of qualitative work. In addition, however, Mathison draws on etic, or what she calls social, theories. These theories have helped her explain testing as a type of ritual and more generally as an expression of utilitarian ethics.

Mathison's research illustrates a complementary use of emic and etic perspectives, each informed by a particular set of theories. Yet, this is not the whole story. Mathison also looks at research in relation to "theories of action." Here her aim is to examine the role of theory in guiding how qualitative inquiry should be used to promote educational reform. Theory in this domain is largely prescriptive. It informs both the conduct of research and the use of research findings to influence policy. Mathison situates these issues within the framework of "critical social science," using her own involvement in political interest groups to illustrate various implications. Although theory is rarely considered by researchers as a guide to their political obligations, Mathison clearly regards doing so as an integral part of her work.

In Chapter 4, Stephen Thornton relates his own use of theory in carrying out a classroom study of beginning social studies teachers. He introduces this study by describing the particular constellation of factors that gave his research its initial focus. By Thornton's account, the early stages of his work were guided by two orienting assumptions. His first assumption is drawn from an assessment of the social studies field and from a general belief that useful knowledge can be learned by closely examining how "good" social studies teachers plan and enact their curriculum. His second assumption stems from recent feminist scholarship in education, specifically scholarship arguing that meaningful accounts of teaching must recognize what teachers share of themselves in the classroom.

Thornton moves on to present two brief case studies of his research participants, doing so in order to ground his discussion of theory in actual descriptions of teaching and, in this case, descriptions of learning to teach. These case studies illustrate the emergence of all

sorts of unanticipated emic theories; that is, theories held by the research participants themselves and indigenous to the context of the
study. Here Mathison's theme regarding the multiple roles of theory
is echoed in Thornton's work. Nevertheless, Thornton finds considerable tension between his orienting assumptions and the emic theories
that emerged over the course of the study. He admits, in particular,
that his initial focus at least partially obscured a full appreciation for
his participants' views of "what was going on." Many researchers in-
vested in a theoretical orientation are apt to forget that a study tends
to take on a life of its own, and this is where Thornton's argument is
most pointed. He contends that for ideas to remain in a state of flux,
and for researchers to refocus their inquiries as they proceed, is precisely the way it ought to be.

Following Thornton are two chapters that recount studies of
planned educational change. In Chapter 5, Joyce Henstrand probes
the theoretical aspects of her doctoral research, a case study of the
suburban high school in which she worked. Henstrand ties the theoretical development of this study in part to her own background and
in part to a graduate course in "Culture Theory." The course came at
a fortunate time, early in the planning stages of her research, allowing Henstrand to "piece together" a conceptual framework from four
different orientations: (1) structural-functional theories, (2) structural analysis, (3) cognitive anthropology, and (4) interpretive anthropology. Henstrand not only critiques each orientation with an eye toward her interest in planned educational change, but she argues that
in different ways each orientation served to guide key aspects of her
research, including the study's focus, unit of analysis, and descriptive
style. Henstrand also describes and illustrates an unanticipated benefit of theory, one that involved helping her manage the conflicts inherent in her role as full participant observer.

Several key issues lie just below the surface of Henstrand's discussion. One issue concerns the manner in which theory informs research. In Henstrand's case, the theoretical orientations from which
she drew guidance did not dictate in any strict sense the specific outcomes of ongoing decisions made in the field or during the analysis
and writing stages of her work. Instead, theory seemed to play a less
scripted role, raising questions and suggesting points of view, but
rarely serving as the last word on any particular matter. Another issue involves the relationship between theory and the researcher's personal background. On more than one occasion Henstrand notes that
her multicultural experience growing up as a first-generation American and her years teaching literature made certain theories more at-

tractive and appealing than others. Finally, although Henstrand offers many reasons to promote the use of theory in case study research, she is also quick to remind us that using theory well is itself a difficult task and that neither public education nor our graduate schools consistently reward efforts to be theoretically self-conscious.

Chapter 6, contributed by Geoffrey Mills, also recounts a case study of planned educational change. The aim of Mills's study, however, was to examine change within an entire district rather than within a single school. He assumed early on in the study that different groups of individuals (e.g., teachers, principals, and district personnel) would perceive and manage change in different ways. The study was also guided by an orienting question: How does change function, and what functions does it serve in an American school district? The importance of this question is closely tied to the literature on educational change, but its emphasis on "functions" is also informed through the application of social theories. Specifically, Mills draws on Merton's classic distinctions among latent functions, manifest functions, and unintended consequences — concepts that help situate the topic of change within a particular frame of reference.

Mills offers concrete examples of how he interpreted the functions of change within the McKenzie school district (the site of his study). The focus of his chapter, however, is not on the functions of change, but on the functions of theory. He recounts how his initial ideas were often challenged by "competing theories" that emerged throughout the course of his work. Different theories offered alternative explanations of the same phenomena, frequently prodding Mills to question his interpretations and rethink earlier assumptions. Mills also borrows several ideas from Louis M. Smith, including the suggestion that theory can be approached at four levels of abstraction: (1) the data level, (2) the level of descriptive narrative, (3) the analytical-theoretical-interpretive level, and (4) the metatheoretical level. Each level of abstraction, Mills contends, opens a different perspective on understanding the functions of theory and its potential contributions to case study research.

Backing up Mills is Chapter 7 by David Flinders, who is also concerned with the functions of theory and its limitations. His aim is to examine theory within the context of educational criticism, a particular approach to qualitative inquiry. This approach is distinctive compared with other forms of case study research in that it takes its lead from the type of work that critics have done in fields such as film, literature, drama, music, and the visual arts. How are the parallels between art criticism and classroom research relevant to theory? Flin-

ders argues that the answer to this question lies in a concept
analogous to theory; that is, the kind of intellectual repertoire and
perceptual acuity that Elliot Eisner has called "educational connoisseurship."

Flinders's thesis is that the notion of connoisseurship offers a perspective from which to highlight the practical uses and limitations of
theory. He develops this thesis by example, describing a classroom
study in which he used educational criticism to examine the day-to-
day professional lives of six high school English teachers. In the context of this study, the most pressing limitations of theory center
around two aspects of qualitative fieldwork: (1) the ability to recognize unexpected patterns of meaning, and (2) the ability to assess the
educational significance of observational findings. Theory is necessary to both of these tasks, but not sufficient because any application
or adaptation of theory automatically becomes an act of imagination.

Laced with its own brand of "dogged rationality," imagination
is also a theme in Chapter 8, contributed by Louis Smith. His account is of his continuing work on a biography of Nora Barlow,
granddaughter of Charles Darwin, author of four books on the Darwin manuscripts, wife, mother of six children, and a member of England's "intellectual aristocracy." Among the problems with theory
that Smith has encountered while working on this biography, he
chooses to focus on what Virginia Woolf aptly phrased the "granite
and rainbow" dilemma. In short, the biographer's challenge is to wed
a granite-like chronicle of facts with a rainbow-like personality in
ways that will capture not just a life but the person of whom the biographer writes. Smith frames this as a problem of theory as well as a
problem of writing, and he offers specific illustrations as he thinks
(and writes) his way through the Barlow project.

Smith's account is remarkably vivid when it comes to describing
the craft-like qualities of this work. Time and again we find Smith
raising a particular example: Nora's friendship with her cousin, her
marriage, her four books on the Darwin manuscripts. And with its depiction, the search for meaning begins. Interpretations are tentatively explored (Are Nora's four books, each written a decade apart,
an example of an "abiding interest," "intellectual commitment,"
"need achievement," or what?). These ideas are tried out and tested
against other "data," connections are drawn, further questions
raised, and then the narrative moves on. At one point Smith notes:
"In a sense, I may be playing word games, but I don't believe so.
Even trying to tell interesting stories about Nora Barlow doesn't preclude the stories having a 'point' or 'moral' to them, and the point can

be a statement about her 'character' as well as other aspects of the situation." If Nora's "abiding interest" tells us something about a person's productivity or mental health, might not it have relevance for classroom teachers, curriculum theorists, and other education professionals?

The final two accounts of "theory at work" look at qualitative inquiry from two perspectives: postmodern and feminist. Ernest Stringer's Chapter 9, representing the first perspective, begins on a pragmatic note. Stringer is among the social and educational researchers who have sought to understand the difficulties experienced by Aboriginal groups as a cultural and racial minority in Australia. He notes that while explanatory theory has become increasingly sophisticated over the past three decades of research, Aboriginal people remain disempowered. Adopting a postmodern view, Stringer argues that the failure of theory and research to improve social conditions is due to the limitations and potentially oppressive applications of expert knowledge.

This chapter, however, is not simply another condemnation of empirical research. On the contrary, Stringer is interested in philosophical ideals primarily for the sake of understanding their implications for community, action-based research and development processes. His aim is to get at the nuts and bolts of an approach to inquiry that is both intellectually rigorous and responsive to desired social outcomes. To this end, Stringer interweaves the threads of postmodern theory with his own "biographic notes," which recount an assortment of development projects conducted at the Center for Aboriginal Studies in Western Australia. The roles of research and researcher are central in Stringer's specific illustrations, again stressing that postmodern views do not eschew science and inquiry, but rather enlist their contributions as a vital, if nonprescriptive, source of knowledge.

In the final chapter of Part II, Petra Munro reflects on some of the continuing dilemmas she encountered in conducting life history research with women social studies teachers. The feminist perspective that Munro brings to this research shapes her aspirations regarding both the methods and focus of her work. One of Munro's aims is to establish a collaborative and reciprocal relationship with her participants. At least initially, she sought to include them as equal partners in the research. Munro also aspires to understand the experience of her participants as women, an aim she tried to pursue not by imposing her own meanings but by allowing her participants to speak for themselves.

As these aspirations are played out, they raise some rather perplexing dilemmas. Munro illustrated this by describing her work with two of her participants: Brenda and Clio. These participants had their own ideas about research, and at times they flatly refused to enter into a collaborative relationship with Munro. Struggling with yet another dilemma, Munro worries that her own ideas may be operating as a self-fulfilling prophesy, allowing her to see only what she wants to see. Concerns of this type lead to challenging questions. Do efforts to collaborate simply mask rather than transform the unequal power between researchers and participants? Can feminist theory itself subvert the meanings that research participants give to their lives? When does the researcher's own story get in the way of the research? These are ongoing questions for Munro, instances of what she describes as the "uneasy" relationship between theory and practice.

These brief summaries of each chapter indicate the range of perspectives that readers will find in this part of the book. We have brought together eight stories of research, each different in the particulars of its setting, main characters, and plot. At the same time, all of these chapters bear a family resemblance that qualitative researchers will not find difficult to recognize. These chapters also point to common experiences regarding the uses and applications of theory. The limitations of theory, for example, tensions between competing theories, or the multiple functions of theory as it enters and exits research at different points—these are recurrent themes. If there is any overarching lesson beyond this, it may simply be to remind us that using theory in research is a human enterprise, subject to many of the same practical logistics, judgments, and struggles on which other social activities depend.

3

From Practice to Theory to Practice

The Roles of Theory in Research on Standardized Testing

SANDRA MATHISON

Theory contributes to qualitative research in multifaceted ways. In this chapter I will discuss the types and roles of theory in an ongoing research program that focuses broadly on the sociology of standardized testing. Over the last half dozen years that I have been conducting research, my interest has focused not on the technical aspects of testing but rather on the role that testing plays in schooling; its effects on teaching and curriculum; and how testing shapes the educational enterprise as a whole. My interest in this topic arose not out of careful consideration of other research, but rather stems from my personal experiences in Canada's educational system and my surprise at the amount of time and effort devoted to testing in American schools. Many Canadian schools now follow in this tradition, but they were different when I was a student. The genesis of my research interests is important, because it does not grow out of a concern for verifying someone else's theory, or a desire to test some theoretical notion, or an intention to develop an abstract theory of my own, or, especially, an interest in discovering what causal propositions might explain and predict the relationship between testing and other school issues. Often these are the espoused reasons for which we conduct research, but more accurately my interests are to understand a puzzling phenomenon and then to use that understanding to make things better. As will be clear by the end of this chapter, my interest in conducting this research is unabashedly reformist, in the realm of what Fay (1987) calls "critical social science."

My research on testing has involved a variety of studies in a variety of settings but represents a coherent program of research. I argue, by example, that theory in qualitative research plays descriptive, analytical, and prescriptive roles, but that at different points in the research process one or another of these roles takes precedence. The chapter is organized around the ideas of lay theories, social theories, and theories of action. I conclude by giving particular attention to theories of action, perhaps the most neglected of the three types.

LAY THEORIES

The first study I conducted on testing was entitled "The Perceived Effects of Standardized Testing on Teaching and Curricula" (Mathison, 1987), which illustrates my fundamental research intention—to explicate the ways in which teachers and school administrators see standardized testing in relation to other aspects of schooling. Case studies of three quite different school districts were based primarily on lengthy interviews with school personnel about what they perceived the role of testing to be in their school/district, the effects of that testing, and for whose benefit the testing was conducted. The focus of the study was on perceptions because it is these perceptions that motivate school personnel to act in certain ways in the context of testing and using information from standardized tests. Some of the findings of that first study were that many people felt tests and test scores were not useful, that testing was frequently harmful, and that testing generally served someone else's needs. Additionally, testing was related to a variety of other variables: changes in curriculum and instruction, uses of time in the school day, and relationships among teachers and administrators. This was particularly the case in high stakes testing situations (those in which important decisions are made based on test scores) but also, to some extent, in low stakes situations. I found the popularity of standardized testing to be puzzling given these perceptions.

To follow up on this initial study, I have been investigating in greater detail educators' conceptions of standardized testing, based on the assumption that there are more foundational beliefs about testing that motivate educators' actions vis-à-vis testing. In a study currently underway, high school seniors and teachers were asked whether the abolition of standardized testing would be positive or negative, and why. The question was merely a catalyst for discussion (what is called an eliciting operation intended to provide opportunities for the respondent to make contrasts), and other prompts could have been used. Naturally, the responses are multidimensional, but I will characterize them along what seems to be at least one important dimension. Based on a content analysis, there appear to be two main views of teachers that underlie the responses: (1) teachers as competent professionals and (2) teachers as potentially dangerous workers. Those who feel the abolition of standardized testing would have positive effects on schooling are more likely to see teachers as caring, competent professionals who would be liberated from unnecessary and punitive constraints on teaching. Those who feel the effects would be negative are more likely to see teachers as workers who need to be constrained and held accountable lest they neglect the interests of students by not teaching the right content or teaching it poorly.

These conceptions illustrate what I would call lay theories. They are firmly held beliefs that motivate individuals to act in certain ways, and to know what is significant, meaningful, accurate, or appropriate. (For discussion of a similar idea but in the context of teaching, see Ross, Cornett, & McCutcheon, 1992.) The empirical evidence in my research on testing thus far suggests that teachers are more likely to hold the "teachers as potentially dangerous workers" conception, thereby accounting, at least somewhat, for the intractability of testing practices. The importance of explicating these conceptions is less to ascertain the "right" conception than to understand how a particular situation is perceived by individuals.

It is accepted that individuals hold certain beliefs and attitudes, and much work in psychology has attempted to describe and explain these. Psychology, on the one hand, attempts to do so by developing abstract general laws of perception that will apply in most, if not all, situations. Phenomenological approaches, on the other hand, describe these beliefs and attitudes, but see the individual's views as part of a conceptualization that gives meaning to the surrounding world and directs how one will behave in that world. In the anthropological tradition this is referred to as the emic perspective (Harris, 1976), and in phenomenology it is attained through *verstehen* (Schutz, 1962). The intent is to obtain knowledge about social reality best characterized as

> the sum total of objects and occurrences within the social cultural world as experienced by the common-sense thinking of men [sic] living their daily lives among their fellow-men [sic], connected with them in manifold relations of interaction. It is the world of cultural objects and social institutions into which we are born, within which we have to find our bearings, and with which we have to come to terms. (Schutz, 1962, p. 53)

The view that we can and should explicate these lay theories is based on eschewing an objectivist epistemological stance, that is, that there is a social world that exists in itself, independent of our apprehension of it. If we wish to understand human action we must do so first from an inside point of view, rather than as an external observer seeing physical objects and manifestations of beliefs and attitudes.

Harris (1976) writes that

> Operationally, emic refers to the presence of an actual or potential interactive
> context in which ethnographer and informant meet and carry on a discussion
> about a particular domain. This discussion is deemed productive to the extent
> that the ethnographer discovers principles that represent and account for the
> way in which that domain is organized or structured in the mental life of
> that informant. (p. 331)

Methodologically this perspective is well explicated by Marton (1988) in
his research characterizing students' conceptions of basic physical phenomena, such as gravity or acceleration. Interviews are used to create the
interactive context to which Harris refers as a means of obtaining the
evidence upon which an analysis of student conceptions can be based.
Marton refers to this research as phenomenography, which can be characterized by its focus on

1. *Relations* — between the individual and some aspect of the world
2. *Experiences* — referring to an interest in describing how things appear to people, rather than describing them as they are
3. *Specific content* — meaning that the categories we have are categories of something and therefore must be understood within some
   particular context
4. *Qualitative understanding* — suggesting that the outcome of the
   research may be a general framework but will not be based on
   strategies of sampling or generalization in the traditional sense

Lay theories should not, however, be understood as simply the idio-
syncratic opinions of natives or social actors. These lay theories exist at
two levels, the subjective level and the intersubjective level (Schutz, 1967;
Taylor, 1982). Each individual holds certain beliefs and conceptions that
tacitly give meaning to his or her actions. At one level these beliefs belong
only to that person, and may be verified or not. However, we learn about
meaning and action in a context that is shared by others. Thus we develop
"intersubjective meanings, ways of experiencing action in society which
are expressed in the language and descriptions constitutive of institutions
and practices" (Taylor, 1982, p. 175). These intersubjective meanings are
not merely the property of an individual but are rooted in social practice,
and as such are crucial theoretical perspectives for understanding any
social phenomenon.

The explication of conceptions is a legitimate product of a qualitative
research study, and issues of validity are often premised on the native's

verification of the conceptions. Guba and Lincoln (1989) take a radical emic viewpoint and assert that member checking is the "single most crucial technique for establishing credibility" (p. 239). This is consistent with a romanticized view of the insider perspective found in the writings of many anthropologists (Harris, 1976) and educational researchers employing ethnographic techniques. The danger in this position is twofold. The first is being caught in hopeless cultural relativism; the second, in thinking that the distinction between emic and etic perspectives is an epistemological one. As discussed in the next section, this is not, in fact, the case. Theoretical notions that derive from the educational research community can also legitimately be employed in conducting qualitative research.

SOCIAL THEORIES

The persistence and growth of standardized testing in schools strike me as inconsistent with my research in which teachers, administrators, and students often see testing as a waste of time and harmful to education. Although I have discussed this issue with study participants, the results of our dialogue have not been satisfactory in explaining this contradiction. I have thus explored the value of conceptions from general social theories (the etic perspective) to understand and explain this phenomenon.

For example, I have borrowed the concept of ritual from anthropology to analyze the practice of standardized testing in schools (Mathison, 1991a). Although schooling practices are not typically thought of as rituals, McLaren (1986) convincingly uses such an analysis to describe what he called the ritual of instruction. A similar approach can be applied to the context of standardized testing. The notion of ritual seems more promising as an analytical strategy than, say, chaos theory, because prior research suggests that testing is a conserving act, one that maintains the status quo. It is not difficult to demonstrate that standardized testing is a repetitive, stylized, performative act, one that is conducted by a designated person at regular intervals and that involves the manipulation of symbols. These are all the essentials of a ritual.

Using this theoretical perspective provides insight into the nature of standardized testing that complements the emic perspective. The interviews in the perceptions study discussed earlier indicate that teachers and administrators think of tests, test scores, and the testing process symbolically, although they did not use such language. It was common for teachers to justify the anxiety and stress the tests caused among children by likening the testing process to "real life" when children would be judged under unfavorable conditions. It was also common for teachers and ad-

ministrators to accept testing as a legitimate practice because all children
were treated the same and thus presumably were being treated fairly.
These emic perspectives provide the empirical evidence with which to
conduct an analysis based on constructs from an entirely different theoretical framework. Symbols are an essential aspect of any ritual, and in the
testing ritual, the testing process, for example, comes to stand for esteemed
American values such as efficiency, equity, fairness, meritocracy, and scientific knowledge. Other symbols can be similarly analyzed.

Another example of drawing on abstract theoretical conceptions is
my analysis of the ethical assumptions underlying the use of standardized
testing as a means to control curriculum and teaching (Mathison, 1991b).
It is apparent to anyone interested in the phenomenon of standardized
testing that increasingly tests have become instruments of policy implementation, but there has been little analysis as to why this is the case.
Within a liberal democratic framework, which is characteristic of contemporary U.S. political culture, utilitarianism tends to dominate as an ethical point of view. Utilitarianism is based on the idea of maximizing happiness, the greatest good for the greatest number. Common indicators of
this happiness include gross national product, the national debt, and standardized test scores. Given this view, means–ends arguments become the
predominate logic. In the case of testing, if the end result is that test scores
go up, then the act of testing is ethically right and justified. Other ethical
frameworks, such as justice as fairness or an ethic of caring, suggest that
testing may not be the way to promote change in curriculum and teaching.

In contrast to the lay theories discussed above, the researcher can
bring to bear "phenomenal distinctions judged appropriate by the community of scientific observers" (Harris, 1976, p. 334). It is unlikely that in an
explication of emic perspectives, educators would suggest that testing is a
ritual or that underlying the uses of tests are fundamental ethical points of
view. This does not, however, make such analyses wrong or less valuable.

In much of the writing on qualitative research the etic perspective is
at worst morally indefensible and at best decidedly inferior to the emic
perspective. This viewpoint confuses the source of the etic perspective,
however. Social theories are developed by researchers — they are the conceptions that give meaning and significance to actions just as surely as
do emic perspectives. Their epistemological status is fundamentally no
different. The difference between emic and etic lies in whose categories
(the native or the researcher) are being used. Moreover, increased literacy
and access to researchers' accounts of social life have increased the likelihood of natives themselves using the researchers' categories, thus making
their perspective etic, not emic as might typically be thought. Clifford

(1986) relates a story of a Mpongwe chief interrupting an interview with an ethno-historian to consult a classic anthropological text on the meaning of a particular word, an excellent example of the confusion in the distinctions between the emic and etic.

Harris (1976) describes the operational meaning of the etic perspective as "defined by the logically nonessential status of actor–observer elicitation" and states that, in fact, these conceptualizations may "be contrary to the principles elicitable from the actors themselves with respect to the manner in which they organize their imaginations, concepts, and thoughts in the identified domain" (p. 331). Marx's notion of false consciousness should encourage us further to consider the value of the researcher's perspective. If the notion of false consciousness is understood to mean that social actors are not conscious of social relations as they are being formed, it is at least reasonable to assert that an observer of those social relations might be conscious of their nature in a perceptive way. Studies of student resistance to schooling are good examples of using social theory to understand social relations in ways that make good sense, but in ways other than those espoused by students' lay theories (MacLeod, 1987; Willis, 1977).

Just as the purpose of an explication of emic perspectives is not particularly to determine which view is right, neither is that necessarily the intent of analyses based on social theoretical constructs. It is not clear, even to me, whether the analysis of the ritual of standardized testing is merely metaphorical or standardized testing is really a ritual. Yet this distinction is less interesting than asking whether such an analysis aids in understanding the role of testing in schools, and I believe the answer to this question is yes. Similarly, the analysis of the ethical theories underlying testing for policy implementation is an opportunity to explicate what the ethical foundations are and might be for important social actions. It is, of course, necessary to decide at some point what the right thing to do is, and this will be the subject of the following section.

THEORIES OF ACTION

Having been engaged in research on standardized testing for several years, I am convinced that much harm is done by testing—harm to students, teachers, and schooling as an institutionalized social practice. This is not to say that students, teachers, and schools should not be evaluated, but rather that standardized tests are often a poor way to accomplish our assessment needs. One of the obvious ways to deal with this understanding of testing is to attempt to reform the practice. The other way would be to revolt against the practice. My research has led, thus far, to actions of the first sort.

As an example of a reform effort, I have been working with a school district in Vermont to develop alternative, more authentic forms of assessment in mathematics. Since Vermont has mandated the use of student portfolios in mathematics and writing, a natural opportunity arises for reform. Working with the mathematics curriculum committee, guidelines and procedures for student math portfolios have been developed for all teachers, as well as planning for inservice on the creation, maintenance, and use of portfolios in this subject area (Mathison, 1991c). The underlying idea in this reform effort is to replace standardized testing with a more viable and productive form of assessment.

Additionally, I have lobbied the mathematics curriculum committee to become actively involved in promoting the replacement, at least in some situations, of the Iowa Test of Basic Skills, the currently administered standardized test, with other forms of assessment and to use the student math portfolios as a model. In the face of school board pressure to test, and with the cooperation of a district administrator, the teachers have begun to develop a variety of compelling arguments for reforming testing practice — the replacement argument being one and a cost effectiveness argument being another. The support I provide to the mathematics curriculum committee consists of knowledge about testing practices and their effects, and knowledge of how these practices might strategically be altered to make life in schools better for both students and teachers.

Another similar reform effort on my part is active participation in the New York Public Interest Research Group (NYPIRG) campaign to eliminate all standardized testing of young children in New York State. NYPIRG conducts research on many public issues, including the uses of tests in schools, and lobbies the state legislature and other policy-making bodies for reform. In an effort to convince the Board of Regents and legislators of the harmfulness of certain testing practices, I have participated in letter writing campaigns and otherwise lent my name and position in this cause. The underlying assumption in these actions is that acts of persuasion will have an effect on policy-making and social practices.

Regardless of the topic of our research, we use the knowledge generated to decide what is good and right. This is never a simple matter of discovering what is good or right, but rather, as Taylor (1961) says, "We must *decide* what ought to be the case. We cannot *discover* what ought to be the case by investigating what is the case" (p. 248; emphasis in original). The criteria by which we discern the good and the right may be different depending on the method, but it is surely the intended and appropriate outcome for research. Naturalistic case studies offer opportunities for naturalistic generalizations of the sort that will aid others in making wise decisions about what ought to be done in some program area in their own social context. Experimental designs are premised on the expectation that we can discover the causal relationships within programs and decide which is the best for all. There appears to be little reason to conduct research if the consequence is not at least the potential improvement, however conceived, of quality of life for someone. Research must therefore make evaluative and prescriptive claims, and researchers do so implicitly or explicitly through the methods and discourse they use.

A theory of action motivates what researchers do with what they have learned in the research process, and there are a multitude of ways to think about this type of action (see, for example, Fullan, 1991; Watzlawick, Weakland, & Fisch, 1974). However, here I wish to take an explicitly political theory of action because I believe schools are political institutions whose practices must be critiqued in order to be reformed. A general framework is suggested by Fay (1987) in his description of a critical social science. This framework consists of four types of theories: (1) a theory of false consciousness, (2) a theory of crisis, (3) a theory of education, and (4) a theory of transformative action. Based on an "activist conception of human beings" (i.e., people are naturally intelligent, curious, reflective, and willful), he outlines each type of theory, the goals of which are to seek rational self-clarity, collective autonomy, and happiness. These goals are sought through education and empowerment.

In my research on testing, education comes hopefully through the research process as well as in the outcomes of the research — certainly to me, but also to those involved in the research. As Fay (1987) indicates, "Social theory is seen as a means by which people can achieve a clearer picture of who they are, and of what the real meaning of their social practices is, as a first step in becoming different sorts of people with different sorts of social arrangements" (p. 89). In Fay's analysis, research must

1. Be translatable into the language of experience if it is to speak to the felt needs of social actors (lay theories or emic perspectives)
2. Provide a critique of the dominant ideology that allows certain social practices
3. Demonstrate viable alternative arrangements

In the first study I conducted of educators' perceptions of the effects of testing, teachers especially had an opportunity during the interviews to think aloud about a practice that they may have taken for granted. Although this is a weak form of education, research can and does alert social actors to the meaning and meaningfulness of certain social phenomena. My current work in Vermont has been more successful in critiquing the ideology within which testing can persist, primarily because of the application of social theoretical constructs to the testing phenomenon, for example, the ritualized nature of testing. And, increased knowledge on my part has created visions of alternative social relations and evaluative structures within schools.

Empowerment is the key idea in change, however, and that means considering the role of power within schooling contexts and in particular the function of testing in power relations. Power, regardless of its form or intensity, is dyadic and depends on the self-understandings of the powerless and the powerful. Consequently, empowerment entails a change in this relationship, first through education but then through action. Primarily, testing serves the interests of administrators (Mathison, 1987), but teachers are often convinced of the necessity for using current forms of testing. Given that administrators have more power in schools, efforts to reform testing practices require that teachers, and perhaps others, must act in concert to disrupt our taken-for-granted assumptions about testing.

Fay (1987) describes a nonviolent model for political emancipation, which underlies the activities described above. Fay also discusses violent social change that occurs in those situations where power is based on coercion through violence. Although schools can be violent places, as an institution they are maintained more by obedience than by coercion. In the nonviolent model the exercise of power is based primarily on obedience, and thus a simple refusal to cooperate can have a decided effect on power relations. Essential to this model is that those with power need not admit to wrongdoing but rather are coerced themselves into doing what they do not want to do by virtue of others' unwillingness to cooperate. Acts of protest, persuasion, noncooperation, and nonviolent intervention are associated with this model. The action theories of Martin Luther King, Jesse Jackson, and Gandhi also come to mind. In the political arena these acts are manifest as marches, boycotts, strikes, sit-ins, manifestos, or the development of parallel organizations. The success of a nonviolent model of empowerment is, of course, dependent on "a genuine solidarity and strong determination among its followers" (Fay, 1987, p. 133).

In the testing example, the actions are primarily ones of persuasion and consist of campaigning, letter writing, and, perhaps most important, presenting viable alternatives. Teachers and/or administrators have not been compelled to actively engage in noncooperation by, for example, refusing to administer the tests.

THEORY IN QUALITATIVE RESEARCH

Doing qualitative research requires the consideration of a complex of theories that are interrelated and essential. These theories reflect the purposes of research, which I perceive to be description, analysis, and prescription, a view that is generally reflected in a critical social science perspective (Fay, 1987). All of these purposes are equally important and integral to the generation of knowledge for the improvement of social life. As I have outlined my research program on the sociology of testing, there is a general progression from the descriptive to the prescriptive, but the use of these theoretical perspectives is not clearly linear. There is a playing back and forth among lay theories, social theories, and theories of action.

In order to improve quality of life, one must first comprehend the self-understandings social actors hold and why. These are the lay theories described in the first section of this chapter and are related to the theory of false consciousness that Fay (1987) describes as essential to a critical social science. But there must also be analyses of how these self-understandings perpetuate oppressive or nonproductive social situations. The application of social theoretical constructs provides a means for demonstrating how the social practices inhibit the values of rational self-clarity, collective autonomy, and happiness, as well as a means for considering the consequences of alternative self-understandings.

Social improvement, however, can occur only if there is a felt need for change. The explication of lay theories and the application of social theoretical constructs may demonstrate the oppressiveness of certain beliefs, but a perceived need for change must also exist. Education in America is generally perceived to be in crisis, although the nature of this crisis is variously conceived. Testing specifically is seen as both a problem and a solution to this crisis, a schizophrenia that is demonstrated by former President Bush's advocacy for a national examination and innovative schools such at the Saturn School of Tomorrow.

The contribution of a theory of action is found in its potential to educate people about the conditions under which social actors can be enlightened about their social relationships. In the case of testing, practices are deeply entrenched, and envisioning changes is not an easy matter. However, some portion of the research community has begun to create alternative visions (National Commission on Testing and Public Policy, 1990), as have some teacher unions (New York State United Teachers, 1991), and advocacy groups such as NYPIRG and Fair Test. In much the same way as Kurt Lewin (1946) conceived of action research, change must be local, particular, and experimental. It is not, as I have argued, atheoretical.

REFERENCES

Clifford, J. (1986). On ethnographic allegory. In J. Clifford & G. E. Marcus (Eds.), *Writing culture: The poetics and politics of ethnography* (pp. 98–121). Berkeley: University of California Press.

Fay, B. (1987). *Critical social science.* Ithaca, NY: Cornell University Press.

Fullan, M. (1991). *The new meaning of educational change.* New York: Teachers College Press.

Guba, E. G., & Lincoln, Y. S. (1989). *Fourth-generation evaluation.* Newbury Park, CA: Sage.

Harris, M. (1976). History and significance of the emic/etic distinction. *Annual Review of Anthropology, 5,* 329–350.

Lewin, K. (1946). Action research and minority problems. *Journal of Social Issues, 2,* 34–46.

McLaren, P. (1986). *Schooling as a ritual performance.* London: Routledge & Kegan Paul.

MacLeod, J. (1987). *Ain't no makin' it: Leveled aspirations in a low-income neighborhood.* Boulder, CO: Westview Press.

Marton, F. (1988). Phenomenography: Exploring different conceptions of reality. In D. Fetterman (Ed.), *Qualitative approaches to evaluation in education* (pp. 176–205). New York: Praeger.

Mathison, S. (1987). *The perceived effects of standardized testing on teaching and curricula.* Unpublished doctoral dissertation, University of Illinois, Urbana.

Mathison, S. (1991a). *The ritual of standardized testing.* Unpublished manuscript, State University of New York, Albany.

Mathison, S. (1991b). Implementing curricular change through state-mandated testing: Ethical issues. *Journal of Curriculum and Supervision, 6*(3), 201–212.

Mathison, S. (1991c). *Guidelines for creating and maintaining student math portfolios* (Technical Report). Manchester, VT: Bennington Rutland Supervisory Union.

National Commission on Testing and Public Policy. (1990). *From gatekeeper to gateway: Transforming testing in America.* Chestnut Hill, MA: Author.

New York State United Teachers. (1991). *Multiple choices: Reforming student testing in New York State.* Albany: NYSUT Task Force on Student Assessment.

Ross, E. W., Cornett, J. W., & McCutcheon, G. (Eds.). (1992). *Teacher personal theorizing: Connecting curriculum practice, theory, and research.* Albany: State University of New York Press.

Schutz, A. (1962). *Collected papers, Volume I* (M. Natanson, Ed.). The Hague: Martinus Niijoff.

Schutz, A. (1967). *The phenomenology of the social world.* Evanston, IL: Northwestern University Press.

Taylor, C. (1982). Interpretation and the science of man. In E. Bredo & W.

Feinberg (Eds.), *Knowledge and values in social and educational research* (pp. 153–186). Philadelphia: Temple University Press.

Taylor, P. W. (1961). *Normative discourse.* Englewood Cliffs, NJ: Prentice-Hall.

Watzlawick, P., Weakland, J., & Fisch, R. (1974). *Change: Principles of problem formation and problem resolution.* New York: Norton.

Willis, P. (1977). *Learning to labor: How working class kids get working class jobs.* New York: Columbia University Press.

4

The Quest for Emergent Meaning

A Personal Account

STEPHEN J. THORNTON

Researchers widely acknowledge that they view the world through a particular lens (Beard, 1934; Eisner, 1991; Spindler, 1982a; Tyack, 1976/1988). Whether it is called theory, conceptual framework, explanatory model, or something else, our observations as researchers are framed in some ways rather than others, which makes perception itself theory-laden. Theory allows seeing what we would otherwise miss; it helps us anticipate and make sense of events. There is considerably less agreement, however, on just what constitutes a "theory" (Kliebard, 1982) and, of concern here, how theory ought to be used by qualitative researchers.

Qualitative researchers are also divided concerning how fieldwork should be conducted. Although the notion that fieldworkers can begin "tabula rasa" is thoroughly discredited (Phillips, 1987, p. 15), some qualitative researchers employ a highly structured approach to fieldwork and data analysis (e.g., Erickson & Mohatt, 1982; Miles & Huberman, 1990), while others rely less on preordained ways of seeing and sense-making (e.g., Barone, 1990; Wolcott, 1990). Researchers still agree, however, that meaning in qualitative research is, to some extent, emergent. That is, unlike with experimental researchers, there is considerable likelihood that qualitative researchers will "find" things they were not "looking" for in the first place. As George Spindler (1982b) put it: "Hypotheses and questions for study emerge as the study proceeds in the setting selected for observation. Judgment on what is significant to study is deferred until the orienting phase of the field study has been completed" (p. 6). For example, in their longitudinal (spanning almost two decades) study of cultural patterns in a German village, George and Louise Spindler (1987) were "surprised" that, despite the modernization of the village and "sweeping educational reform" (p. 143), the villagers actually grew "more traditional" in their outlook (p. 147).

Issues of emergent meaning and new hypotheses surfacing during a study, of course, raise significant questions about the proper conduct of fieldwork: Where do theoretical perspectives come from? How are they shaped by the subjectivity of the researcher? How do they help shape what is "found"? How are they modified by the observer's experiences in the field? In sum, how is theory actually used by qualitative researchers?

I address this last and overarching question by examining a preliminary study conducted with three beginning social studies teachers, two of whom are described below. The study illustrates how a theoretical perspective can change, and may continue to change, during fieldwork and analysis, and through retrospective analyses of the study (see also Spindler & Spindler, 1982; Wolcott, 1990). As the study proceeded, I soon realized that my original ideas were too narrow; there were meanings emerging in interviews, participant journals, and observations that were outside the scope of my study as I had initially conceived it. In particular, I grew increasingly aware that my observations were selective. Heeding Alan Peshkin's (1988) warning that "one's subjectivity is like a garment that cannot be removed" (p. 17), I attempted to ascertain exactly what was guiding my observations and interview questions. For example, what images did I have in mind of good social studies teaching and learning? What did I consider to be appropriate behavior in teacher–student exchanges? By what criteria was I appraising the curriculum's substance and its relevance to the students? By posing such questions, I hoped to complete and refine what Harry Wolcott (1990) has called "the critical sentence": "The purpose of this study is . . . " (p. 30).

THE BEGINNINGS OF A THEORETICAL FRAMEWORK

At the beginning of my project, I did, of course, have a general notion of what I wanted to study. Like all other researchers, I had to begin my investigations somewhere. The very act of entering the field presupposes that a setting has been identified and that the researcher expects that something worth studying—however vaguely defined—is going on there. Thus, as Elliot Eisner (1991) points out, inquiry is partly a normative enterprise from its very inception.

Specifically the original ideas for my study resulted from the convergence of two streams of thought. First, I wanted to pursue an ongoing line of research on social studies instruction (see, e.g., Thornton, 1988, 1992; Thornton & Wenger, 1990). In this work, I had sought to understand how teachers planned and taught, and the effects of this on their students. This is an important concern because teachers are a key determinant of the social studies experiences of their students (Shaver, Davis, & Helburn, 1980; Thornton, 1991). What teachers believe shapes the curriculum that ultimately makes a difference — the one enacted in classrooms. While there has long been criticism of the dullness and mediocrity of much social studies instruction, there has been until recently relatively little research aimed at identifying the teacher beliefs underlying it (Shaver, 1987). Rather, most research was focused on isolated parts of the problem. As Hazel Hertzberg (1985) observed:

> Concentrating on only one or two elements of the art of teaching — at present the favorite seems to be upgrading teacher's knowledge of content — is necessary but not sufficient. It is a simplistic solution to a complex problem. All the elements of the art of teaching history and, above all, their interconnections have to be addressed. (p. 39)

One possible remedy for the problems of social studies instruction is to learn from what "good" teachers believe and do. There is certainly no shortage of strictures about poor teaching, but generations of condemnation have accomplished few fundamental changes in the ways social studies is taught (Cuban, 1991). There seemed little point in further documenting where things go awry. Thus, I set out to study good teachers in the hope that their experiences might hold lessons for others.

In the last several years a few researchers have shown a growing interest in the beliefs of good teachers (e.g., Brophy, in press; Levstik, in press; Thornton, 1988, in press; Wineburg & Wilson, 1991). Although there have been a number of studies of beginning social studies teachers' beliefs (e.g., Bennett & Spalding, 1992; Goodman & Adler, 1985; Johnston, 1990; Ross, 1987; Wilson & Wineburg, 1988), their primary focus was not on individuals who showed particular promise early in their careers. Therefore, I decided to study beginning teachers from their first experiences as education professionals. Specifically, I started with their first term of graduate education courses. This would mark their formal entry to the study and practice of teaching. What were these preservice teachers' beliefs? How would these beliefs eventually be conveyed to their students? How would these beliefs change under the impress of the daily grind of classrooms? How would these novice teachers be changed by their classroom encounters?

The preservice teachers with whom I worked seemed a promising group to study. From a practical standpoint, access to them and their beliefs could be relatively easily arranged. I began with six volunteers, but time constraints soon forced me to scale back to three if depth was not to be sacrificed. More important than the number studied, however, the beginning teachers with whom I worked seemed anything but dull and uncritical. On the contrary, they were eager to make a difference in the classroom. They had gained admission to a highly selective program, and were idealistic, academically talented, and creative. Perhaps most important, they voiced a powerful, implicit message for their own students: "Education can make a difference in your lives." In other words, they approached what Philip Jackson (1986) calls a "transformative" view of teaching. As one of them put it, "[I want to ask] students to relate their own experiences . . . connect their own lives to their schoolwork." They did not just want to transmit information; they wanted their students to see the world in new ways, to recognize that they could act on the world, not merely be acted on by it.

This was the rationale for my investigation of good social studies teaching. As I mentioned above, however, a second concern also motivated this study: the narrow conceptions of teaching and teachers evident in the literature. Teachers have often been studied as if their lives inside the classroom were hardly affected by their lives outside it. The publicly visible teacher and his or her privately held beliefs, motivations, satisfactions, and expectations have too often been studied separately. The possibilities inherent in the teaching profession for intrinsic satisfactions and the integration of one's personal values and public career are precisely why many talented people enter the profession (Boston Women's Teachers' Group, 1983; Noddings, 1987, 1990; Zumwalt, 1988). Thus, separating the public and the private distorts our view of both teaching and teachers.

Teachers bring to the classroom more than pedagogical skills (Flinders, 1989; Jersild, 1955; Lightfoot, 1983; Noddings, 1990). Speaking even more broadly, Dewey (1916/1966) condemned a "double standard of reality" (p. 177) between the private and public. In his view, teacher beliefs must be situated in the context of their lives. We cannot explain, as Nel Noddings (1987) has shown, why bright, dedicated young teachers want "to make a difference" with one-dimensional explanations. Rather, we need to explore their motivations and expectations in all their richness. As feminist scholars (e.g., Noddings, 1990; Witherell & Noddings, 1991) have underscored, teaching is a complex interplay of teachers' private lives and the public forums in which they teach. For all its public character, teaching remains a deeply personal undertaking. The personal shapes why people come to teaching, what they do in teaching, and why they stay in teaching (Stark, 1991; Zumwalt, 1988).

In sum, I began this study with two separate but interrelated concerns serving as a theoretical framework. The first theoretical concern was the beliefs of "good" beginning teachers. The second theoretical concern was to understand how their personal lives and their public behaviors were interrelated. Both my reading of the research literature and my previous research studies testified to the importance of these two concerns for making sense of teachers and teaching. I knew from research on beginning teachers that survival concerns often dominate one's early teaching (e.g., Nemser, 1983; Ryan, 1970), muting both the idealism and dimensions with which I was concerned. Would these teachers be different, however, starting out under what might be viewed as the best conditions to be expected?

I suspected so, but my focus required "getting inside teachers' heads." Through a combination of their journals, multiple formal and informal interviews, analysis of their instructional plans and materials, and classroom observations, I believed that over a nine-month period I would be able to secure some valuable insights into the concerns I had raised.

CASE STUDIES

I now turn to two brief case studies of participants whom I shall call Lorraine and Paul. These, as the reader will well recognize, are not full-blown studies, but rather preliminary sketches to provide a sense of context within which to discuss the study as a whole. While my aim is not to report this study, it is nevertheless important for qualitative researchers to provide sufficient evidence so that a reader has enough information to assess the credibility of the researcher's interpretations.

Lorraine

Lorraine believed that "learning social studies opens up the world" and that by "examining the history, economics, and politics of other cultures, we can learn more about ourselves and perhaps learn a little more tolerance, or at least respect for one another." Her hope was to use stories, skits, art, music, film, and novels to "bring social studies alive" and "show students that their problems in today's world have happened before."

Meaningful learning, Lorraine argued, is impossible without free expression. She said that she would feel no compunction abut sharing her strong personal beliefs about social and political issues as long as there was an atmosphere of free exchange. Lorraine thought it feasible to reveal her beliefs without imposing them on her students. The difference between sharing beliefs and indoctrination, she said, lay in making sure that those who disagree are respected. Education ends when students cannot express their points of view. With these caveats in mind, she had no qualms about arranging the curriculum to include issues important to her, such as "peace, social justice, [and] respect for other people and their ideas."

It had been 15 years since Lorraine had graduated from high school and her first few classroom observations shocked her: "The most blatant thing I observed — and this is even in a predominantly white, middle class, suburban high school [near New York City] — was a general lack of respect. Students ignored teachers' requests for quiet, were unprepared, were disruptive, didn't care that a visitor was in the room."

Nevertheless, Lorraine was "energized by watching good teachers" and saw "possibilities and alternatives" when watching not-so-good teachers. She reacted especially strongly to a teacher who did not seem to give students credit for being able to figure out complex situations. With evident frustration, Lorraine declared: "I don't think it is beyond even ninth graders' abilities to present them with [fine distinctions]."

When she began student teaching, Lorraine tried to put some of her ideas into action. For example, on being assigned to duties in a "structured" study hall, she thought she could use the opportunity to develop more personal relationships with students: "I've managed to have conversations with them about music and sports. I'm working my way around to history to see if I can't fool them into conversing about the history of some of their hobbies."

In her regularly assigned tenth-grade global studies classroom, Lorraine was given the opportunity to teach a unit on conflict and change in the Soviet Union and eastern Europe. This was a ready opportunity for Lorraine to include subjects on which she had strong personal beliefs. She divided the class into research groups, and each group was assigned the task of investigating a challenge to Soviet authority in eastern Europe during the Cold War, such as the Hungarian uprising of 1956 and the more recent Polish Solidarity movement. Consistent with her aims, Lorraine worked hard to present multiple viewpoints and encouraged the students to take on the roles of the group they were researching. She also tried to counter the oversimplistic belief that associates everything good and reasonable in the Cold War with the West and everything evil and unreasonable with the Soviet Union. She worked hard to show that there were rational and historical reasons for Soviet behavior.

After several days' preparation, the day arrived for the student presentations. Lorraine's expectations were low; she usually was her own harshest critic. She felt sure that she "had not given them enough information to work with . . . and positive . . . all the oral presentations would be just lousy." To Lorraine's surprise most of the presentations were lively and informed. The students often "got inside" their roles, the "Soviets," for example, complaining that the "Hungarians" were ungrateful for the millions of Soviet dead spent in "liberating" eastern Europe from the Nazis. A few students who had complained about the difficulty of the assignment made the best presentations. Several students went to sources beyond what Lorraine had given them.

Lorraine's personal beliefs were even more evident when she dealt with a topic that drew directly on her own experience. She had been to Central America twice and was eager to share what she had seen and learned. It is most important, she believed, that students "understand that these places are different in many ways from the way we live our lives but in many ways we're [all] people, very often [with] the same worries and concerns."

Several months into her student teaching assignment, Lorraine was invited by a ninth-grade global studies teacher to give a slide presentation on Central America in his class. Lorraine described some of the problems that Central America has experienced, such as earthquakes, recurrent U.S. interventions, corrupt leaders propped up by the United States, and poor health care. She mentioned Nicaraguan war widows who had warned her that the United States should not fight in the Persian Gulf, "otherwise your husbands will be coming back in plastic bags like ours did." Throughout her presentation, she spoke clearly and with passion. She had a keen eye for comparisons and contrasts that would make sense to ninth graders, including the state of the roads, sanitation, and housing in Central America versus suburban New York. The students appeared interested and attentive throughout.

Although Lorraine's presentation on Central America was forceful, she provided a sufficiently rich description so that students would be able to draw their own conclusions on matters such as U.S. policy in the region. After she had finished her student teaching assignment, I asked her: "Why didn't you just come out and say [what you really think] that U.S. policy in Latin America has for a long time been misguided if not morally wrong?" "I think I implied it," she answered. She added, however, that she worried about being too explicit and that the possibility of "dictating in a power position" made her "nervous." Care must be exercised because "kids will buy it!" A teacher should "stroke their interest" and get students to "reach their own conclusions." Overall, while Lorraine often felt preoccupied with surviving the day, it was never to the "extent that it prevented [her] from covering things [she] felt important."

Paul

The personal beliefs that Paul brought to teaching were well thought through but less focused on controversy than those of Lorraine. Paul's three main reasons for wanting to teach were, first, a desire to teach students "the basic knowledge of social organizations and cultures at home and abroad so they will have a sense that today's world is a global village." Second, he wanted students to meet the "demands of citizenship" by learning the "ability to think critically about modern life and the effects of the past," as well as to "think analytically and communicate their opinions effectively." Finally, he simply found history and the social sciences intrinsically interesting.

Paul's announced aims in the fall did not seem particularly evident when I observed his teaching in the spring. For example, he had written in one of his earliest journals, long before he had even observed in the classroom, of his great interest in "material culture studies." In detail he explained this as the "study through artifacts of the beliefs — values, ideas, attitudes, and assumptions — of a particular community or society at a given time." Paul felt that material culture studies could be a corrective to the "orientation of social studies [which] has not only been toward the European white male, but also toward literate testaments." Although Paul never said specifically that he would use material culture studies in his own teaching, it seemed plain that he would like to. After his first few journals in the fall, however, he never again raised the topic.

Inevitably, opportunities for Paul to share his personal beliefs arose during his student teaching at a public junior high school in New York City. More so than with Lorraine, Paul's opportunities for sharing his personal beliefs originated with the students. For example, early on the morning of Ash Wednesday Paul had attended a church service. By the time he arrived at school he had forgotten about the smudge of ashes on his forehead. Some of the students recognized the significance of the ashes but most did not. Paul explained that the ashes were from palm leaves, not from a cigarette butt. He further explained that he was an Episcopalian, but "did not feel it proper to go into further explanations because I thought it might introduce an improper degree of religion into the classroom." Paul did not appear to question this conclusion and summed up his thoughts on the episode with characteristic humor and resilience: "I did learn that you have to explain Ash Wednesday repeatedly in the course of the school day and that a late-afternoon [church service] might be more practical than an early-morning service."

When Paul more deliberately set out to share his personal beliefs, he was not always successful. This was partly because of his inexperience in the classroom. No doubt it also reflected the almost antithetical backgrounds of Paul and his students. They were nearly all from underprivileged, urban backgrounds and of Latino and African-American heritages, while Paul's background was rural, Ivy League, white, and middle class. Understandably, a period of adjustment transpired on both sides. As Paul noted early in his student teaching experience, he found himself "two steps behind the students on almost every occasion." Similarly, the vehemence with which students insulted each other stunned him at first and prevented him from addressing problem situations as effectively as he would have liked: "Part of it is my amazement at what I am hearing; part of it is a disinclination to confrontation." Often Paul would move to "cool the situation down but took no decisive action on the spot with regard to [the] personal invective." Disappointment with being "behind" the students continued to haunt Paul: "The overwhelming feeling of frustration that I have comes from the fact that I am always reacting to [situations of] this kind. This makes it difficult to pick out parts of myself that I am sharing with kids. Often they exercise an indirect control of the agenda."

As already noted, Paul was less inclined than Lorraine to arrange the curriculum to address his personal beliefs. He sometimes found, however, that students' reactions to subject matter provoked a reaction in him that probably made his personal beliefs evident. For instance, a unit on the Civil War included a debate over the right of the South to secede from the Union. Many students sided with the South. Paul was surprised that it was mostly African-American students who defended the right of the slave-holding South to secede. The students had less sympathy for Lincoln's constitutional duty to hold the Union together and the southerners' obligation to abide by the Constitution.

Thus, Paul found himself trying to persuade the youngsters that there was reciprocity between citizens having rights and having responsibilities — as both citizens of a nation and members of this class: "They pick up much faster on rights, much faster than responsibilities." Paul also recalled in this regard that one student had asked to bring a sleeping bag to school for occasions when fellow students were making presentations. Although presumably the student was speaking at least partly tongue-in-cheek, in response Paul tried to emphasize that as students in the school they had a "responsibility to tune in." He suspected that this made his personal beliefs evident: "They can probably detect that I'm frustrated with their lack of understanding of . . . responsibility. In that way, they see what I value more."

WHAT BECAME OF THEORY IN THE FIELD?

As we have seen, before their student teaching experiences began, my participants expressed idealistic hopes, albeit with some trepidation about how all this would work in real classrooms with real adolescents. Although I tended to downplay their trepidations, they were not unwarranted, as it turned out. Virtually from the moment their classroom experiences began, their concerns about the practicability of their hopes emerged with cogent force and urgency in cases such as Paul's concern about the lack of civility his students exhibited toward one another.

The primacy of "survival" concerns, often documented in the literature on beginning teachers (e.g., Nemser, 1983; Ryan, 1970), was a stronger influence on the participants than my implicit theories or ideas of good teaching had led me to suspect. The participants wondered: Is it possible to teach as I want in today's public schools? They also often confessed that they found themselves unable to implement some of their best ideas. Their frustrations, most of all, boiled down to the feelings that their own voices were too often lost in classroom encounters.

As I have suggested, I had anticipated that the participants would encounter frustrations in their initial classroom experiences, but I had underestimated the intensity of these frustrations. I had been confident that the obvious talent these beginning teachers brought to their work would overcome the worst problems of classroom survival. Whereas Frances Bolin's (1988) study of "Lou" revealed that he construed teaching as primarily action devoid of reflection, the participants in my study viewed teaching as a reflective and interactive enterprise. These were people not merely interested in keeping order and adhering to the teacher's guide. Thus, I had felt some assurance that I could simply screen out what seemed irrelevant to my purposes: their learning to teach. After all, learning to teach was not a central focus in this study.

More specifically, what I had not anticipated was the degree to which the participants' concerns with classroom survival would make it difficult to study other factors. Yet, it appeared possible that their concerns with survival could alter their prior conceptions of their role as teachers. In other words, the initial theoretical guides I had employed were obscuring parts of what was going on. The participants were, for the time being at least, often more interested in getting through the next lesson with their classes than in reflecting on what they had shared of themselves. One sign of their priorities was that their previous almost exemplary punctuality with their journals stopped. Instead, there were constant apologies about lack of time and energy to write. As Lorraine put it in her final journal near the end of her three months in the classroom: "I know I have been horribly delinquent in keeping up with this journal for you — My only excuse is that I have been *very* busy — completely underestimating how exhausting teaching is." And, perhaps most revealing of all, the content of the journals took on an immediacy most concerned with day-to-day classroom and planning concerns they encountered.

As Wolcott's (1990) earlier-quoted aphorism about a study's "critical sentence" suggests, the focus of my study had changed — whether I liked it or not. Although obviously the participants were still sharing their personal selves with their students, it was often a sharing of "let's get through the day" rather than their more transformative views. I finally realized that these were not just case studies of what promising teachers share of themselves; they were also studies of how beginning teachers get to a point where they can be sufficiently proficient and comfortable in the classroom so that they *can* share what they wish of themselves.

IMPLICATIONS OF THE USE OF THEORY

I began this study with two theoretical foci: (1) what could be learned from good teachers and (2) what these teachers shared of themselves with their students. Both brought into focus important facets of teaching. My first focus on the participants' qualities of perseverance, dedication, and academic talent helped predict the direction of their development as teachers—they were slowly learning not only how to teach but also how to learn from teaching. There was ample evidence for the utility of the second focus too, such as Lorraine sharing her beliefs on Central America and Paul on reciprocity between rights and responsibilities. Perhaps more significant, however, it seemed that the participants' growing proficiency as teachers made possible greater sharing of themselves. If teachers are to be transformative, they must also be proficient in their classroom craft.

Despite the utility of my initial theoretical framework, it proved to be too narrow and was applied prematurely. Most particularly, my framework needed broadening to include the teachers' novice status. Further, it is entirely possible that additional frameworks would capture meanings I have neglected. For example, I suspect that a cultural analysis of Paul's interactions with his students would yield fresh insights.

As Spindler and Spindler (1982) have shown with their study of "Roger Harker," the application of additional theoretical perspectives to even decades old data can yield fresh insights and meanings.

> The translation of Roger Harker has changed over three decades. . . . In 1952–1960 I saw personality factors as more important. . . . Since about 1958 . . . what loomed as more and more important—though it had been there from the start—was the selectivity with which Harker's culture . . . was projected into his interactions. (p. 28)

This changing translation or theoretical frame enriches the initial analysis; it does not discredit it. Moreover, as the Spindlers observe, the data for the newer translation were always there, but a shifting theoretical perspective made them "loom" larger.

The shifting theoretical framework the Spindlers describe is not unusual, although writers of educational research textbooks seldom dwell on it. Consider, for example, dissertation work or funded projects that call for reports by a particular date. At some point the dissertation has to be signed off and filed or the report submitted to the funding agency. Does this end the study?

Perhaps it does in a formal sense, but we continue informally talking about it with friends and colleagues. Or we might decide to write up the findings for a particular journal, retelling the research for a particular audience. What is striking about these and related processes is that with each retelling of the research the story changes. Different ideas receive different emphases, and different interpretations take on new importance in the light of changing times and policy concerns. For instance, how might Peshkin (1991) reinterpret his study of ethnicity in "Riverview," California, in the light of 1992 upheavals in Los Angeles? It surely makes a difference whether one read Peshkin's account before or after the Los Angeles riots. In trying out different ways of recounting what a study was about, we gain new insights into what it means.

So what have we learned about the role of theory in qualitative research? Our theoretical perspectives on the meaning of research reports are constantly in flux. During the conduct of my study, my ideas broadened, informed by the immediacy of the information I was gathering. But the story does not end there. The retelling and reinterpretation of the research has and will continue into the future. Far from an aberration or an embarrassment, researchers would be more honest and true to the spirit of inquiry if they were to celebrate that the quest for emergent meaning is perennial.

REFERENCES

Barone, T. E. (1990). Using the narrative text as an occasion for conspiracy. In E. W. Eisner & A. Peshkin (Eds.), *Qualitative inquiry in education: The continuing debate* (pp. 305–326). New York: Teachers College Press.

Beard, C. A. (1934). *The nature of the social sciences in relation to objectives of instruction*. New York: Scribner's.

Bennett, C., & Spalding, E. (1992). Teaching the social studies: Multiple approaches for multiple perspectives. *Theory and Research in Social Education, 20,* 263–292.

Bolin, F. S. (1988). Helping student teachers think about teaching. *Journal of Teacher Education, 39,* 48–54.

Boston Women's Teachers' Group (Freedman, S., Jackson, J., & Boles, K.). (1983). Teaching: An imperilled "profession." In L. S. Shulman & G. Sykes (Eds.), *Handbook of teaching and policy* (pp. 261–299). New York: Longman.

Brophy, J. (in press). Mary Lake: Introducing fifth graders to American history. In J. Brophy (Ed.), *Advances in research on teaching* (Vol. 4). Greenwich, CT: JAI Press.

Cuban, L. (1991). History of teaching in social studies. In J. P. Shaver (Ed.), *Handbook of research on social studies teaching and learning* (pp. 197–209). New York: Macmillan.

Dewey, J. (1966). *Democracy and education*. New York: Free Press. (Original work published 1916).

Eisner, E. W. (1991). *The enlightened eye: Qualitative inquiry and the enhancement of educational practice*. New York: Macmillan.

Erickson, F., & Mohatt, G. (1982). Cultural organization and participation structures in two classrooms of Indian students. In G. Spindler (Ed.), *Doing the ethnography of schooling* (pp. 132–174). New York: Holt, Rinehart & Winston.

Flinders, D. J. (1989). *Voices from the classroom*. Eugene, OR: ERIC Clearinghouse on Educational Management.

Goodman, J., & Adler, S. (1985). Becoming an elementary social studies teacher: A study of perspectives. *Theory and Research in Social Education, 13*(2), 1–20.

Hertzberg, H. W. (1985). Students, methods, and materials of instruction. In M. T. Downey (Ed.), *History in the schools* (pp. 25–40). Washington, DC: National Council for the Social Studies.

Jackson, P. W. (1986). *The practice of teaching*. New York: Teachers College Press.

Jersild, A. T. (1955). *When teachers face themselves*. New York: Bureau of Publications, Teachers College, Columbia University.

Johnston, M. (1990). Teachers' backgrounds and beliefs: Influences on learning to teach the social studies. *Theory and Research in Social Education, 18*, 207–233.

Kliebard, H. M. (1982). Curriculum theory as metaphor. *Theory into Practice, 21*, 11–17.

Levstik, L. S. (in press). Building a sense of history in a first grade class. In J. Brophy (Ed.), *Advances in research on teaching* (Vol. 4). Greenwich, CT: JAI Press.

Lightfoot, S. L. (1983). The lives of teachers. In L. S. Shulman & G. Sykes (Eds.), *Handbook of teaching and policy* (pp. 241–260). New York: Longman.

Miles, M. B., & Huberman, A. M. (1990). Animadversions and reflections on the uses of qualitative inquiry. In E. W. Eisner & A. Peshkin (Eds.), *Qualitative inquiry in education: The continuing debate* (pp. 339–357). New York: Teachers College Press.

Nemser, S. F. (1983). Learning to teach. In L. S. Shulman & G. Sykes (Eds.), *Handbook of teaching and policy* (pp. 150–170). New York: Longman.

Noddings, N. (1987). *The school environment*. Unpublished manuscript, Stanford University.

Noddings, N. (1990). Feminist critiques in the professions. In C. B. Cazden (Ed.), *Review of research in education, 16* (pp. 393–424). Washington, DC: American Educational Research Association.

Peshkin, A. (1988). In search of subjectivity — One's own. *Educational Researcher*, *17*(7), 17–21.

Peshkin, A. (1991). *The color of strangers, the color of friends*. Chicago: University of Chicago Press.

Phillips, D. C. (1987). Validity in qualitative research: Why the worry about warrant will not wane. *Education and Urban Society*, *20*, 9–24.

Ross, E. W. (1987). Teacher perspective development: A study of preservice social studies teachers. *Theory and Research in Social Education*, *15*, 225–243.

Ryan, K. (Ed.). (1970). *Don't smile until Christmas: Accounts of the first year of teaching*. Chicago: University of Chicago Press.

Shaver, J. P. (1987). Implications from research: What should be taught in social studies? In V. Richardson-Koehler (Ed.), *Educators' handbook: A research perspective* (pp. 112–138). New York: Longman.

Shaver, J. P., Davis, O. L., Jr., & Helburn, S. W. (1980). An interpretive report on the status of precollege social studies education based on three NSF-funded studies. In *What are the needs in precollege science, mathematics, and social science education? Views from the field*. Washington, DC: Government Printing Office.

Spindler, G. (1982a). Concluding remarks. In G. Spindler (Ed.), *Doing the ethnography of schooling* (pp. 489–496). New York: Holt, Rinehart & Winston.

Spindler, G. (1982b). General introduction. In G. Spindler (Ed.), *Doing the ethnography of schooling* (pp. 1–11). New York: Holt, Rinehart & Winston.

Spindler, G., & Spindler, L. (1982). Roger Harker and Schönhausen: From the familiar to the strange and back again. In G. Spindler (Ed.), *Doing the ethnography of schooling* (pp. 20–43). New York: Holt, Rinehart & Winston.

Spindler, G., & Spindler, L. (1987). Schönhausen revisited and the rediscovery of culture. In G. Spindler & L. Spindler (Eds.), *Interpretive ethnography of education* (pp. 143–167). Hillsdale, NJ: Erlbaum.

Stark, S. (1991). Toward an understanding of the beginning-teacher experience: Curricular insights for teacher education. *Journal of Curriculum and Supervision*, *6*, 294–311.

Thornton, S. J. (1988). Curriculum consonance in United States history classrooms. *Journal of Curriculum and Supervision*, *3*, 308–320.

Thornton, S. J. (1991). Teacher as curricular-instructional gatekeeper in social studies. In J. P. Shaver (Ed.), *Handbook of research on social studies teaching and learning* (pp. 237–248). New York: Macmillan.

Thornton, S. J. (1992). How do elementary teachers decide what to teach in social studies? In E. W. Ross, J. W. Cornett, & G. McCutcheon (Eds.), *Teacher personal theorizing: Issues, problems and implications* (pp. 83–95). Albany: State University of New York Press.

Thornton, S. J. (in press). Towards the desirable in social studies teaching. In J. Brophy (Ed.), *Advances in research on teaching* (Vol. 4). Greenwich, CT: JAI Press.

Thornton, S. J., & Wenger, R. N. (1990). Geography curriculum and instruction in three fourth-grade classrooms. *Elementary School Journal*, *90*, 515–531.

Tyack, D. B. (1988). Ways of seeing: An essay on the history of compulsory schooling. In R. M. Jaeger (Ed.), *Complementary methods for research in education* (pp. 24–58). Washington, DC: American Educational Research Association. (Original published 1976)

Wilson, S. M., & Wineburg, S. S. (1988). Peering at history through different lenses: The role of disciplinary perspectives in teaching history. *Teachers College Record, 89,* 525–539.

Wineburg, S. S., & Wilson, S. M. (1991). Subject-matter knowledge in the teaching of history. In J. Brophy (Ed.), *Advances in research on teaching* (Vol. 2; pp. 305–347). Greenwich, CT: JAI Press.

Witherell, C., & Noddings, N. (Eds.). (1991). *Stories lives tell: Narrative and dialogue in education.* New York: Teachers College Press.

Wolcott, H. F. (1990). *Writing up qualitative research.* Newbury Park, CA: Sage.

Zumwalt, K. K. (1988). Are we improving or undermining teaching? In L. N. Tanner (Ed.), *Critical issues in curriculum* (pp. 148–174). Chicago: University of Chicago Press.

5

Theory as Research Guide

A Qualitative Look at Qualitative Inquiry

JOYCE L. HENSTRAND

In winter of 1988 I began the search that doctoral students dread: finding an interesting, yet workable, research project for my dissertation. After trying out several small pilot projects, I decided that my personality preferences and intellectual skills lay in the general area of qualitative inquiry. Although I was confident I had made the right decision, the next steps were far more difficult. Would I follow what Haller (1979) has cited as the national trend for education administration doctoral students and use a questionnaire to measure attitudes and opinions related to a specific administration-related topic? Or, would I follow the example of most of my fellow doctoral students and use some combination of interviews and questionnaires to answer some preconceived questions?

I was comfortable with neither of these choices because they seemed suspended somewhere between qualitative and quantitative research. On the one hand, I lacked both the interest and the resources to conduct a large questionnaire study. On the other hand, conducting a limited number of two-hour interviews did not take me far enough into what I regarded as the heart of qualitative work—the opportunity to know a few people or a social system really well. I was interested in exploring the full complexity of a situation and placing it in the broader context of education (Wolcott, 1988). Ultimately, I decided against the first two options in favor of a third. I decided to write a descriptive case study of attempts at planned change in a suburban high school (Henstrand, 1991). Choosing to gather data through ethnographic research strategies, I returned to my teaching position at a comprehensive high school and engaged in active participant observation for one year.

That decision led to yet another question. What theory or combination of sociological and/or anthropological concepts would guide my gathering of data and analysis? Although I was a relative newcomer to sociology and anthropology, my status as a first-generation American living in multicultural neighborhoods, combined with my experiences teaching literature, made me sensitive to the idea that our thoughts and actions are determined in part by preconceived frameworks. I was particularly concerned about the biases inherent in my research role. So, I began my search for theory. My first encounter with anthropological theory was in a class taught by Harry Wolcott at the University of Oregon. Called Culture Theory, the seminar focused on the major anthropological theories that have been popular in the past 100 years. My work in that class resulted in a paper that explored the appropriateness of using various theories in educational research.

Once I began this exploration, I found what seemed like multitudes of theories or models from which I could choose. Often confused and sometimes impatient with what Philip Salzman (1988) calls "the demidecadal trade-in of models" (p. 32), I realized that no one theory or model would be satisfactory for my study. I thus considered abandoning my search. David Kaplan and Robert Manners (1986), however, claim, "To have some theoretical knowledge is better than to have none. A partial explanation is better than no explanation at all" (p. 90). They reason that when knowledge is organized according to a theory, there is a "potential for growth and development" (p. 11). Similarly, Robert Bogdan and Sari Biklen (1982) state, "Theory helps data cohere and enables the research to go beyond an aimless, unsystematic piling up of accounts" (p. 30). For these reasons, I decided not to ignore theory. Indeed, I continued to search for appropriate theoretical models.

This chapter, then, is a description of how I pieced together the theoretical models I eventually used as a framework for gathering data and writing my analysis. The first section is an exploration of major theories, my assumptions regarding their possible application, and a synthesis of the ideas I planned to use. Much of it was written before I went into the field and was then revised in the early months of fieldwork. It provides a record of my early thinking about major theories and models, and how I would use them in a study of organizational change. The second section discusses how theory helped and hindered my progress in the study. I look at the usefulness of each of the ideas and at my own ability to use them. I also reveal what went as planned and what surprised me as my work developed.

FINDING A THEORY

What, then, were the theoretical approaches that guided my early thinking about school change? I have grouped these approaches into four categories: (1) structural-functional theories, (2) structural analysis, (3) cognitive anthropology, and (4) interpretive anthropology.

Structural and Functional Theories

Structural-functional theories have largely dominated social research in the twentieth century. They trace their origins to Emile Durkheim, who took society as the unit of analysis. Durkheim explained elements of society (e.g., roles, social events, and customs) in terms of the purpose or function they serve and how they contribute to society at large (Hansen, 1970). This functional approach assumes that social systems are "highly integrated" (Abrahamson, 1978, p. 6) and tend to resist change. Because all the system parts are integrated, change that occurs in one part of the system has an impact on other parts. To endure, customs and practices in this context must make a vital contribution that functionalists believe can be understood only by "theoretically sophisticated observers." One task of such observers is to differentiate between the function as stated by the natives and the function "inferred from the comparative analysis of [the] ceremonies" (p. 17).

Although all structural-functionalists tend to share the same general perspective, Abrahamson (1978) notes that subtle differences exist among the ways individual anthropologists and sociologists have interpreted and used functionalism. Durkheim's (1961b) brand of functionalism focused on society as the unit of analysis in social research. He visualized society as having both a body and soul. The soul is represented by "the composition of collective ideals" (p. 1310). Individuals alone cannot construct the ideals of a society; instead, "society forces the individual to transcend himself and to participate in a higher form of life" (p. 1309). An example of this viewpoint is Durkheim's (1961a, 1961c) analysis of suicide. He depicted it not in terms of individual life stories but as general types that exist in a society. In one type of suicide, anomic suicide, a person finds him- or herself in a state of anomic when society, in a crisis such as a major change of moral values, leaves the individual without a force to regulate his or her passions. For Durkheim, then, the societal forces that create the potential for suicide are more important than individual cases.

Radcliffe-Brown's brand of structural-functionalism contrasted with Durkheim's in that he looked at how certain mechanisms in society served to "connect individuals into an integrated whole" (Abrahamson, 1978, p. 29). For Radcliffe-Brown (1987), people exist simultaneously as separate biological beings and as part of the whole social structure. He believed that the best way to find out about a social structure is to observe directly the actions of individual human beings and their "complex network of social relations" (p. 122). Further, he argued that social structures are constantly being renewed from within by the actions of individuals, but "even in the most revolutionary changes some continuity of structure is maintained" (p. 125). Rather than ask how systems change, Radcliffe-Brown asked, How do they persist? When Radcliffe-Brown discussed change, however, he did so in terms of the structure of a whole social system rather than of the individual.

Theoretically aligned with sociologist Max Weber rather than Emile Durkheim, anthropologist Bronislaw Malinowski (1987) interpreted the functions of various social phenomena based on the needs of individuals, not on the whole social system. He insisted that individuals be considered a "biological reality" and become the unit of analysis. He also studied the culture of social groups as part of change because "individuals never cope with, or move within, their environments in isolation, but in organized groups" (p. 116). Culture, Malinowski argued, is a "vast instrument reality . . . which allow[s] man to satisfy his biological requirements through cooperation and within an environment refashioned and readjusted" (p. 119). Ultimately to understand individuals, the researcher must also understand how the culture of the individuals' society molds and conditions them (Malinowski, 1961; cited in Kaplan & Manners, 1986).

Although structural-functional theories have dominated twentieth-century social research, their weaknesses have been described by many anthropologists. Roger Keesing (1981) claimed that in "stressing how the system fits together [and] how elements are functionally interconnected, one is prone to depict 'the system' as in timeless equilibrium. . . . [This impedes] our view of the structure of ideational systems" (p. 353). I. C. Jarvie (1968) echoed this concern, arguing that functionalism is limited because its explanations are capable only of explaining unchanging systems. Jarvie also stated that despite this limitation, functionalism has heuristic merits in its emphasis on the "unintended consequences of action and its assumptions that social systems are rational" (p. 200).

Because my concern was to examine the process of planned change in a suburban high school, I viewed the tendency of functional analysis to stress continuity as one of its limitations. If the social system of the high school proved to be resistant to change, however, the theoretical assumptions of functional analysis promised to be useful in determining the sources of stability in the school's system. For example, an examination of the hierarchical structure of the organization could raise questions about the role of official and unofficial power, such as, What roles will teachers play in institutionalizing or rejecting structural changes mandated by the principal? In this context, functionalism could contribute to my analysis, but it would not account for the variety of individual reactions among teachers.

Structural Analysis

Claude Levi-Strauss's structural analysis promised additional insights. According to Levi-Strauss (1963), "the object of social-structure studies is to understand social relations with the aid of models" (p. 289). A model must (1) "exhibit the characteristics of a system," (2) be able to be reproduced, and (3) be predictable in terms of "how it will react if one or more of its elements are submitted to certain modifications" (p. 289).

Levi-Strauss differentiated his own brand of structural analysis from the structuralism of Radcliffe-Brown, who emphasized the role of components that stabilize a social system. Levi-Strauss praised Radcliffe-Brown as "an incomparable observer, analyst, and classifier" but criticized him for being "disappointing when he turned to interpretations" (p. 304). Levi-Strauss's (1963) structural analysis, in his own words, "has nothing to do with empirical reality but with models" (p. 279).

H. Applebaum (1987) explains that the interpretation emerging from Levi-Strauss's use of models is that there is a "dialectical relationship between human beings and their natural environment" (p. 401). Drawing on linguistic analysis as his inspiration, Levi-Strauss (1963) argued that "the unconscious activity of the mind consists in imposing forms upon content" (p. 21). A person's reality is thus dependent on the perception of the mind. Since all minds, "ancient and modern, primitive and civilized," are the same, it is possible to grasp universal meanings by examining and analyzing individual institutions and customs. Each case may be different, but universal types can be found. Levi-Strauss argued that by understanding the universal types, an anthropologist can come to know the relationship between humans and the world.

Levi-Strauss (1963) also believed that paying close attention to the language of the participants of a culture is of utmost importance in doing structural analysis. He explained that the relationship of language and culture is extremely complex in that language can be a result of culture, a part of culture, or a condition of culture. He did not establish a causal relationship, but saw both language and culture as products of the human mind. He argued that to know either language or culture, the scholar must study both.

Although Levi-Strauss's main use of structural analysis was to examine myths, it can be used in other types of study as well. For example, in *Teachers Versus Technocrats*, Harry Wolcott (1977) depicted the social system of schools as a moiety system with the same universal characteristics that can be found in primitive societies. Wolcott also used language as a tool for understanding the ideational system of each group. Wolcott's use of structural analysis suggested the usefulness of an examination of how teachers create reality in a different way than administrators, students, or parents.

Cognitive Anthropology

The two major theoretical orientations described thus far emphasize discovering patterns or models that can be used to understand all social groups. In contrast, cognitive anthropology "focuses on discovering how different peoples organize and use their cultures" (Tyler, 1969, p. 3). Like structuralists, cognitive anthropologists perceive that culture is in the minds of people rather than in the material phenomena of the system. When they study a culture, cognitive anthropologists ask, "What material phenomena are significant for the people?" and "How do they organize these phenomena?" (p. 3).

Cognitive anthropologists are interested in both differences between cultures and differences *within* cultures (Tyler, 1969). According to Anthony Wallace (1970), "human societies may characteristically require the nonsharing of cognitive maps," and this lack of uniformity serves two purposes in a complex system: "(1) it permits a more complex system to arise than most, or any, of its participants can comprehend; (2) it liberates the participants in a system from the heavy burden of learning and knowing each other's motivations and cognitions" (p. 35).

Like Levi-Strauss, cognitive anthropologist Ward Goodenough (1981) argued that a study of language is integral with the study of a culture because people gain much of their knowledge of culture through language. Just as every individual has a personal ideolect or version of the language, each person also has a private version of the shared culture. Goodenough labeled this individual outlook "propriospect," and used the term *culture pool* to mean the "sum of the contents of all of the propriospects of all of the society's members" (p. 111). Furthermore, the Culture of a society (with a capital *C*) includes those values and traditions that are both known to all members and true only of one or more subgroups in the society. Just as the culture pool contains the sum of many individual propriospects, each propriospect can contain bits and pieces from many different cultures. The concept of propriospect not only allows for differences between individuals but also accounts for an individual person being multicultural and choosing an appropriate operating culture at any particular time.

Goodenough's idea of Culture includes a conceptual model for culture change, including gradual change, rapid change, innovation, and response to change. One type of slow change, cultural drift, is change that occurs over time when proponents of a tradition within the culture pool die, causing the tradition to disappear. Change can also result from a re-evaluation of the ideas, beliefs, recipes, skills, and traditions that are accepted in the Culture. Change in Culture happens smoothly if it is on a small scale, while large-scale changes can cause a crisis in the system. A crisis may emerge if people's declared beliefs (those they appear to accept) are in conflict with their private beliefs. A change in social rules can cause a crisis if some members are deprived of rights or privileges or if a member chooses not to honor the rules. Changing recipes or formulas of behavior when people do not have an accompanying understanding of the principles involved in the changes can also create turmoil. Goodenough (1981) claimed that public commitment to customs can be so great that the customs "acquire value as ends in themselves," and people demand "cooperation from one another in their performance, and . . . prohibit behavior that . . . jeopardizes the arrangements . . . on which performance of these customary routines depends, investing them with moral rightness and even sanctity" (p. 90).

Harry Wolcott (1987) has argued that Goodenough's concept of propriospect offers a valuable tool in the field of education and anthropology, particularly as it relates to the study of cultural acquisition. Propriospect, according to Wolcott (1987), draws our attention not to universal processes, but "to the individual acquisition of cultural competencies in which each of us is engaged throughout the course of a lifetime" (p. 51). Wolcott's discussion defines cultural acquisition in terms of the children who attend school. In my own study, however, I planned to use Goodenough's concept of culture, and particularly the concept of propriospect, to analyze planned change in an educational system. Propriospect offered a model for studying both the individual teachers and the culture pool of the school's social system.

An advantage of using the concept of propriospect, according to Wolcott, is that it avoids an evaluative stance. In looking at the differing ideational systems of teachers and administrators, for example, the concept of propriospect in itself does not evaluate the relative worth or appropriateness of either group's actions or ideas. Wolcott (1987) states that when using propriospect, "comparisons are better made in terms of the range and quality of experiences to which each human is exposed. One's propriospect is a function of those experiences" (p. 28). This view accommodated my interest in what people believe and why, rather than whether I agree or disagree.

Another advantage of using propriospect is that it draws attention to the idea "that multiculturism is exhibited in *normal human experience*" (Wolcott, 1987, p. 32). This allows the researcher to acknowledge the multiple cultural competencies of individuals in the system. For example, it would not force me to label department heads as either teachers or administrators. Instead, I could simply acknowledge their need to swing from teacher to administrator as each situation demands.

According to Goodenough (1981):

> When we speak of the cultural evolution of societies, whether they are simple or complex, we speak of the processes governing the content of culture pools and governing the selective use people make of the content of culture pools and governing the selective use people make of the contents of their own society's culture pool. (p. 119)

Thus, Goodenough's approach suggested that I focus on how planned change in a school social system is mediated by the culture pool, which is, in turn, determined by individual propriospects.

One recent study using the analytical perspective of cognitive anthropology to examine the process of change in three different schools was conducted by Gretchen Rossman, Dickson Corbett, and William Firestone (1988). They argued that those who seek to reform schools must pay close attention to the belief systems of the individuals within schools. Their study showed that those changes challenging beliefs held sacred by individuals will be difficult to institutionalize. Alan Peshkin, in the introduction to the Rossman, Corbett, and Firestone book, placed the study's value in moving from the general to the specific and back to the general. This is exactly the value of using the cognitive approach in my study. The concept of propriospect allowed me to acknowledge the varied effects of the system's culture on individuals and, in turn, examine how individuals affect the total system.

Interpretive Anthropology

Perhaps now the most influential theoretical approach to ethnography, interpretive anthropology refers to both a theory of culture and the practice of studying culture. It has its roots in the sociology of Parson and Weber, phenomenology, structuralism, structural linguistics, semiotics, and hermeneutics. Interpretive anthropologists study individuals or institutions or both. They avoid both the typical chapter categories of the functionalist and Levi-Strauss's search for universal truths for all cultures. The only reality that interpretive anthropologists claim is that of their own interpretation of what they are describing. Discussions of the texts themselves, and the way they are written, are central to this movement.

G. E. Marcus and M. M. Fischer (1986) credit Geertz's (1973) *The Interpretation of Cultures* for a shift in the emphasis of anthropological analysis. Geertz focused on symbols, meanings, and mentality rather than social structure or behavior. Borrowing Weber's idea that "man is an animal suspended in webs of significance he himself has spun," Geertz (1973, p. 5) claimed that those webs are culture and that the analysis of culture is an interpretive science in search of meaning rather than laws or universals. Geertz disagreed with both Radcliffe-Brown's notion that culture can be viewed as an organism and Goodenough's view that culture is located in the mind. Instead, Geertz argued that cultural analysis is "guessing at meanings, assessing the guesses, and drawing explanatory conclusions from the better guesses" (p. 20). He believed writing ethnography is "an elaborate adventure in . . . 'thick description'" (p. 6) in which the writer seeks to advance to more incisive descriptions rather than create seminal interpretations.

Melford Spiro (1984) has stated that there are dangers inherent in the interpretive approach. One danger is its relativism. Interpretive anthropologists often claim that it is impossible to judge any society even for its extreme behavior and that one society cannot be compared with another. A second danger is implying that creating an adequate description of another society is impossible. In contrast, Geertz (1973) argued that a strength of the interpretive approach is that it provides a framework for understanding change. Because interpretive anthropology differentiates between patterns of social action and systems of meaning, interpretive anthropologists can thereby recognize the difference between change that emanates from the human need to make the world more meaningful and change that results from changes in the function of some aspect of the social system. This distinction also seemed to me relevant to my research topic.

Creating a Synthesis

I planned to use cognitive anthropologist Ward Goodenough's ideas as the basis of my analysis because they offered opportunities to understand the role of teachers both in creating a school's culture and in accepting or rejecting planned change. I was also attracted to Clifford Geertz's idea of "thick description," for I set out to record the words and actions of the participants in an effort to understand the meanings they attach to events in the planned change.

Though not central, the ideas of functionalism and structuralism also influenced my thinking. Functionalism reminded me to look beyond the obvious in determining the purpose served by some action or some other material aspect of a cultural system. It also offered me a means for looking at elements of social structure that serve to prevent change. In addition, structural analysis aided my understanding of the development of cognitive anthropology. Levi-Strauss's emphasis on linguistic analysis as the basis for understanding culture as a product of the human mind served as a bridge for me to understand Goodenough's concept of two elements that form culture: (1) propriospect and (2) the interdependence of the individual and the social system.

Cognitive anthropology, used as a framework for analysis, suggested a way to deal with the politically sensitive areas that could emerge in the study. Using this framework, I could describe events and individual attitudes as components of a cultural system rather than as successful or unsuccessful attempts at change. For instance, a decision made by the principal could be described in terms of how it corresponded to or contradicted teacher values rather than whether or not it was a "good" decision.

Bringing the ideas of Geertz and Goodenough together did raise concerns about synthesizing two apparently contradictory theories: (1) Geertz's notion that we know only public culture, and (2) Goodenough's view that culture is essentially private. Though cognitive anthropologists have looked at culture as private, they are "beginning to develop an understanding of cultural systems as public, socially established symbolic systems rooted in the individual" (Dougherty, 1985, p. 9). On the one hand, Geertz's thick description is a way to picture the public aspects of the individual and the system. On the other hand, Goodenough offers the means to use each description for the purpose of understanding both the individual propriospect and the Culture.

REFLECTING ON THE USE OF THEORY

To attend to theory is not always common in educational administration research. The tendency of researchers simply to choose a major orientation (such as qualitative or quantitative), and the queries from my friends who wondered why I was going through all the extra trouble, prompted me to question the wisdom and practicality of studying and using theory as part of my research and analysis. When I first investigated and worked out the synthesis of anthropological and sociological theories that would frame my interpretation, my goal was to use theory to help data "cohere and enable the research to go beyond an aimless, unsystematic piling up of accounts" (Bogdan & Biklen, 1982, p. 30). I wanted concepts that would unify the work. As I now look back at my expectations and the way they worked out in the study, I would say that, in general, my expectations were met. The theories did provide me with ways of looking at things and clarifying my ideas. In some areas, the usefulness of theory went beyond my expectations by providing me with a means to deal with the difficulties associated with my role as a researcher. Bringing a theoretical orientation into the study, however, was not without its difficulties. Not only did I need to defend my interpretation of the data, but I was also forced to defend the way the study made use of theory. Although theory helped me formulate ideas, I had to be ready to show how these ideas and theory fit together. My success at this was mixed, and the remainder of the chapter is devoted to an examination of the specific ways in which my use of theory helped or hindered me in completing the study.

Theory and the Study

Choosing an anthropological orientation meant that I would emphasize description over statistics. Beyond that, however, what I described and how I described it grew out of the theoretical framework I chose. I say "grew out of" because I do not claim to be a purist in using theory, and it was not my purpose to use the case to prove the veracity of any particular social theory. My interest in the study was the social situation. Theory was a guide in my observations and analysis and a gentle reminder to me when I was getting off track. The theories that guided my thinking were those I described in the first half of this essay, and now I will discuss how they actually influenced the study.

The structural-functional models of Weber (1961), Durkheim (1961a, 1961b, 1961c), and Parsons (1951, 1964) were important early in my data gathering as I tried to decide on the unit of analysis for the study. At first, however, they caused me more confusion than clarity. Initially, I decided to look at the entire social system of a high school going through planned change and, as I will explain in the next paragraph, to consider it a moiety system made up of administrators and teachers. I soon grew uncomfortable, however, with the idea of explaining the social system in terms of a composite personality. In my daily observations I saw teachers who were leaders in changes as well as those who resisted. Some teachers started out supporting changes but ended up opposing them when the changes did not materialize in the same form as originally planned or when unanticipated issues interfered with the original proposals. Because I was aware of the variety of individual responses that teachers made to the system, I believed I would miss one of the advantages of being an insider if I did not acknowledge that individuality. I started to lean toward the individual teacher as the unit of analysis, but that did not work well either. There was no denying that the various individual personalities came together to form a unique culture for the school I studied. Talcott Parsons's (1964) discussions of interplay between the individual and the social system led me to my decision to study "individuals in the system," the interactions between them, and the group as a whole.

Although I did not use the models per se of Levi-Strauss or perform formal linguistic analysis, his structural analysis was partially responsible for my developing emphasis on language as the way to examine meanings people attach to their worlds. Most of the evidence I present consists of the words of the participants rather than their actions. In addition, Harry Wolcott's (1977) moiety model in *Teachers Versus Technocrats* was important throughout my study from initial planning and observations to the final analysis. Being able to acknowledge that in the social structure of the high school, teachers experience a different reality than administrators helped to move me away from puzzling over the existence of their differences. Instead, I spent my time analyzing the effects of those differences on the social system and the potential for successful efforts at planned change.

My understanding of Ward Goodenough's (1981) work in *Culture, Language, and Society* influenced the final organization for my analysis. More specifically, by choosing Ward Goodenough's concept of Culture, culture pool, and propriospect, I framed my observations and interpretations into three major categories: the social group as a whole, the smaller groups functioning for special purposes within the larger social group, and the individual propriospect. Goodenough's approach also increased my sensitivity to language as a vehicle for understanding each person's version of the culture. This was a natural extension of my early decisions regarding unit of analysis. As the study turned out, my final analysis discusses the teachers in the school as a group, smaller subgroups of teachers, and one teacher operating within the larger group.

Goodenough's model of culture also enabled me to deal with an unexpected issue that emerged during my fieldwork. I found that it was not enough to analyze the group and an individual. Operating within the social system of the school were several groups or subcultures, each of which possessed a unique personality and way of interacting with individuals and with the large system. In addition, individuals who worked in different subcultures often acted in different ways in each. Because Goodenough's model accounts for such variation, I felt comfortable in my decision to include a section on individual teacher committees by considering them subgroups of the school's social system. Like individuals, the subcultures contributed to the culture pool. In my own mind, at least, the discussion had cohesion.

Goodenough's influence went further than providing me with a way to structure my analysis. Goodenough's (1981) definition of propriospect and Wolcott's (1987) discussion of it influenced the way I approached my observations and analysis. I did not use Goodenough's formal model or follow Wolcott's suggestions that the model be used to explain how individuals gained competency in the social group I studied. Instead, I used propriospect as a way to frame the observation and analysis, and Wolcott's article suggested some of the ways in which this worked out. First, the concept of propriospect helped me to justify my research role (see next section) and "see my competence [in the system] as a research tool rather than a research objective" (p. 27). Second, propriospect provided a way to analyze the operating culture of individuals without being overly evaluative. As Wolcott suggests, I could compare the range of experiences of teachers and administrators in order to explain their individual propriospects without discussing the relative worth of each person's world view. Here the emphasis is on what exists rather than what should exist. Third, propriospect enabled me to account for the partial overlap in viewpoint between administrators and teachers. Because all administrators in my case had also been teachers at one time, I could explain their similarities in terms of shared experiences. The differences in experiences between administrators and teachers, however, account for their diverse social competencies and perspectives.

Did my study also make use of interpretive anthropology and the work of Geertz? I owe to Geertz a more general approach as revealed on three counts. First, I tried to emulate Geertz's (1973) concept of "thick description" in my presentation of data. I hoped that by doing this, my interpretation would be clearly supported and readers would be able to arrive at their own interpretation. Second, my emphasis was on arriving at meanings related to what happened in the case rather than laws or a universal understanding of schools. And, third, like the interpretive anthropologists, I have reflected on the way I have written my account. In particular, I have acknowledged that the only truth I can claim in the study, or this essay for that matter, is my own.

Theory and My Research Role as Participant Observer

I had correctly anticipated that theory would be useful in framing my observations, data gathering, and analysis. There was, in addition, an equally useful, but unanticipated, benefit from explicitly considering the theoretical orientation of my study. Having theory enabled me to manage several problems associated with my membership role as an active participant observer. Traditionally, anthropologists and sociologists alike have advocated the position that researchers who engage in participant observation should be outsiders who are able to avoid becoming overinvolved with the natives and thus lose their analytical perspective (Agar, 1980; Becker, 1958; Goetz & LeCompte, 1984; Gold, 1958; Lofland & Lofland, 1984; Pollard, 1985; Wax, 1971; Whyte, 1951).

Recently, however, a number of researchers have taken the position that full involvement in the social system being studied can be an advantage (Adler & Adler, 1987; Jorgensen, 1989; Peshkin, 1988; Wolcott, 1988). With that justification in mind, I engaged in ethnographic fieldwork as a complete member of the social system I studied. Labeled by Adler and Adler as the "complete member role" (CMR), it is potentially the most subjective of all research positions. As a full-time English teacher who had taught in the school for three years, I was not only involved with the natives, I was one of the natives! From the beginning, establishing and maintaining a research stance was a major issue for me, and I worried about my ability to operate with any distance. Alan Peshkin (1988) points out, however, that it was not necessary "to exorcise my subjectivity" (p. 17). Peshkin argues cogently that subjectivity is a "garment that cannot be removed." The best we can do in any role is to "manage it — to preclude it from being unwittingly burdensome" (p. 17).

I found that establishing a theoretical framework played a major part in helping me manage the subjectivity of my researcher role. When I started the fieldwork, I fully expected to record a very successful process of planned change that might be useful for other educators. As I participated in the events of daily life in a suburban high school, however, I inevitably observed and recorded teachers, administrators, and students engaged in conflicts or making what I perceived as poor decisions. Specifically, I found an organization struggling with poorly understood efforts to help at-risk students stay in school. As tension mounted and staff members suffered from stress, more than a few teachers and administrators spoke and acted in ways that tended to divide rather than bring the organization together. Even though I had explained my research to the staff, I suffered conflicts of conscience at the thought of publishing their words and actions in a public document.

Theory was useful in helping me cope with these conflicts of conscience. It was, in fact, the chief means by which I was able to turn on and off "my analytic function" and "switch back and forth between the insiders' perspective and an analytic framework" (Jorgensen, 1989, pp. 84–85). When I was in my teaching role, my relationships with colleagues and students were likely to play a dominant role in determining my responses. When I moved to my research role, however, I consciously stepped back to consider the questions important to analyzing the situation. More often than not, the questions I asked myself were guided by anthropological theory. Let me explain.

For the entire year of the fieldwork, I was a nonvoting member of a committee called the School Improvement Team, an elected group of teachers who worked with administration to determine school goals and carry out the activities to reach these goals. The chair of the committee had asked me to work with them to plan and carry out a survey of the staff's reaction to school improvement efforts. I saw it as an opportunity to reciprocate (Gouldner, 1960; Wax, 1952) by offering my researcher services in return for the opportunity to observe teachers and administrators working through issues related to planning changes in an organization. The experience turned out to be a challenge for me both as a teacher in the school and as a researcher.

Like the other teachers, I was torn between believing in the school goals and the frustrations of carrying them out. For example, I believed in the goal of keeping at-risk students in school, but, like other teachers, I felt frustrated when students were not suspended or expelled for extremely destructive behavior. As a researcher, I worried about recording the conflicts that emerged among committee members during the course of the year. I felt professional respect for the teachers and counted two of them among my circle of friends. In addition, I had a good working relationship with the principal and understood the difficulties he faced. Recording the frustrations of teachers and the conflicts between teachers and administrators often placed me in emotional turmoil. At those times, I was able to slip into the role of researcher by thinking about the situation in terms of my theoretical model. If, for instance, I applied Goodenough's (1981) concept of Culture to the situation, I looked for the public culture, the "standards the group's members expect of one another to operate in their mutual dealings" (p. 106). In trying to understand the group's public culture, I also would look at the individual versions, or propriospects, that came together. Then I would ponder the interaction of the committee in the school Culture. Thus, the theory allowed me to step back from my personal relationships and emotions in order to perform an analysis as a researcher. Instead of betraying friends, I tried to interpret an interesting social situation.

Problems with Using Theory

Before I go too far in my recitation of the ways theory can be helpful in conducting qualitative research in schools, I must raise a flag of caution for those who would use it in the ways I have just suggested. By introducing anthropological and sociological theory into my study, I was able to cope with a number of problems. Emphasizing the use of theory, however, also created two problems that any researcher should seriously consider before following my lead.

Time. Bringing anthropological and sociological theory into a study takes lots of time, especially if the researcher has not previously studied these areas. I spent nearly a year of intense reading and writing before I was able to develop the initial synthesis that appears in this chapter. In part, it took me that long because I was a novice (and still consider myself barely beyond that stage) in the areas of anthropology and sociology. Looking back at my colleagues in graduate school, however, I do not believe that I was an unusual case. Few of my peers were well versed in theory, regardless of their subject area backgrounds, and thus chose to conduct studies not dependent on a close understanding of theory or how to use it. In addition, many students had set strict completion deadlines for their research. Anxious to return to administrative positions in public education, they were more interested in finishing the degree and applying research findings than in analyzing their own theoretical framework. The environment of public schooling into which many of us return after graduate study affords little opportunity for worrying about theory.

Being accountable. In addition, the decision to emphasize theory gives the researcher just one more issue to worry about. Although theory gave me a framework from which to observe and analyze the case, it also forced me to be conscious of the way in which I was using it or not using it. Once I decided to use the concept of propriospect, I struggled with finding a way to represent the Culture, culture pool, and propriospect. I decided to write one chapter depicting the Culture (as defined by Goodenough, 1981), another depicting groups of people who contribute to the culture pool (an example of Wolcott's idea that all social systems are multicultural), and a third describing one individual, or one propriospect, that contributed to the culture pool.

I felt rather pleased with what I saw as my cleverness in using theory as a way to organize the case. That feeling came to a sudden end when Harry Wolcott suggested I cut the explanation of propriospect from the theory synthesis because I didn't use it very well anyway! Salvaging my ego after the initial shock of not being lauded for my work, I went back to Goodenough's (1981) book *Culture, Language, and Society* and the article in which Wolcott argues in favor of using the concept of propriospect in educational research. I found that my use of propriospect was much more superficial than that suggested by Wolcott. I had used it as an organizer and justification for including the story of an individual within the organization. Wolcott (1987), however, argues that the concept of propriospect can be used to examine and explain such complex issues as "cultural acquisition, multiculturalism, and the distinction between cultural and private knowledge" (p. 23). Although I did not extensively rework my analysis, I returned to my manuscript to clarify exactly what use I would make of the term *propriospect*. I also became acutely aware of the necessity of returning periodically to the text in order to renew my understanding of theory and to be clear about how I would use it.

CONCLUSION: TO THEORIZE OR NOT TO THEORIZE

Using theory, then, is a mixed blessing for educational researchers. Theory adds another layer of accountability because the methodology, data, and analysis must be consistent with the theoretical models framing the research. Outside of the possibility of theory becoming an end in itself, however, I believe that qualitative research and, especially highly descriptive studies, benefit from the infusion of theoretical models. I have tried to demonstrate how using theory benefited my case study on both a personal and professional level.

Using theory was personally beneficial in two major ways. First, writing a theoretical review clarified my own thinking and aided me in developing a relatively coherent synthesis of several theories and models. Until I committed myself on paper, I felt "stuck" in planning and conducting the study. Although I would not claim to be anything near a purist in using theory, I was able to establish a basis for working through issues as they arose. The second personal benefit was in having a tool for working through my role as a researcher. As I have discussed, the problems associated with my role as a member of the organization I studied were made manageable by my use of theory to gain distance and perspective.

I also believe that more conscious use of theory benefits the cause of qualitative research in education. In the introduction to *Ethnography and Qualitative Design in Educational Research*, Judith Goetz and Margaret LeCompte (1984) suggest that one reason they wrote their book was that they "grew weary of defending the work done by [their] research peers, [their] students, and [themselves] against charges from some quarters that ethnography is easy, lacking in rigor, or just not science" (p. ix). Later, they argue the importance of establishing a theoretical framework for qualitative research, especially ethnographic studies. They claim that using theory increases vigor and makes the studies "intelligible across disciplines" (p. 35). I believe their arguments ring true. Although I make no assumptions on the ultimate worth of my own case study, working

through the issues associated with using anthropological theory has provided me with a foundation on which to defend and improve my work as
well as an avenue to develop future research.

The debate over the relative worth of quantitative versus qualitative
inquiry will surely continue in years to come. Although qualitative research is no longer taboo in most universities, and thus enjoying an increase in popularity among educational researchers, researchers must
answer the challenges made regarding the conceptual rigor of their work.
Theory here, too, will play a critical role.

REFERENCES

Abrahamson, M. (1978). *Functionalism*. Englewood Cliffs, NJ: Prentice-Hall.
Adler, P. A., & Adler, P. (1987). *Membership roles in field research*. Beverly
    Hills, CA: Sage.
Agar, M. H. (1980). *The professional stranger: An informal introduction to eth-
    nography*. New York: Academic Press.
Applebaum, H. (Ed.). (1987). *Perspectives in cultural anthropology*. Albany:
    State University of New York Press.
Becker, H. S. (1958). Problems of inference and proof in participant observation.
    American Sociological Review, 23(6), 652–660.
Bogdan, R. C., & Biklen, S. (1982). *Qualitative research for education: An intro-
    duction to theory and methods*. Boston: Allyn & Bacon.
Dougherty, J. W. (Ed.). (1985). *Directions in cognitive anthropology*. Urbana:
    University of Illinois.
Durkheim, E. (1961a). Anomic suicide. In T. Parsons, E. Shils, K. D. Naegele, &
    J. R. Pitts (Eds.), *Theories of society: Foundations of modern sociological
    theory* (pp. 916–929). New York: Free Press.
Durkheim, E. (1961b). On the process of change in social values. In T. Parsons,
    E. Shils, K. D. Naegele, & J. R. Pitts (Eds.), *Theories of society: Foundations
    of modern sociological theory* (pp. 1305–1311). New York: Free Press.
Durkheim, E. (1961c). Types of suicide. In T. Parsons, E. Shils, K. D. Naegele,
    & J. R. Pitts (Eds.), *Theories of society: Foundations of modern sociological
    theory* (pp. 213–218). New York: Free Press.
Geertz, C. (1973). Thick description: Toward an interpretive theory of culture.
    In C. Geertz, *The interpretation of cultures* (pp. 3–30). New York: Basic
    Books.
Goetz, J. P., & LeCompte, M. D. (1984). *Ethnography and qualitative design in
    educational research*. New York: Academic Press.
Gold, R. L. (1958). Roles in sociological field observations. *Social Forces, 36*,
    217–223.
Goodenough, W. H. (1981). *Culture, language, and society*. Menlo Park, CA:
    Benjamin/Cummings.

Gouldner, A. W. (1960). The norm of reciprocity: A preliminary statement. *American Sociological Review, 25*(2), 161–178.

Haller, E. J. (1979). Questionnaires and the dissertation in educational administration. *Educational Administration Quarterly, 15*(1), 47–66.

Hansen, J. F. (1970). *Sociocultural perspectives on human learning: An introduction to educational anthropology.* Englewood Cliffs, NJ: Prentice-Hall.

Henstrand, J. (1991). *Teacher culture from the inside: A case study of planned change from the perspective of active participant observer.* Unpublished doctoral dissertation, University of Oregon, Eugene.

Jarvie, I. C. (1968). Limits to functionalism and alternatives to it in anthropology. In R. A. Manners & D. Kaplan (Eds.), *Theory in anthropology: A sourcebook* (pp. 196–203). Chicago: Aldine.

Jorgensen, D. L. (1989). *Participant observation: A methodology for human studies.* Newbury Park, CA: Sage.

Kaplan, D., & Manners, R. A. (1986). *Culture theory.* Prospect Heights, IL: Waveland Press.

Keesing, R. M. (1981). *Cultural anthropology: A contemporary perspective* (2nd ed.). New York: Holt, Rinehart & Winston.

Levi-Strauss, C. (1963). *Structural anthropology.* New York: Basic Books.

Lofland, J., & Lofland, L. (1984). *Analyzing social settings: A guide to qualitative observation and analysis* (2nd ed.). Belmont, CA: Wadsworth.

Malinowski, B. (1961). *Argonauts of the Western Pacific.* New York: E. P. Dutton.

Malinowski, B. (1987). The group and individual in functional analysis. In H. Applebaum (Ed.), *Perspectives in cultural anthropology* (pp. 116–120). Albany: State University of New York Press.

Marcus, G. E., & Fischer, M. M. J. (1986). *Anthropology as cultural critique: An experimental moment in the human sciences.* Chicago: University of Chicago Press.

Parsons, T. (1951). *The social system.* New York: Free Press.

Parsons, T. (1964). A functional theory of change. In A. Etzioni & E. Etzioni (Eds.), *Social change: Sources, patterns, and consequences* (pp. 83–97). New York: Basic Books.

Peshkin, A. (1988). In search of subjectivity — One's own. *Educational Researcher, 17*(7), 17–21.

Pollard, A. (1985). Opportunities and difficulties of a teacher ethnographer: A personal account. In R. Burgess (Ed.), *Field methods in the study of education* (pp. 217–234). London: Falmer Press.

Radcliffe-Brown, A. R. (1987). On social structure. In H. Applebaum (Ed.), *Perspectives in cultural anthropology* (pp. 121–135). Albany: State University of New York Press.

Rossman, G. B., Corbett, H. D., & Firestone, W. A. (1988). *Change and effectiveness in schools: A cultural perspective.* Albany: State University of New York Press.

Salzman, P. C. (1988, May). Fads and fashions in anthropology. *Anthropology Newsletter, 1,* 32–33.

Spiro, M. E. (1984). Some reflections on cultural determinism and relativism with special reference to emotion and reason. In R. A. Shweder & R. A. LeVine (Eds.), *Culture theory: Essays on mind, self, and emotion* (pp. 323–346). Cambridge: Cambridge University Press.

Tyler, S. (1969). *Cognitive anthropology*. New York: Holt, Rinehart & Winston.

Wallace, A. F. C. (1970). *Culture and personality* (2nd ed.). New York: Random House.

Wax, R. H. (1952). Field methods and techniques: Reciprocity as a field technique. *Human Organization, 11*(1), 34–37.

Wax, R. H. (1971). *Doing fieldwork: Warnings and advice*. Chicago: University of Chicago Press.

Weber, M. (1961). Types of social organization. In T. Parsons, E. Shils, K. D. Naegele, & J. R. Pitts (Eds.), *Theories of society: Foundations of modern sociological theory* (pp. 218–229). New York: Free Press.

Whyte, W. F. (1951). Observational field-work methods. In M. Jahoda, M. Deutsch, & S. W. Cook (Eds.), *Research methods in social relations* (pp. 493–514). New York: Dryden Press.

Wolcott, H. F. (1977). *Teachers versus technocrats: An educational innovation in anthropological perspective*. Eugene, OR: Center for Educational Policy and Management.

Wolcott, H. F. (1987). *The acquisition of propriospect*. Unpublished manuscript. Eugene: University of Oregon.

Wolcott, H. F. (1988). Ethnographic research in education. In R. M. Jaeger (Ed.), *Complementary methods for research in education* (pp. 185–250). Washington, DC: American Educational Research Association.

6

Levels of Abstraction in a Case Study of Educational Change

GEOFFREY E. MILLS

Louis Smith (1978) argues that in order to develop useful and potent theories of descriptive research, we need to share the stories that accompany the evolution of a researcher's work. In part, this chapter is a retrospective account of the development of theory in my doctoral research (Mills, 1988). It is also an account of my continuing struggle with "theory" and the increasing levels of abstraction that have accompanied this struggle. I address the implicit and explicit theories underlying a case study approach to an investigation of directed educational change.

One of the problems with talking about "theory" is the ambiguity associated with its definition. David Kaplan and Robert Manners (1986) allude to this difficulty:

> In general, if a proposition or a body of propositions explains, predicts, retrodicts or leads us to "new" avenues of research it is likely to be called a theory. In short, theories are defined pragmatically rather than strictly in terms of their formal properties. (p. 12)

For the purposes of this chapter, I will use the following definition of theory: an analytical and interpretive framework that helps the researcher make sense of "what is going on" in the social setting being studied. This pragmatic definition is in keeping with Louis Smith's (1978) conservative view of theory as "novel, comprehensive, internally consistent, and func-

---

Parts of this chapter are based on a paper presented at the annual meeting of the American Educational Research Association (Mills, 1990). I wish to thank Harry F. Wolcott for his comments on an earlier draft of this work.

tional" (p. 360). It provides a frame of reference for the "theory," "concepts," and "hunches" discussed in this chapter.

Throughout my graduate studies I was concerned primarily with issues related to the methodology of qualitative research. Practical "how to do it" questions were foremost in my mind. My previous attempts at qualitative research (cf. Mills, 1985, 1987) had aimed at describing social settings involving transient (highly geographically mobile) children, and sorority girls. Yet, in doing this research I did not explicitly consider the underlying assumptions that guided what I chose to report and the manner in which I developed my report. The work I will recount in the following pages tells a different story, as I tried to be more conscious of my work's underlying assumptions. Louis Smith (1978) has described this process as a "somewhat tortuous route . . . in searching for a theoretical-methodological rationale" (p. 326). It is such a tortuous route that I have chosen to describe as I continue to struggle with several competing theories — none of which is working perfectly.

FORESHADOWED PROBLEMS

My case study of planned educational change began with a set of beliefs and propositions that may more accurately be described as "foreshadowed problems" in contrast to "preconceived ideas."

> If a man sets out on an expedition, determined to prove certain hypotheses, if he is incapable of changing his views constantly and casting them off ungrudgingly under the pressure of evidence, needless to say his work will be worthless. But the more problems he brings with him into the field, the more he is in the habit of molding his theories according to facts, and of seeing facts in their bearing upon theory, the better he is equipped for the work. Preconceived ideas are pernicious in any scientific work, but foreshadowed problems are the main endowment of a scientific thinker, and these problems are first revealed to the observer in his theoretical studies. (Malinowski, 1922, pp. 8–9)

This distinction between "foreshadowed problems" and "preconceived ideas" I view as a critical factor in doing case study research. The researcher's ability to enunciate foreshadowed problems ("propositions") provides a foundation for questioning the evidence that is uncovered in the course of the research.

I first began to consider my own "foreshadowed problems" in a course assignment that required me to examine the literature on educational change and develop a list of propositions I held to be true. Given that these propositions were the basis of my beliefs about the nature of change, an attempt to fit them into a particular theoretical position may help my search for a theory of best fit. I should also note that the focusing questions of my study (How does change function, and what functions does it serve in an American school district?) provide further clues about the theoretical perspective with which I am most closely aligned. Smith (1978) proposes that the explicit identification of theoretical concerns taken into the field is one way to combat concerns about selectivity of data, seeing what one wants to see, and implicit theoretical biases. What follows is an analysis of my implicit theories, concepts, and hunches that accompanied me into what I have called the McKenzie school district.

LATENT FUNCTIONS, MANIFEST FUNCTIONS, AND UNINTENDED CONSEQUENCES OF CHANGE

Important to my study of the McKenzie school district were the concepts of "process" and "function." These dimensions of the change process were evident in my list of change propositions, and were a focus during the development of the research proposal. Robert Merton (1967) defines functions as follows:

> Functions are those observed consequences which make for the adaptation or adjustment of a given system; and dysfunctions, those observed consequences which lessen the adaptation or adjustment of the system. There is also the empirical possibility of nonfunctional consequences, which are simply irrelevant to the system under consideration. In any given instance, an item may have both functional and dysfunctional consequences, giving rise to the difficult and important problem of evolving canons for assessing the net balance of the aggregate consequences. (p. 105)

Of particular interest in my research were Merton's complementary dimensions of latent function and manifest function because they provided an important distinction between what the participants in the change process considered to be the intended and unintended consequences of change.

> Manifest functions are those objective consequences contributing to the adjustment or adaptation of the system which are intended and recognized by the participants in the system. Latent functions, correlatively, being those which are neither intended nor recognized. (Merton, 1967, p. 105)

Further, Merton distinguishes between the "unintended consequences" of action and "latent functions." Merton considers that the unintended consequences of action are of three types.

> (1) those which are functional for a designated system, and these comprise the latent functions;
> (2) those which are dysfunctional for a designated system, and these comprise the latent dysfunctions; and
> (3) those which are irrelevant to the system which they affect neither functionally nor dysfunctionally, i.e., the pragmatically unimportant class of nonfunctional consequences. (Merton, 1967, p. 105)

One aim of my study was to discuss change in an American school district in terms of manifest and latent functions. In considering the "lessons" or themes of the case, I borrowed Merton's terms "manifest function," "latent function," and "unintended consequences" to summarize the managing and coping strategies used by personnel at different levels within the school district, and to view the functions these strategies might serve in promoting educational change.

This use of theory, however, was emergent. As Smith (1978) suggests, "foreshadowed problems represent initial and partial analyses of the problem, the tenor of thinking of people who are working in related and relevant areas, and provisional modes of thinking" (p. 331). So, when did these concepts of manifest function, latent function, and unanticipated consequences crystalize in my study as a thesis about educational change? For an answer to this question I must return to the period of my fieldwork. Data were collected utilizing a variety of techniques, including participant observation, interviewing, written sources of data, and nonwritten sources of data. The process of data analysis and interpretation was ongoing and dialectic. With the fieldwork completed, there was time during the writing of the descriptive report when I could reflect on the common patterns that had emerged during the study and that appeared to account for much of the behavior observed and discussions recorded. Opler (1945) refers to these common patterns as "cultural themes" (p. 198). Yet it would seem that these concepts of manifest and latent functions emerged during the latter days of my fieldwork as I was comparing and contrasting themes that were emerging from my fieldnotes. Smith (1978) considers this process of comparing and contrasting, looking for antecedents and consequences, as the essence of concept formation. "As items appear in the perceptual images, as verbal comments are recorded, as situations appear, as events come and go, one asks a simple two-sided question: How are they alike, and how are they different?" (p. 338). In my study of the McKenzie school district, I pursued this process of comparing events and grouping clusters of concepts that eventually led to a taxonomy of managing and coping strategies.

MULTIPLE LEVELS OF MANAGING CHANGE

I was also interested in how my case study of the McKenzie school district illustrates the multiple levels at which efforts to manage and cope with change are played out. I suspected that personnel at different levels in a school district employ different strategies. Further, the "level" of the change effort—whether state or district mandated, based on "soft" or "hard" money, instigated by central office personnel or growing out of personal interest at a building level—is likely to elicit different managing and coping strategies from central office personnel, principals, and teachers.

In order to demonstrate the process I engaged in as I worked through these ideas, I will present some examples from my study. These examples provide a picture of a neophyte qualitative researcher searching for a theory that would best explain the managing and coping strategies utilized by central office personnel, principals, and teachers. Consider first the "players" at various levels in the system in which my fieldwork was conducted.

The Superintendent

I had few opportunities during the year to observe the superintendent as he went about his work. In part, I believe that this was a reflection of the manner in which he delegated responsibility within the district, choosing to be a public relations person and assigning the work of monitoring the curricular and instructional aspects of the district to the assistant superintendent. However, there were indicators during the year suggesting that the superintendent was performing his duties in a manner that gained him favor with the McKenzie School Board. This culminated with a headline in the local McKenzie newspaper that he was "Rated 'Excellent' by Board."

The superintendent employed his own managing and coping strategies during the course of the school year. In the face of steadily declining test scores over the four years he had been at McKenzie, the "posture" presented to the school board was one strategy of coping with a changed emphasis on the district's testing program. At a mid-January meeting of the board, the superintendent assured board members that everything possible was being done to ensure that the district's children were receiving, and would continue to receive, the best possible curriculum and instruction available. Similarly, the story released to the local McKenzie newspaper represented a picture that was in contrast to the reality of improvement plan development and implementation. In spite of assurances that improvement plans targeted at halting the tide of declining test scores were being developed and implemented at the school level, there was a lack of evidence for the superintendent's claims to be found among principals and teachers.

This scenario provides an example of the struggle I faced in searching for a theory that would best fit the events I observed in the McKenzie school district. My graduate studies had introduced me to a number of "theories" that possibly could have explained the actions of the McKenzie school district superintendent. For example, Louis Smith and Pat Keith (1971) discuss this kind of administrative posturing by introducing the concept of "facade," the "formal doctrine as it was presented to the public." According to Smith and Keith, the doctrine includes "an elaborated system of concepts, spelling out the entire structure of means and ends within an organization" (p. 21). The superintendent's presentation of the "means and ends" that were to be the focus of the district's improvement plans, represent a "facade" that was different from the district's operation. Similarly, the story released to the local newspaper represented another facade that stood in contrast to plan development and implementation. The news story was more a collection of "special instances and fond hopes" (p. 21) than an accurate representation of what was going on.

However, there were competing theories (concepts, hunches) that I struggled to rationalize in my search for an increasing level of abstraction. For example, Anthony Wallace's (1956) notion of the "charismatic leader" in a revitalization movement appeared to provide another way of viewing the role of the superintendent as he managed and coped with a changing emphasis on test scores. Similarly, Robert Merton's concepts of "process" and "function" as applied to latent functions, manifest functions, and unintended consequences of change provided a level of abstraction beyond the "facade" and "charismatic leader" concepts. This "theory" appeared to help explain the managing and coping strategies used by personnel at other levels in the McKenzie school district. Merton's theory was not a perfect fit, if indeed such a perfect theory exists to explain any social setting. Based on my immersion in the cultural and educational change literature, however, the concepts did appear to be those of "best fit" for what I observed.

Principals

An example of how I applied Merton's theory can be seen in the following scenario involving the elementary school principals and teachers in the McKenzie school district. Following the superintendent's increased emphasis on improving district test scores, the principals were directed by the assistant superintendent and director of elementary education to improve the levels of "academic excellence" in their schools (as measured by scores on a standardized test). The principals were also informed that their efforts at dealing with "at-risk" children may have represented misguided priorities, as the new focus for the school year would be the development and implementation of improvement plans.

In spite of the evidence presented to the board, the general reaction among the principals toward the testing and improvement plan process was cynical. The following comments reflect the barrage of concerns that central office personnel had to deal with:

> The tests don't test what it is that the curriculum being used in our schools teaches.
> The results of these tests will drop my staff on their butts. I'm really concerned about the impact all of this will have on morale.

However, the underlying message to the principals from the central office personnel was clear: "It's not the tests or curriculum that is at fault, but the emphasis that has been given in the teaching of the curriculum."

In response to the central office directive to develop and implement improvement plans, many of the principals adopted a "fine tuning of instruction" stance. That is, they considered it important that teachers not overreact to test scores. The message to teachers was simple: "We are going to fine tune what we are already doing in the school. We aren't going to make sweeping changes." The principals viewed their jobs in handling the improvement plans as "fine tuning" instructional programs, or writing plans that will "keep the folks downtown happy" but remain in the principal's office.

Applying Merton's theory to this scenario provided the following analysis. The manifest function of fine tuning was to improve instructional programs without overemphasizing the importance of test scores to teachers. The expectation of fine tuning was that test scores would improve without teachers making major changes to their instructional programs. The latent function of fine tuning was to validate ongoing programs that were proving satisfactory, thus putting principals in the role of "advocates of constraint." Adopting directives from the central office was overshadowed by the adaptation of an innovation and the priority it was awarded in a school. The unintended consequences of fine tuning was stability of instructional programs.

Teachers

Teachers interpreted the comments made by principals as supportive of an attitude of doing little to change programs. The manifest function of the development of improvement plans was to provide teachers with "hard data" on which to base instructional improvement. It was a process the McKenzie school district had been committed to for nearly a decade. The latent function of developing improvement plans was to validate the critical role of the teacher as the person who knows best how to improve the education of children. In spite of central office efforts to change instructional programs, it was the status of the teacher that was validated. However, the unintended consequences of the accountability placed on teachers to develop and implement improvement plans were not expected by the central office administrators. Teachers were skeptical of the test results and questioned the validity of scores as a measure of the curriculum being taught in the McKenzie schools and as the basis for instructional improvement. Teachers went through the motions of plan development without becoming advocates of the approach. Principals went along with district directives, and teachers went along with the principals' directives.

Given these brief examples, how did theory help me tell the story of the McKenzie school district? And having told the story, how would theory help with the reporting of the case study?

THEORY, STORYTELLING, AND INCREASING LEVELS OF ABSTRACTION

Theory serves a number of important roles in the development and reporting of any descriptive narrative, but I do not believe that a theoretical perspective will tell the story. Instead, it influences the choices we make and the emphasis we give to particular events. As Kaplan and Manners (1986) contend, "in practice, anthropological theorizing is a matter of emphasis" (p. 90). But an important element in this cognitive process of theory generation is creative thinking. It includes

> the generation and construction of concepts, perspectives, and theories from an initial set of problems, through a long period of sought and unsought percepts and experiences in the field setting, to some final kind of order

> which appears as a written report. Its open-ended quality frightens some
> novices and critics and exhilarates others. (Smith, 1978, p. 335)

In search of increasing levels of abstraction, it is particularly important
not to lose sight of the elements that enrich the descriptive narratives at
the heart of qualitative research. Smith (1978) proposes that descriptive
accounts "hold" in the face of data, and the ideas developed during analysis should result in a structure that reflects three major dimensions: integrity, complexity, and creativity.

According to Smith, integrity means a theme, a thesis, or a point of
view that allows all the pieces of the account to fit together in an interrelated way. In my study of the McKenzie school district I proposed the
thesis that personnel at different levels in a school district employ different
strategies for managing and coping with change. This theme provided a
framework that allowed the story pieces to fit together in a cohesive account that included central office personnel, principals, and teachers.

Complexity refers to the ability of the major themes and minor nuances to do justice to the system being studied. The major themes of my
study related to specific managing and coping strategies used at different
levels in the school district. However, the complexity of the McKenzie
school district was also discussed in terms of the manifest functions, latent
functions, and unintended consequences of the change processes.

Finally, in Smith's view, creativity is the conveyance of novel and
important ideas to the audience. I believe that my application of Merton's
theoretical framework is a creative attempt to convey important change
process concepts to readers of the account. The descriptive account is
written with, to use Alfred Smith's (1964) words, a "high ratio of information to explanation" (p. 257) in order to present the participants' perceptions of the change process.

Louis Smith (1978) maintains that in judging research reports there
are four areas of concern representing increasing levels of abstraction:
(1) data, (2) descriptive narrative, (3) analytical-theoretical-interpretive,
and (4) metatheoretical. At the data level, a series of questions can be
asked concerning the information and how it was collected.

> The resulting cluster of dimensions — direct on-site observation, freedom of
> access, intensity of observation, triangulation and multimethods, sampling,
> and attention to muted cues and unobtrusive signs — seems to comprise the
> major conditions assuring valid data. (p. 341)

In my study of the McKenzie school district, data were collected utilizing
a variety of techniques, including participant observation, interviewing,
written sources of data, and nonwritten sources of data. An important

aspect of this approach is the utilization of fieldwork modes that permit the researcher to check the findings from the application of one technique against the findings of another. That is, my aim was to "triangulate" data by obtaining information in many ways.

Secondly, Smith (1978) describes narrative as "telling the story of the characters, settings, incidents, and on occasion the drama of conflict, crisis, and denouement" (p. 350). In his discussion of the descriptive narrative and the commitment of qualitative researchers to the narrative as one of the outcomes of their research, Smith brings in the implications of the kind of sociological and psychological theory one generates and uses. The theories that guide one's work exert an influence on the nature of the narrative. As Smith writes, "the data problems, the metatheoretical dilemmas, and the theoretical stance all contribute a context to the narrative" (p. 353).

My descriptive narrative of the McKenzie school district was written around the themes that emerged during the fieldwork. Clearly, these themes (and hence, the story) were influenced by the "foreshadowed problems" that accompanied me to the field. My focus on the "process and function of change" shaped the descriptive narrative and its organization around the theme that there are multiple levels at which efforts to manage and cope with change could be examined when looking at the dynamics of a school district. These different levels and functions provided narrative structures.

At the next level of abstraction, the theoretical-analytical-interpretive level, Smith discusses the process of moving beyond "telling the story of a group" to the more abstract activity of developing theory, analysis, or interpretation. This is a matter of asking: What is your theory a theory of? I was confronted with this question at various times during my graduate research as I grappled with different theoretical questions related to educational and cultural change, and culture theory. Little did I realize at the time the importance of these endeavors to the long-term goal of developing theoretical coherence in my analysis and interpretation of the McKenzie school district. Again, Merton's (1967) theoretical framework incorporating the concepts of latent function, manifest function, and unintended consequences of change provided the theory of "best fit" for my analysis and interpretation of the efforts of central office personnel, principals, and teachers to manage and cope with change efforts.

I would argue that the task of challenging qualitative researchers to make explicit their theories about the fields they are studying is the responsibility of our research community. Many neophyte qualitative researchers, such as myself, have difficulty with the notion of "theory generation" as part of qualitative research. Yet, if the aim of qualitative research is to understand the social setting under investigation, then the generation of theory can hardly be avoided. Smith (1978) suggests five ideal criteria that focus at the theoretical level. A study should strive to provide

1. Insightful distinctions that tell something new about the phenomena
2. Clear definitions of new concepts at the theoretical, operational, or concrete example levels
3. A cumulative glossary of these ideas within a specific project
4. The interrelations of ideas into patterns or concatenations
5. Findings that are helpful in solving problems in the same broad domain

These five criteria promise to provide guidance in thinking about "theory generation" at a practical level.

Finally, Smith considers metatheoretical issues related to what has been learned from a qualitative study. That is, what rationale exists for the manner in which the researcher has phrased the results of the study? Here Smith identifies six metatheoretical issues he considers important to educational researchers:

1. What are the metaphors that guide the researcher's thinking about the phenomenon under investigation?
2. Has the researcher adopted an emic or etic perspective in an attempt to provide the subject's point of view, the outsider's point of view, or some combination of the two?
3. What is the scope of the theory that informs the researcher's work? For example, the researcher might be working with a "miniature" theory that in some way will contribute to a more "general" theory.
4. At what level of abstraction is the researcher working? Is the researcher's focus on description through the use of concrete examples or at a more abstract level?
5. Is the researcher influenced by educational rather than social science theory? Further, do the outcomes of the research have application to a significant educational problem?
6. Is the researcher concerned with describing "what is" or clarifying "what should be"? That is, is the researcher working with an "action oriented" or "analytical" theory?

The main point for qualitative researchers is the notion that the individual's position in relation to these metatheoretical issues separates his or her research from the research of others. For example, my use of Merton's framework helps make explicit my position on several of these issues. I viewed the organization of a school district as structural and attempted to portray an "insider" perspective on how participants managed and coped with change. At the same time, my use of Merton's theory is limited in scope and time to the local context of the McKenzie school district. Any attempt to a level of abstraction is restricted to concrete, descriptive examples in the interpretation of the case study.

My difficulty with the role of theory in the presentation of a descriptive account is linked to the trouble I have with the word *theory*. I feel more comfortable with labels such as concept, assumption, and maybe even the term *hunch*! However, it is important to recognize that my assumptions (ideology, world view, theory, idea . . .) about how best to make sense of a social setting influence the way I report my experiences. There are no definitive "right" or "wrong" ways to go about using theory, but there are clearly different ways. And each way makes a different contribution.

The message for me — someone who has tried to be basically "atheoretical" in previous work — is that I have always been influenced by a theory (assumption, concept, hunch, idea . . .) all along. Although I still cannot categorically classify myself as a proponent of one theoretical school or another, I can acknowledge that certain underlying assumptions have provided me with perspective in my work. This perspective is evident in my propositions about change and in the way in which I have told the story of the McKenzie school district. I would also argue that the theoretical perspectives that have emerged in my work thus far will influence my future research efforts. However, these theories will have to compete with new theories that become internalized as I read current research and return to read "old favorites" through different lenses — lenses tainted by experience.

CONCLUSIONS

In closing, let me review what I see as the major reasons for considering the roles and uses of theory in qualitative research.

1. Identification of theoretical concerns taken into the field helps the researcher combat concerns about selectivity of data and implicit theoretical biases.
2. Concern for theory helps the researcher acknowledge the competing nature of alternative theories, and encourages an internal struggle for the theory of "best fit" while acknowledging the limitations of any singular perspective.

3. Adopting a theoretical perspective provides the researcher with a framework for the problem and questions to be addressed in the study.
4. Exposure to competing theoretical perspectives in the academic preparation of qualitative researchers allows for the development of "foreshadowed problems" and an initial analysis of a research problem, but the "crystallization" of a researcher's theoretical perspective is likely to occur at a later time during and after the fieldwork.
5. Theory allows the researcher to search for increasing levels of abstraction, to move beyond a purely descriptive account. Further, I would propose that it is the increasing levels of abstraction we seek in qualitative work that allow us to communicate the essence of descriptive work to our colleagues at research meetings. How else can we encapsulate many hundreds of pages of description into a 20-minute oration or 10-page preface?
6. The manner in which researchers apply a theoretical perspective to their work provides a means for judging qualitative research. Smith (1978) has suggested four areas of concern that represent increasing levels of abstraction: data, descriptive narrative, analytical-theoretical-interpretive, and metatheoretical.
7. The struggle endured by a qualitative researcher searching for a theory of best fit promotes the exercise of imagination. Hence, one outcome of qualitative research is a creative, interesting account. The search for increasing levels of abstraction leads to enriched descriptive accounts, and this remains at the heart of qualitative research.

REFERENCES

Kaplan, D., & Manners, R. A. (1986). *Culture theory*. Prospect Heights, IL: Waveland Press.

Malinowski, B. (1922). *Argonauts of the western Pacific*. London: Routledge.

Merton, R. K. (1967). *On theoretical sociology: Five essays, old and new*. New York: Free Press Paperback.

Mills, G. E. (1985). *The transient child: Some case studies*. Unpublished master's thesis, Curtin University of Technology, Perth, Australia.

Mills, G. E. (1987). *The effects of posting on the children of service personnel*. Canberra, Australia: Report to the Commonwealth Schools Commission.

Mills, G. E. (1988). *Managing and coping with multiple educational change: A case study and analysis*. Unpublished doctoral dissertation, University of Oregon, Eugene.

Mills, G. E. (1990, April). *Theory and concepts in qualitative research: A theory of methodology in a study of directed educational change*. Paper presented at the annual meeting of the American Educational Research Association, Boston.

Opler, M. E. (1945). Themes as dynamic forces in culture. *American Journal of Sociology, 51*(3), 198–206.

Smith, A. G. (1964). The Dionysian Innovation. *American Anthropologist, 66,* 251–265.

Smith, L. M. (1978). An evolving logic of participant observation, educational ethnography, and other case studies. *Review of Research in Education, 6,* 316–377.

Smith, L. M., & Keith, P. M. (1971). *Anatomy of educational innovation: An organizational analysis of an elementary school.* New York: Wiley.

Wallace, A. F. C. (1956). Revitalization movements. *American Anthropologist, 58,* 264–281.

7

From Theory and Concepts to Educational Connoisseurship

DAVID J. FLINDERS

In this chapter I will examine theory from the arts-based perspective. My own research takes the form of educational criticism and connoisseurship, an approach that draws its conceptual guidance from the type of work critics do in fields such as literature, film, drama, and the visual arts (Eisner, 1985, 1991). Connoisseurship refers to the particular repertoire of knowledge that critics bring to their work, and as such it offers an alternative to conventional perspectives on theory. However, because connoisseurship is rarely used as a frame of reference in formal discussions of educational research, I want to begin at the level of basic assumptions. The first questions are simple enough. What is connoisseurship? Who are connoisseurs?

The word *connoisseur* stems from the Latin root *cognosere*, meaning "to know" or "to understand," the same root from which we derive the words *cognizant* and *cognition*. A connoisseur is someone who knows, who is knowledgeable and informed within a particular field. A wine connoisseur is someone who knows about wine; an art connoisseur is someone who knows about art. Connoisseurs also "know" in another respect. That is, they know what to look for. Their perceptual acuity is highly attuned to the phenomena they seek to understand. This ability to see and hear is not physiological, but rather learned. Indeed, connoisseurship is a cultural achievement. It must be actively pursued through a combination of direct experience and reflective inquiry.

Researchers who have been trained in and practice educational criticism do not have exclusive rights to connoisseurship. On the contrary, we find connoisseurship or some analogous concept as a relevant consideration in all forms of social research. And more to the point at hand, connoisseurship serves as a complement to theory in each case. The reasons for this are threefold. First, there is much to experience in any domain that theory cannot fully encompass. Theory, by its nature, is abstract. It can contribute to the refinement of our sensibilities, and thereby deepen our understanding of experience. But theory cannot replace or substitute for any given experience, whether it is listening to a symphony, visiting a classroom, or, for that matter, analyzing statistical data.

Second, theory alone does not tell us when or how to use it, and thus cannot in and of itself adequately guide either the assessment or the overall practice of research. On this point, Joseph Schwab (1969) offers a similar argument in terms of curriculum. He reminds educators that curriculum practice "requires arts which bring a theory to its application" (p. 12). These "arts" include the ability to recognize when a theory is relevant, whether it fits a given set of circumstances, and how well it stacks up against competing theories. To paraphrase Schwab, the practice of research requires, at the very least, an ongoing modification and adaptation of theory as it is applied to setting problems and defining the focus of research.

Third, the folklore of research accommodates if not demands notions comparable to connoisseurship. Our professional norms, for example, ask that researchers keep up-to-date with the scholarship in their areas of study. To put this another way, good research requires a knowledge base as well as theoretical and methodological competence. In addition to being broadly informed, we also expect the best of our research to be imaginatively conceived and adroitly carried out. This too implies connoisseurship. It makes sense to speak of a "well-crafted" case study, "elegant" theory, or an "inventive" sampling procedure, not because these artistic metaphors interject an element of mystery into our work, but because no other language is capable of capturing the genuine complexities of research.

My thesis, then, is that connoisseurship makes a vital if not indispensable contribution to theory, and vice versa. I will develop this thesis by example, describing a study of classroom teaching in which I used educational criticism as my primary research methodology. My account of this work gives particular attention to the interactions between theory and connoisseurship at various points during the study. Finally, I will draw on this study to illustrate some of the limitations of theory. Before doing so, however, I first want to clarify my use of the term *theory*.

DEFINING THEORY

Our everyday meanings of theory span a wide range of semantic possibilities. At one end of the continuum, theory includes the ideas or reasons we use to account for a particular action at a particular time and place. Such "theory" is often informal and context-specific. I might have a "theory," for example, about why Herb and Alice split up. At the other end of the continuum are grandiose and broadly conceived orientations to understanding how the world operates. These theories are what Stephen Pepper (1942) calls "root metaphors," or what William Foote Whyte (1984) terms "orienting theory." More modest than grand theories yet less context-specific than daily accounts of behavior are the formal explanations that act to consolidate a set of ideas. Robert Merton (1957) labeled these attempts to explain a given type of experience as "theories of the middle range," describing them as "intermediate to the minor working hypotheses evolved in abundance during the day-to-day routines of research, and the all-inclusive speculations comprising a master conceptual scheme" (pp. 5–6).

The full range of meaning implied in the word *theory* is important because it calls attention to the "theory-dependence" of all research (Papineau, 1979). This dependence is certainly evident in the research described below. Yet, unless otherwise noted, I will use the term *theory* to specify a formal "body of interconnected propositions about how some portion of the social world operates" (Kidder, 1981, p. 9). This "middle range" definition highlights a number of points. First, theory generally takes the form of propositional statements that explain the relationships among observed actions (Lin, 1976, pp. 15–17). Second, these propositions are more closely joined by the logic of definition and classification (Hempel, 1952) than are hunches or intuitive feelings. Third, formal theory is always simpler than the parts of the world that it seeks to explain (Agnew & Pyke, 1969). And finally, theory both shapes and is shaped by empirical research; their interaction is a two-way street.

A PERSONAL ACCOUNT OF THEORY AT WORK

The study I will describe was completed some years ago (Flinders, 1987). At that time, I was glad to have the project "finished and done with." Then almost two years later, I was asked to write up the study's finding as a monograph for the ERIC Clearinghouse on Educational Management (Flinders, 1989). This occasion to revisit the study and to write about it in retrospect brought forward some previously unrecognized lessons on the role that theory plays in guiding my own research. Looking back, I also came to realize that this particular study is the closest that my work has come to representing a "textbook case" of educational research.

However, even this "closest case" scenario does not mean that the study always proceeded in a highly orthodox fashion. Its research questions, for example, were derived neither from a close examination of theory nor from the research literature within my particular field. Instead, they originated from a nagging suspicion that in an even earlier study, I had not gotten things right. A part of this first study involved interviewing a sample of high school teachers about their various curriculum and instructional practices. The teachers politely answered my questions but showed much more interest in talking about how the conditions of their work made their own professional survival extremely difficult. These concerns were so pervasive among the teachers I spoke with that I began to feel I had asked the wrong questions. As a result, I decided to do a second study, this time looking at the practical concerns that teachers identified as most relevant to their professional lives.

It was only after I had formulated the basic questions and the overall design for my study of "professional life in schools" that any formal notion of theory arrived on the scene. And even at this late stage, its entrance was somewhat arbitrary. This is how it happened. I shared a proposal of my study with a colleague who advised me that in order to help focus the study, and simply as a matter of conventional wisdom, I should "get a theory." My response was naively pragmatic: "Where do I get one?" Without even so much as missing a beat in the tempo of our conversation, my colleague unceremoniously picked up a copy of Michael Lipsky's *Street-Level Bureaucracy* (1980), and quite literally handed me a theory.

Theory and Its Application

My fortuitous introduction to Lipsky's theory of street-level bureaucracy was not quite as simple as I make it sound, for I had no way of knowing at that time how well it would explain particular aspects of classroom teaching. Sorting out its implications is part of the complicated process I will describe next, but first let me summarize some of the main points of Lipsky's theory. This theory attempts to locate the place of the individual within institutional settings where public service workers interact directly with clients and have substantial discretion in determining precisely how this interaction takes place. Street-level bureaucracies include public agencies such as welfare offices, police departments, the lower courts, and schools. Lipsky describes the work environment within these agencies as characterized by inadequate resources, ambiguous goals, vague performance standards, and nonvoluntary clients. Faced with these conditions, street-level bureaucrats (e.g., teachers) develop work strategies that are adaptive to their own professional survival. These strategies include rationing services, controlling clients, and conserving resources. They lead public service workers to what Lipsky calls a "processing mentality."

Lipsky's theory does not leave us with a particularly flattering image of street-level bureaucrats. However, I was fascinated by the parallels between Lipsky's conditions of work and the nature of professional life in schools. Resources, particularly time, do seem largely inadequate for classroom teachers relative to what we generally want these teachers to accomplish with their students. The more teachers do, the more there is to do, and thus demands increase to meet the availability of services. Educational goals are noted for their ambiguity, and a teacher's work performance is difficult or impossible to evaluate in any definitive sense. Finally, compulsory education laws situate students, strictly speaking, as nonvoluntary "clients."

I also recognized that Lipsky's theory was able to bring into focus several aspects of teaching that we often fail to recognize. In particular, the theory highlights the survival function of certain teaching routines. Worksheets, multiple-choice exams, and a heavy reliance on textbooks are examples of how practice, while justified (we hope) in terms of educational goals, is also responsive to the practical demands and crowded conditions of classroom life. Even the isolation of teachers documented by other classroom researchers (Goodlad, 1984; House & Lapan, 1979) can be understood from this perspective as a survival strategy that allows teachers to conserve time and energy (Flinders, 1988).

In bringing these issues forward, Lipsky's theory alerted me to patterns (e.g., resource conservation) in how teachers went about organizing their day-to-day work. In other words, the theory told me what to look for. It guided my observations at both an explicit and implicit level by suggesting what particular aspects of teaching experience deserve close attention. This is the conventional use of theory in research. Yet on these grounds, I believe we are tempted to overstate the importance of theory. There are, after all, limits to theory whenever it is applied in the context of research.

The Limitations of Theory

In my particular study, theory proved inadequate on two counts. First, it fell short of capturing the rich complexities and intricate dynamics of the participating teachers' everyday professional lives. As I sat in classrooms week after week, I could not ignore the motives and identities of "real" people. In a sense, I saw and heard too much. This was frustrating at first because many of my observations of teachers' day-to-day work readily fit

Lipsky's theory. But it also seemed that many observations would not have been predicted. All I could do was sort out my information into a broad set of categories. In doing so, what I learned was that my observations in support of Lipsky's theory were by and large focused on curricular concerns. Reviewing text materials, preparing lessons, and grading homework or exams are activities that I came to label the "task demands" of teaching. In relation to these demands, it was quite easy to identify strong patterns of conservation. The teachers in my study had developed, as Lipsky's theory would predict, a "work-processing mentality."

However, I found that other dimensions of the teachers' work simply did not support Lipsky's theory. These dimensions tended to focus on the interpersonal demands of working with students. When it came to facilitating a class discussion, directing small groups, or providing individual assistance, the teachers I observed tended to demonstrate "nonbureaucratic" strategies. Examples of these strategies range from bending school rules in the students' interest to providing opportunities for individual recognition. Negotiation and flexibility, not conservation per se, guided teachers in these particular patterns of work. In short, the teachers I observed had not developed a "client-processing mentality."

Why was it that I found "work" processing but not "client" processing? In pondering this question, I went back to Lipsky's assumptions about the salient work conditions in street-level bureaucracies, reconsidering each assumption in light of the circumstances in which teachers work. One assumption in particular seemed questionable: the nonvoluntary status of clients. If student participation in day-to-day classroom life was indeed nonvoluntary, why did teachers negotiate with students on an ongoing basis, and why were teachers flexible in responding to student concerns even when such flexibility did not serve in the conservation of scarce resources? The issues surrounding the students' nonvoluntary status now seemed more complex than I had first considered. Students could be considered nonvoluntary participants in some but not all ways. To put this another way, the image of student involvement implied in Lipsky's theory is less dynamic than would be needed to account for the relational dimensions of teaching that I observed.

In looking back on my research, I have also learned that theory alone offers an inadequate basis for assessing educational significance. All theory rests on ideological assumptions, and thus theory and values become inextricably interwoven. Theory attempts to explain what we believe is worth explaining, but our judgments of worth go beyond theory per se. I can best illustrate this point by referring to my example of work-processing versus client-processing patterns of teaching. I regarded the abundance of work processing that I observed as "the bad news" of my study. While these processing strategies (e.g., multiple-choice exams, point systems, and routinized use of the text) can be understood as adaptive to the immediate practical demands of classroom instruction, they lead to problematic consequences for both teachers and students. First, these strategies give rise to clerical demands that can co-opt and even overwhelm any opportunities the teachers have for continued learning within their subject areas. Second, processing strategies tend to fragment the curriculum, thus making it difficult for students to derive substantive meaning from their classroom experiences.

In contrast, I came to regard my inability to document client processing as "the good news" of the study. In support of this judgment, I argued not only that teachers realize job satisfaction from their interpersonal strategies (e.g., orchestrating class discussions, providing individual recognition, bending school rules), but also that these strategies model for students implicit "lessons" about cooperation, negotiation, and human interdependence. But I made these normative assessments as an educational critic, not as a theoretician. At least in the field of education, the question "So what?" is more than theoretical; it is a question of cultural and educational values.

BEYOND THEORY

My discussion to this point can be summarized by saying that Lipsky's theory played an important but secondary role in my study of professional life in schools. The theory was sometimes illuminating, sometimes simply irrelevant, and sometimes relevant but less satisfying than I would have liked. In pushing this analysis a step further, I will now try to identify what guided my work when theory proved inadequate. In particular, I wish to address two questions: (1) How was I able to recognize patterns of teaching that did not fit Lipsky's theory? and (2) What, if not theory, informed my judgment of these patterns as educationally significant?

Casting a Broad Net

The first question concerns recognizing what I did not expect to find. This was not a matter of ignoring theory or of trying to enter the field empty-headed. Rather, it was a matter of making careful observations. In my fieldnotes and daily summary sheets, for example, of course I recorded information about the types of teaching patterns that Lipsky's theory would predict. Yet, I also recorded as much as I could of any instance, behavior, interaction, and so on that participating teachers and students

seemed to regard as important. Moreover, I went out of my way to sched-
ule observations and interviews so that they would afford opportunities to
revisit themes and concepts that emerged over time. I also pored over my
fieldnotes throughout the study, rereading them dozens of times while still
in the field, and then returning to them constantly while analyzing and
writing up individual cases. I even found myself rereading them yet again
in order to write the ERIC monograph more than two years after the actual
fieldwork.

I intended my observations to follow the type of heuristic advice
that Harry Wolcott (1990) offers ethnographers and others engaged in
qualitative research. Wolcott's recommendations include several points,
some of which I have summarized below.

1. While doing fieldwork, try to spend much more time listening
   than talking.
2. Record fieldnotes during observations or as soon as possible there-
   after.
3. In writing descriptive accounts, let those you observe "speak for
   themselves" as much as possible.
4. Share descriptive accounts with others who are knowledgeable
   about the particular setting.
5. Use subsequent observations to check the balance, fairness, com-
   pleteness, and sensitivity of descriptive accounts.
6. Give close attention to details in revising descriptive accounts.

I believe these recommendations should be viewed broadly. Rather
than a methodological bag of tricks, they suggest an underlying regard for
the role of connoisseurship in qualitative research. At issue here is the
enhancement of perception, and the connoisseur's methodical approach to
avoid what Walter Pater called "the roughness of the eye that makes any
two persons, things, situations, seem alike" (Abrams, 1974, p. 1640).

Making Judgments

My second question asks about the criteria used in assessing educational
significance, and therefore brings into focus a different set of issues. Evaluation, rather than perception or understanding, is the process I wish to
emphasize at this point. Again, however, evaluating the significance of
what researchers see and hear leads them beyond theory. Wine connoisseurs, to draw an analogy, are not only interested in why a particular
wine possesses certain qualities; they are also interested in how good the
wine is relative to other wines. Theory plays a role here; the wine connois-

seur may have a theory about how, for example, regional climatic differences influence the taste or bouquet of a given vintage. Yet, this theory by itself does not tell the connoisseur whether the influence is good or bad, a virtue or a vice. To make that assessment, the connoisseur draws on a combination of past experience, a discerning palate, *and* culturally defined expectations for what constitutes good wine.

In my own study, evaluative judgments of good teaching involved a process of situating instructional patterns in relation to historically and culturally grounded value orientations. Work processing, for example, I found important not because Lipsky's theory makes it important, but because it shapes the educational value of what students learn in the classroom. When a work-processing mentality dominates instruction, the clerical demands of teaching become an end in themselves, the curriculum is fragmented into easily managed bits and pieces, and coherence suffers. At the same time, we have reasons to value coherence in this context because it fosters the likelihood that students will be able to find meaning in what they study.

My point, I hasten to add, is that the evaluative dimensions of research are not simply a matter of personal taste. Whether in education or in art, all of us have likes and dislikes, but not all of us are connoisseurs. In education, this means developing a conscious recognition of the values that one is willing to embrace, the history of those values, how they have been articulated by past and contemporary proponents, where they stand in relation to alternative values, and what they look like in practice. This is where experience in educational settings and broadly based knowledge from the foundations of education make an essential contribution to research.

Distinctions Between Theory and Connoisseurship

Placing my own study in the background for a moment, I want to briefly summarize some of the main differences between theory and connoisseurship. First, while theory strives toward general explanations that will apply across different settings, connoisseurship is domain-specific. That is, a connoisseur's knowledge and skills are recognized only within a particular area of expertise. A wine connoisseur, for all we know, might be a completely incompetent judge of music or art or film, just as educational connoisseurship will not necessarily help us assess the qualities of a particularly good wine.

Second, while theory is an explicit and distinct form of knowledge, readily described, connoisseurship eludes differentiation by building on a gestalt of information accumulated across time and from multiple sources.

Many researchers view this gestalt knowledge as a form of implicit theory. Yet, unlike formal theory, it works behind the scenes, roughly corresponding to the nontechnical processes that Donald Schön (1983) calls "reflection-in-practice." In short, connoisseurship is to theory what background is to foreground.

Third, while the functions of theory emphasize explanation and prediction (telling us what leads to what), the functions of connoisseurship stress the application and modification of theory in use. To put this another way, connoisseurship plays a heuristic role in how we manipulate or set ideas into motion. It facilitates and guides the formulation of questions that theory proposes to answer.

Fourth, while theory relies on the nominal logic of definition and classification, connoisseurship is more of an alloy that blends logic with firsthand experience. For the wine connoisseur, knowledge in the abstract cannot replace the act of sitting down, pouring a glass of wine, and drinking it. Conversely, one does not become a wine connoisseur simply by drinking a lot of wine. Experience and the informed understanding of that experience must come together.

Finally, theory is expressly instrumental. It explains how and why things work as they do. This same instrumentality is what often prevents us from recognizing that theory is also inherently value-laded. In contrast, connoisseurship is both inherently *and purposefully* value-laden. That is, the connoisseur strives explicitly toward understandings of "goodness."

WHAT MAKES FOR GOOD THEORY?

I hope the distinctions I have briefly outlined above do not obscure the complementary relationship between theory and connoisseurship. Theory in the absence of connoisseurship is analogous to having highly sophisticated tools but with absolutely no ability or knowledge of how to use them to one's advantage. If theory is to inform qualitative research at all, it must be used with an appreciation for the context in which the theory is to be applied. The potential contributions of theory to connoisseurship are also important. Without theory, connoisseurship would have little or no opportunity to develop.

Even in the study I have described, where a theory was somewhat arbitrarily introduced, the evaluation and adaptation of that theory became increasingly central to my work. Where the theory broke down or proved inadequate, I was forced to seek out alternative explanations. Doing so was guided, however vaguely, by notions of what constitutes good theory. What, then, are the characteristics of good theory? Neil Agnew and Sandra Pyke (1969) recommend that good theory be (1) simple, (2) testable, (3) novel, (4) supportive of other theories, (5) internally consistent, and (6) predictive.

I suspect that all six of these criteria should play a role in evaluating theory. However, in doing my own research, I have learned to be increasingly tolerant of theoretical complexity, varying degrees of untestability, old and seemingly obvious ideas, unorthodoxy, internal inconsistency, and low predictive ability. The level of this tolerance depends on the extent to which a given theory provides insightful distinctions and ways of understanding classroom life. If a theory makes otherwise perplexing observations intelligible, I will put up with a great deal. This is to say that I find theory most attractive and useful when it contributes to increasingly sophisticated levels of educational connoisseurship.

My tolerance of imperfect theory is largely pragmatic, but it also seems well matched to the exploratory stance of qualitative research in contrast to the theory-verification stance of quantitative research. Qualitative forms of inquiry, to the degree that they are exploratory and approached open-mindedly, demand that theory be used with imagination and flexibility. In this respect, a researcher's satisfaction with any given theory may be tied to a fundamental aspect of human curiosity — the desire, as John Dewey (1934) put it, to re-educate our perceptions.

REFERENCES

Abrams, M. H. (Ed.). (1974). *The Norton anthology of English literature* (Vol. 2). New York: Norton.

Agnew, N. McK., & Pyke, S. W. (1969). *The science game.* Englewood Cliffs, NJ: Prentice-Hall.

Dewey, J. (1934). *Art as experience.* New York: Perigee.

Eisner, E. W. (1985). *The educational imagination* (2nd ed.). New York: Macmillan.

Eisner, E. W. (1991). *The enlightened eye.* New York: Macmillan.

Flinders, D. J. (1987). *What teachers learn from teaching: Education criticisms of instructional adaptation.* Unpublished doctoral dissertation, Stanford University, Stanford.

Flinders, D. J. (1988). Teacher isolation and the new reform. *Journal of Curriculum and Supervision, 4*(1), 17–29.

Flinders, D. J. (1989). *Voices from the classroom.* Eugene, OR: ERIC Clearinghouse on Educational Management.

Goodlad, J. I. (1984). *A place called school.* New York: McGraw-Hill.

Hempel, C. G. (1952). *Fundamentals of concept formation in empirical science.* Chicago: University of Chicago Press.

House, E. R., & Lapan, S. D. (1979). *Survival in the classroom*. Boston: Allyn & Bacon.

Kidder, L. H. (1981). *Research methods in social relations* (4th ed.). New York: Holt, Rinehart & Winston.

Lin, N. (1976). *Foundations of social research*. New York: McGraw-Hill.

Lipsky, M. (1980). *Street-level bureaucracy: Dilemmas of the individual in public services*. New York: Russell Sage Foundation.

Merton, R. K. (1957). *Social theory and social structure*. Glencoe, IL: Free Press.

Papineau, D. (1979). *Theory and meaning*. Oxford: Clarendon Press.

Pepper, S. C. (1942). *World hypothesis: A study in evidence*. Berkeley: University of California Press.

Schön, D. (1983). *The reflective practitioner*. New York: Basic Books.

Schwab, J. J. (1969). The practical: A language for Curriculum. *School Review*, 78, 1–24.

Whyte, W. F. (1984). *Learning from the field*. Beverly Hills, CA: Sage.

Wolcott, H. (1990). On seeking—and rejecting—validity in qualitative research. In E. W. Eisner & A. Peshkin (Eds.), *Qualitative inquiry in education: The continuing debate* (pp. 121–152). New York: Teachers College Press.

8

Notes Toward Theory in Biography

Working on the Nora Barlow Papers

LOUIS M. SMITH

THE PROBLEM

I am writing a biography of Nora Barlow, granddaughter of Charles and Emma Darwin, daughter of Horace and Ida Darwin, wife of the eminent civil servant Alan Barlow (who himself was the son of the pediatrician to Queen Victoria's children), mother of six children, one of the founders of what is now called "the Darwin Industry," and author/editor of four books on the Darwin manuscripts (the first of which was published as she turned fifty, the second in her sixties, the third in her seventies, and the fourth in her eighties), among a number of other things. And I believe that one of my problems is in the nature of the theory—social, psychological, and personality—that will underlie the book.

The struggles with that problem, the nature and role of theory, especially personality theory, is what I want to raise in this chapter. I believe the issue has been part of the intellectual world of biographers, at least implicitly if not explicitly, since the first stories of people were recited and written down. The phrasing of the issues has varied dramatically. Sixty-five years ago, Virginia Woolf (1927/1960) presented, in her usual elegant style, apt phrasing that could have been written yesterday or today. She opened her essay on "The New Biography" with her "granite and rainbow" dilemma. She commented:

> "The aim of biography", said Sir Sidney Lee, who had perhaps read and written more lives than any man of his time, "is the truthful transmission of personality", and no single sentence could more nearly split into two parts the whole problem of biography as it presents itself to-day. On the one hand there is truth; on the other there is personality. And if we think of truth as something of granite-like solidity and of personality as something of rainbow-

like intangibility and reflect that the aim of biography is to weld these two into one seamless whole, we shall admit that the problem is a stiff one and that we need not wonder if biographers have for the most part failed to solve it. (p. 149)

The granite-like and the rainbow-like. She develops her argument by commenting that Mr. Lee wrote awful biographies; "dull" and "unreadable" were two of her adjectives. She turns the problem into a failure in writing, which is a large part of the truth, I believe. But I want to explore another reason for the difficulties, the nature of the theory of personality that one uses explicitly or implicitly.

In the late eighteenth century, Boswell's (1791/1991) *Life of Johnson* became a turning point. Now not only actions and works stood for the man, but his words symbolized his personality. And Johnson was a man of words.

In the early twentieth century, another kind of liberation occurred with Strachey's (1918) briefer, focused, and often more critical than laudatory biographies. In Woolf's (1927/1960) words, the biographer "has ceased to be the chronicler; he has become an artist" (p. 152). But the artist and the chronicler, in her view, are forever in conflict. The chronicler captures the truth, even as the artist catches the "character," the "private life," and the "reflections" of the individual through manners, dramatic stories, and the relations of the biographer with his or her friends. She concludes with mysteries yet to be solved: "Nor can we name the biographer whose art is subtle and bold enough to present that queer amalgamation of dream and reality, that perpetual marriage of granite and rainbow. His method still remains to be discovered" (p. 155).

I propose to rephrase her emphasis on "method" to an emphasis on "theory." But my account of Nora Barlow is not finished, nor is my conceptualization. And the latter may never "really" be over. On an earlier and different occasion, Martin Hammersley (1991) described my ethnographic education and social science orientation as "disciplined eclecticism." I believe that that was what I was about then and there, and that is what I am about here in biography. And I don't believe that "disciplined eclecticism" is too bad a place to be.

A WORKING PROBLEM/ILLUSTRATION

In the spring of 1990, I spent three months in Cambridge, England, working on the biography. I have written a long monograph about that experience. It carries the title *Doing Ethnographic Biography: A Reflective Prac-*

titioner at Work During a Spring in Cambridge (1992). In early May I had been reading two sets of letters, different "pools of data" to use an earlier phrasing of mine (Smith, 1990). One set was the 1910 and 1911 engagement letters between Nora Darwin and her husband to be, Alan Barlow. The second set was between Nora and her first cousin, Gwen Darwin, later Gwen Raverat. In addition, about the same time, I had a brief tour of the biochemistry laboratory of the university with a young friend from Israel who was a postdoctoral student in the lab. We were engaged in a series of discussions about the nature of inquiry in ethnography, biography, and biochemistry. (You really need to read the whole 270-page monograph for the complexity of my life there that spring.) On May 10, I wrote the beginnings of a memo on some of the methodological problems I was having with the letters. The memo illustrates one of the issues I want to raise today. It began this way.

> Reading Latour and Woolgar (1979) [*Laboratory Life, the Social Construction of Scientific Facts*] this morning and their emphasis on constructing seems so relevant as I go back to the Nora to Gwen letters. The writing of a life seems to be one continuous process of construction.

And now the critical sentences.

> I am rethinking how to present the Nora and Gwen relationship. In the ethic of the Victorian and Edwardian world their relationship seems best construed as an intimate friendship. It came before, paralleled, and then lost out to Nora's marriage to Alan. (5/10/90) (Smith, 1992, p. 106)

My evolving and partially conscious personality theory, in this illustration, contains the concept of relationships, of which I noted two kinds—intimate friendship and marriage. And then I noted that the Nora and Gwen relationships "came before, paralleled, and then lost out" to the engagement and later marriage to Alan, and, I might add, also Gwen's marriage to Jacques Raverat. Even now, I am compelled by the implicitly theoretical insight of coming before, paralleling, and losing out. As I tell this brief anecdote, I am sure it has its commonplace quality and resonates to the personal experience of many of you, and that similar illustrations run rampant through the fiction of novelists and playwrights. But what does one, as a qualitative researcher, in this instance a biographer, do theoretically with Nora, Gwen, and Alan and relationships of two kinds that overlap in time and lose out? And if that were not difficult enough, how does one write about it as part of life story, a biography? As author, do I write then sequentially, or do I fuse them in some way? Is one a more major theme than the other, and hence does it assume a superordinate rather than a subordinate place in the biography? And to which of my psychological gurus do I turn for guidance?

At a minimum, as a first step, I seem to need someone who has a conception of a total person, an integrated personality. Second, this personality must be seen as changing over time. Third, the conception must have a social or interpersonal dimension. Fourth, some kind of compartmentalization of events must be possible if the friendships come before and run parallel. Fifth, the "losing out" phrase seems to imply elements of choice and perhaps tragedy, as elements of personality theory. And then lurking behind all this should be a body of psychological research that should help me think through, perhaps do a better job with, this part of my biography of Nora Barlow. Calvin Hall and Gardner Lindzey's (1970) *Theories of Personality* suggests an array of possibilities.

And by thinking through, I don't mean a simple set of rules that I might "apply" in some easy, one-to-one fashion, although some statements of the "application of psychological theory to practical educational problems" seem just that, a part of the educational psychology literature in its relationship to the teacher's problems in the classroom (Schön, 1983). Do personality theorists have the same relationship to biographers? And are those relationships "equally as effective" as the psychologists' relationships to the educational practitioners? Major questions for me.

SEVERAL ITEMS FROM THE BOOK OUTLINE

Now I would like to backtrack a bit and present several of the issues I encountered and the concepts that arose as I thought through a prospectus and outline of the biography. Issues in the personality of the subject, the author, and the audience are front and center.

In the first chapter, I present a series of anecdotes of Nora at different stages of her life. These illustrations come from her letters and the letters and comments of her friends and family. My intention here is to develop an overall image of Nora Barlow over her life-span. The overall image is, I would argue, a pattern of traits, dispositions, or characteristics that show some stability and change over the years, yet are age related. Character is an early, more literary label; personality tends to be the psychologist's term.

One of these illustrations is a summary one indicating that Nora Barlow published four books on the Darwin papers over a 40-year period: from her late forties to her early eighties. What should I call that phenomenon? An "abiding interest" seems closer to the mark than need Achievement or need Cognition, or need Autonomy, although they surely seem a part of the phenomenon as well. Research serial might be a label from Henry Murray's (1938) personological theory, yet that seems to stress more the cognitively planned and implemented set of actions and less the motivational aspects.

Another item integrates with, yet shades off from, this interpretation. It is a comment Nora made in a letter to Gregory Bateson when she was 60 years old: "My Ivory Tower has been a nice little old sailing ship called the Beagle. So remote, so irrelevant, but O so pleasant" (1946, p. 1). The major focus of her Darwin intellectual work—the *Diary* (1933), the letters from the Beagle (1946), the Henslow letters (1967), and the ornithology monograph (1963)—was from the five years he spent on the H. M. S. Beagle. But in the eyes of a nonacademic, an "Ivory Tower" is a retreat, a haven. It is "remote" presumably from a family of six children, a husband inordinately busy with government civil service work, and World War II underway for the prior half dozen years. "Irrelevant" suggests understatement, in the form of potentially unimportant to anyone except herself. But 40 years on an irrelevancy? Finally, the "but O so pleasant" comment returns to the emotional satisfaction present, apparently a huge amount. My label "abiding interest" vies, obviously, with other possible labels, such as "intellectual commitment." It seems reasonably arguable that "intellectual commitment" might be a subclass of "abiding interests." In a sense, I may be playing word games, but I don't believe so. Even trying to tell interesting stories about Nora Barlow doesn't preclude the stories having a "point" or "moral" to them, and the point can be a statement about her "character" as well as other aspects of the situation. In my view, theories are supposed to play this kind of role, thinking about an individual case and moving toward the understanding of other cases, in psychology and presumably in biography done by psychologists.

As soon as a general category is isolated, then attention can be turned to judgments of value of the characteristic and to the antecedents and consequences of the phenomenon. As a psychologist turned educationist, I am not arguing for a hard causality or determinism, but I am arguing for a kind of value-laden theory. I believe that individuals who have several "abiding interests," whether these be gardening, fishing, genealogy, playing sports, doing psychological research, or even writing books, have more meaning in their lives, are judged to be more interesting people, and maybe are more healthy psychologically than people who don't have abiding interests. Some years ago Marie Jahoda (1958) struggled with several concepts of positive mental health. If some of these beliefs are empirically demonstrable, and they are testable propositions, then educators should have some interest in "abiding interests." An obvious next set of questions resides in antecedents — what can a teacher or a school do to enhance, make more probable, the occurrence of a child's "abiding interests"? Whether all biographers have such curiosity, I don't know. But this one does! My students find speculating on such a question a fascinating piece of curriculum.

One more illustration follows along from this one. As children, Nora and her cousin Gwen Darwin (later Gwen Raverat) grew up in Cambridge and later attended the Levana School, a boarding school for young ladies in Wimbledon, South London (Raverat, 1952). Gwen went there first and urged Nora to attend, for she was in dire need for support in an alien environment. In their adolescence, Nora and Gwen wrote a large number of letters back and forth. During those years they were both writers and artists. Both perceived themselves to be intellectuals; rationality, not emotionality, was the supreme value. Nora turned to science, passionately I might add, and Gwen continued with art, also passionately. But the point I want to make is that each married a few years later. Nora was the first to have a child. That experience was a major event. She had not expected to be the first of the female cousins of their generation to have a child; both her sister and Gwen had indicated more interest. But she found the experience to be so surprisingly important that she wanted more children. She had six children in the first 10 years of her marriage. The first child had multiple physical and mental disabilities, and a long and interesting story within the biography resides here. But the point I want to make is that motherhood "brought out," "developed," or "created" a nurturing dimension to her personality. A dimension not visible before. For the rest of her life, "nurturing" vied with "intellectual autonomy" and with "abiding interests" in Darwiniana — especially the Beagle voyage — as significant aspects of her personality.

Writing about these kinds of events, that is, constructing the biography per se, has its own kind of difficulties, but underlying the writing problem is the theoretical problem, how does one think about such items? To return to Virginia Woolf, whether one resolves the issues intuitively or more doggedly rationally, a resolution is needed if the biography is to have coherence, sense, and interest. Each of the dozen chapters has posed similar problems of underlying ideas about personality.

ONE MORE TROUBLING PROBLEM

When I, as a social scientist, turned my hand to biography, I found myself in a strange new world peopled by humanists and literary scholars. And when I as a male began writing a biography of a woman, I found myself, as you might imagine, in another world as well. Also, as you might suspect, I have tried to tread cautiously and carefully. I would like to raise now a theoretical problem that surfaced early and that has been troubling throughout. Early on I was struck by, and impressed with, what I called Nora Barlow's late in life intellectual productivity—the four books from just before fifty to her mid-eighties. More recently, I have been intrigued with, but also puzzled by, Carolyn Heilbrun's (1988) *Writing a Woman's Life*. Today I want to begin an integration of the two puzzlements.

The social scientist in me suggests that Heilbrun's last chapter is in part a theoretical chapter, and one that fits, perhaps explains, Nora Barlow's late in life productivity. Consider the first paragraph of that chapter.

> For women who have awakened to new possibilities in middle age, or who were born into the current women's movement and have escaped the usual rhythms of the once traditional female existence, *the last third of life is likely to require new attitudes and new courage.* Virginia Woolf is an example of a woman who found a new and remarkable courage when she was fifty. *This is, I believe, an achievement uniquely female.* (p. 124; emphasis added)

"New attitudes and new courage" and "an achievement uniquely female" are powerful empirical statements. In her elaboration, Heilbrun raises further implications—fears of the patriarchy and fears from one's own deepest beliefs, as these relate to the expression of anger. Old age becomes a time for the possibility of freedom. And Heilbrun's "theory" takes on a valuational quality: "Instead, we should make use of our security, our seniority, to take risks, to make noise, to be courageous, to become unpopular" (p. 131). "Should's" are troublesome for some scientific theories, although I find myself, as an educator, in her camp. Educational theory, by definition, I believe is a practical theory and has value components as premises. But that is a complication, not the core of what I want to dwell upon here.

My problem is that the substance of Heilbrun's theorizing doesn't seem to fit the data and my understanding of Nora Barlow. So, what do we have—bad or limited theory? data? or biographer's understanding? Or some of each?

One step in thinking my way through the issue is to return to the question being asked. Am I especially interested in explaining that a woman wrote four books late in life? Probably not, for usual explanations abound with the concerns of marriage, children, and husband's career receiving priority. Woolf early on and Tillie Olsen (1983) in *Silences* graphically make the case. The better questions might be, Why did this woman, Nora Barlow, write any books? and Why did she write these particular ones? And perhaps, "Why four?" My notion of explanation has a traditional ring to it: I went looking for antecedent events, potential causes, and developed them into pictorial models, what Zetterberg (1965) called an inventory of antecedents.

Consider these events: In the late 1920s as Nora moved into her forties, William Bateson died. He was her first, continuing, and major connection to research in genetics, the field of her early scientific publications. That avenue, nearly closed for a long time, now was definitely at an end. She declined a later offer from R. A. Fisher to return to her early work, and her unsolved problem, but it was too distant. Second, her Uncle Frank, Sir Francis Darwin, the keeper of the Charles Darwin files, records, and assorted materials, also died in 1925. His son Bernard, who inherited most of the material, was singularly uninterested in Darwiniana. The contents of the black boxes were slowly decomposing in his cellar. Nora took an active interest in their resurrection, and that's a long story in itself. Up until that time no one had been permitted to work on the original documents except Francis himself. In the 1920s death also took all of the surviving Darwin children except for Leonard — Elizabeth in 1926, Henrietta (Aunt Etty) in 1927, and Nora's father Horace in 1928. In that generation Aunt Etty was the only likely candidate for assuming the family historian role. She had published a two-volume work, *The Letters of Emma Darwin*, her mother's correspondence. She had a lively and vigorous intellect. Of Nora's generation, the nine grandchildren of Charles Darwin, she was the only one trained in biology. The only other scientist was the eminent physicist, her cousin Charles Galton Darwin. Also she was the only one to have written materials about Darwin (and Galton) for an *Encyclopedia* or other such publications. If you like, the "abiding interest" had been about for a long time. And it was not a merely adulatory kind of interest, for Bateson had said years before that only a Darwin could have gotten away with saying some of the negative things about Charles Darwin that Nora had said early in her genetics career. Finally, I would return to the adolescent definition of herself as an intellectual. The importance of that is evidenced in her teenage and early twenties correspondence with her cousin Gwen. I would argue that never left her, in spite of family, husband and children, separation from Bateson and his laboratory and gardens, and the nearly two decades of frustration in not solving the problems in the genetics of trimorphic flowers.

As I recite these facts and tentative interpretations, I find that they do not sound like the interpretations made by Heilbrun. Fear of the patriarchy was not a fear of Nora's, as best as I can determine. Nor was anger and the going against her basic beliefs a key factor. She wrote once to Gregory Bateson late in life, wishing she had more training in zoology, "animal physiology," as she termed it, so that she could participate more fully in discussing some of the issues he was raising toward the end of his career. But that seems different from Heilbrun's analysis. A kind of non-fit seems apparent between Nora's life and Heilbrun's interpretations and explanations of the later periods in women's lives. In short, I need to think some more about any kind of general theory of women's lives and the writing of a particular woman's life. I hope and believe I have provided enough of an account of the life of a fascinating individual to open the discussion another step or two.

BY WAY OF A TENTATIVE CONCLUSION

Conclusions are a bit hard to come by when one is only part way through a project. But several along-the-way ideas seem worth emphasizing.

First, I have attacked the biography much as I have done the more ethnographic field studies in education that I have carried out over the last couple of decades. Essentially, this is our variant of Glaser and Strauss's (1967) conception of the discovery of grounded theory. Here as before, I have a continuing strong interest in a detailed narrative, as Paul Pohland and I (1976) argued some years ago. Among qualitative studies, I remain drawn to the case study variant. Biography seems ideally suited to that.

Second, and more often implicit in the present essay, I find that the kind of biography I am doing has a flavor of symbolic interactionist theory. I want to see and report Nora Barlow as she interacts with significant others—friends, family, relatives, and intellectual colleagues. Perhaps most significant, I am trying to argue for a personality theory that goes well beyond the more limited, though valuable, self-theory. Nora was a beautiful child and young woman, by the usual Western standards. She was highly intelligent as would have been determined by any intelligence tests if they had been available and she had taken them. Her colleague in the "Darwin industry," Sydney Smith, commented that she had the "best Darwin mind since Charles," a casual observation but one, in less extravagant form, supported by innumerable other pieces of evidence. And as I tried to argue here, she had major "abiding interests" and "intellectual commitments." In the best sense, these were stable personality structures. I agree with David Hargreaves (1986) in his "Whatever Happened to Symbolic Interactionism?" that it is alive and well, but needs to be continually worked upon.

Third, as Hargreaves also argues, some of the macro issues that symbolic interactionism does not handle so well will, I believe, appear in the

Nora Barlow biography. Noel Annan (1955), the English social historian, raised a major conception in the analysis of English culture when he began his studies of "the intellectual aristocracy," that part of upper middle class society which over the last two centuries has come to dominate the intellectual life of England. The Darwins (and the Huxleys, Keynes, Macaulays, Trevelyans, etc.) were a part of this. And as developed briefly and implicitly here, Nora Barlow is also a part of this world, in spite of the fact that Annan omitted her by name, though including her sister and son. Issues in social class and gender are writ large in her life. And what to make of that — from the point of view of personality theory and a theory of biography?

Fourth, I find myself enamored with the literary biographers. I am not sure whether I am a frustrated would-be student of English, or whether I am overly impressed with the quality of thought and writing style, but Boswell, Strachey, Woolf, to mention just a few, write significantly to key issues. Perhaps it's their craft perspective I find so significant, for they are fine artists and reflective practitioners of that art.

Fifth, I have been reading a host of women writers and critics, Woolf (1929) again, but also Heilbrun (1988), Mary Catherine Bateson (1990), and Tillie Olsen (1983), among others. As I try to integrate their ideas into my social science perspective, I find a lively kind of controversy possible. Opportunities and constraints, death, family position, and resources all seem very important in my data. In the present discussion I have mainly illustrated dilemmas posed by Heilbrun's generalizations. Keller, author of the biography of Barbara McClintock (1983) and other essays (1985), would take the analysis another step or two.

As I indicated earlier, a few years ago Martin Hammersley (1991) called my approach to studying classrooms and schools "disciplined eclecticism." Upon reflection, that seemed to fit my self-perception of what I was doing. Now I find the idea reappearing as I think my way through the biography of Nora Barlow. Specifically, when it was initially conceived, I thought that this chapter would be an analysis, synthesis, and evaluation of the Henry Murray (1938, 1954) position. In looking for one of his books in our library, I found Gordon Allport's (1965) *Letters from Jenny*. That book was so much closer to the work I had been doing, that I started exploring more of Gordon Allport (1942, 1960). His "structural dynamic" approach, which I hadn't read much of for years, resonated to what I seemed to be doing intuitively. His references to the idiographic and nomothetic dilemma lies at the heart of much of my efforts. It may well be that the "personality" of the biographer is almost as important as the personality of the subject of the biography. The historian Jack Hexter's

(1971) distinction between the first record and the second record seems inescapable. But all this belongs in another chapter for another time.

In brief, I find that biography is a fascinating kind of qualitative research. It poses all kinds of theoretical sub-issues that more traditional ethnography, and history as well, often tends to gloss over. I have tried for a beginning here, while midway in doing a particular biography, *Nora Barlow and the Darwin Legacy.*

REFERENCES

Allport, G. W. (1942). *The use of personal documents in psychological science.* New York: Social Science Research Council.

Allport, G. W. (1960). Personality: A problem for science or a problem for art? In G. W. Allport (Ed.), *Personality and social encounter* (pp. 3–15). Boston: Beacon Press.

Allport, G. W. (1965). *Letters from Jenny.* New York: Harcourt, Brace.

Annan, N. (1955). The intellectual aristocracy. In J. H. Plumb (Ed.), *Studies in social history: A tribute to G. M. Trevelyan* (pp. 243–287). New York: Longmans Green.

Barlow, N. (1913). Preliminary note on heterostylism in oxalis and lythrum. *Journal of Genetics, 3,* 53–65.

Barlow, N. (Ed.). (1933). *Charles Darwin's diary of the voyage of the H. M. S. Beagle.* Cambridge: Cambridge University Press.

Barlow, N. (1946). Letter, Gregory Bateson Archives, University of Santa Cruz Library, Santa Cruz, CA.

Barlow, N. (1946). *Charles Darwin and the voyage of the Beagle.* New York: Philosophical Library.

Barlow, N. (Ed.). (1958). *The autobiography of Charles Darwin 1809–1882.* London: Collins.

Barlow, N. (1963). Darwin's ornithology notes. *Bulletin of the British Museum (Natural History) Historical Series, 2*(7), 201–278.

Barlow, N. (Ed.). (1967). *Darwin and Henslow: The growth of an idea. Letters 1831 1860.* Berkeley: University of California Press.

Bateson, M. C. (1990). *Composing a life.* New York: Plume/Penguin.

Boswell, J. (1991). *Life of Johnson.* Oxford: Oxford University Press. (Original work published 1791)

Glaser, B., & Strauss, A. (1967). *The discovery of grounded theory.* Chicago: Aldine.

Hall, C. S., & Lindzey, G. (1970). *Theories of personality* (2nd ed.). New York: Wiley.

Hammersley, M. (1991). *Classroom ethnography.* Milton Keynes, UK: Open University Press.

Hargreaves, D. (1986). Whatever happened to symbolic interactionism? In M.

Hammersley (Ed.), *Controversies in classroom research* (pp. 135–152). Milton Keynes, UK: Open University Press.

Heilbrun, C. G. (1988). *Writing a woman's life*. New York: Norton.

Hexter, J. (1971). *The history primer*. New York: Basic Books.

Jahoda, M. (1958). *Current concepts of positive mental health*. New York: Basic Books.

Keller, E. F. (1983). *A feeling for the organism: The life and times of Barbara McClintock*. New York: Freeman.

Keller, E. F. (1985). *Reflections on gender and science*. New Haven: Yale University Press.

Latour, B., & Woolgar, S. (1979). *Laboratory life, the social construction of scientific facts*. Beverly Hills, CA: Sage.

Murray, H. A., & Kluckhohn, C. (1954). Outline of a conception of personality. In C. Kluckhohn, H. A. Murray, & D. Schneider (Eds.), *Personality in nature, society, and culture* (2nd ed.) (pp. 3–52). New York: Knopf.

Murray, H. A., et al. (1938). *Explorations in personality*. New York: Oxford University Press.

Olsen, T. (1983). *Silences*. New York: Laurel.

Raverat, G. (1952). *Period piece*. London: Faber and Faber.

Schön, D. (1983). *The reflective practitioner*. New York: Basic Books.

Smith, L. M. (1990, April). The experience of biography: Coming to know Nora Barlow. Paper presented at the annual meeting of the American Educational Research Association, Boston.

Smith, L. M. (1992). *Doing ethnographic biography: A reflective practitioner at work during a spring in Cambridge*. Unpublished manuscript.

Smith, L. M. (in process). *Nora Barlow and the Darwin legacy*. Ames: Iowa State University Press.

Smith, L. M., & Pohland, P. (1976). Grounded theory and educational ethnography: A methodological analysis and critique. In J. Roberts & S. K. Akinsanya (Eds.), *Educational patterns and cultural configurations* (pp. 264–279). New York: Harcourt, Brace.

Strachey, L. (1918). *Eminent Victorians*. New York: Harcourt, Brace.

Woolf, V. (1929). *A room of one's own*. New York: Harcourt, Brace.

Woolf, V. (1960). *Granite and rainbow*. London: Hogarth Press. (Original work published 1927)

Zetterberg, H. (1965). *On theory and verification in sociology* (3rd ed.). Totowa, NJ: Bedminster Press.

9

Socially Responsive Educational Research

Linking Theory and Practice

ERNEST T. STRINGER

In the 1960s and 1970s I was among the social scientists and educators searching for solutions to the social problems experienced by Aboriginal people as a cultural and racial minority in Australia. Research projects proliferated during this time, and explanatory theory became more sophisticated. In the same period, however, the problems of Aboriginal people multiplied. Solutions designed by experts, legitimized by governments, and imposed by a growing bureaucracy appeared to have little positive impact on the lives of Aboriginal people and were, in many cases, destructive. I eventually realized that the knowledge gained by "us" — expert scholars and professionals — was not only ineffective as it was applied to "them" — Aboriginal people — but that the processes of research and development work were fundamentally flawed; that they reinforced a social system that maintained Aboriginal people in disempowered, dependent, and impoverished circumstances.

The consciously critical perspective of this chapter explores how research processes themselves contribute to the reproduction and maintenance of sometimes destructive social norms. In particular, the chapter uses insights derived from postmodern theory to illuminate ways in which problematic features of social life are embedded in everyday, institutionalized research practices. A topology of the postmodern provides the basis for a set of underlying principles for a socially responsive approach to educational research. Practical frameworks for enacting these principles are described, portraying research processes that are not only intellectually rigorous but also responsive to the broader social outcomes of intellectual inquiry.

Biographic Notes appear in this chapter as an overt commentary connecting analyses and arguments with my own personal and professional experiences. This approach to writing highlights the fact that *all* the text is, in one way or another, derived from the perceptions and interpretive frameworks of the author. It is my attempt to take seriously the work of Derrida (1976, 1978) and Ulmer (1989) by consciously integrating the diverse social texts upon which this chapter is based and presenting them as a collage or montage of ideas.

Biographic note. The frameworks that follow are derived from many years of working with Aboriginal people in West Australia. Learning, with them, to deal with the harsh realities of institutional ethnocentricism and racism has sensitized me to the ways in which cultural practices, acted out in the ordinary, everyday private and institutional lives of educators, are often disempowering and destructive to those whose cultural perceptions and practices are different. Lessons learned from Aboriginal colleagues and community members have been complemented by study and teaching in the foundations of education, particularly sociology, anthropology, and philosophy.

Knowledge derived from experiences outside the broad mainstream of society have accentuated the underlying mechanisms that maintain the social life of communities in which I have worked. Just as ethnomethodologists purposely violate common rules of interaction in order to expose the underlying mechanisms of social life, the "violation" of mainstream Australian cultural rules by Aboriginal people has served to reveal the cultural rules that are implicit in the everyday, ordinary organization and operation of mainstream social life.

In the following sections of the chapter, experiences drawn from my work in schools and with Aboriginal community groups and organizations are used to illustrate a variety of points. These illustrations serve to emphasize general features of social life and to suggest ways to implement changes that have the potential to enhance our work. I will make the assumption that what works well in the Aboriginal arena provides insight into educational and social practices more broadly. Experience at the Centre for Aboriginal Studies has indicated, for instance, that education and training processes designed specifically for Aboriginal people are equally successful when adapted to the training of non-Aboriginal workers and students.

The voices of my Aboriginal friends and colleagues, therefore, provide a silent counterpoint to the arguments incorporated in this paper. They provide both the challenge to engage in socially liberative educational work and the means whereby we may together accomplish a common sense of purpose.

THE LIMITS OF SCIENTIFIC APPROACHES

For the greater part of this century educational research has been largely influenced by paradigms that look to the physical sciences. Research has been envisioned as a search for new knowledge, expressed in the form of law-like statements about human behavior, that enables greater prediction and control of educational activity. It has been an integral part of an era characterized by postmodern scholars as a period of faith in the application of rationality, science, and technology to the improvement of the human condition. This faith is given credibility by the many advances in scientific knowledge that have had a positive impact on people's lives. The control of disease and the curative powers of modern medicine have resulted in greater longevity; the harnessing of agricultural production has helped reduce the destructive impact of widespread famine; and mechanization associated with technological advances has eased the labor of many people.

The rewards of the modern era, however, have been matched by the development or aggravation of huge and intractable social problems. Human alienation in the form of increased levels of drug use, depression, stress, street violence, and domestic discord are compounded by widespread environmental problems, and ecological destruction continues as an ongoing accompaniment to modern social life. In the international arena, the proliferation of weapons of destruction taxes the meager resources of third world countries and places enormous pressures on the everyday lives of people. A genre of writers, as diverse conceptually as they are in disciplinary background, has provided a critique of the cultural life of the modern world. Collectively labeled as "postmodern," these writers have contributed to the development of a perspective that is critical of some of the major tenets of the modern world, especially its faith in rationality, science, and technology. Writers such as Foucault (e.g., 1972, 1984), Derrida (e.g., 1976, 1978), Jameson (1990, 1991), Lyotard (1984), Baudrillard (1983), and Huyssons (1984) have emphasized the need for people to change the ways in which they conceptualize the social world and, by extension, to formulate new directions for the regeneration of social and political life.

Applied to the educational arena, the postmodern critique suggests the fallacy of relying solely on "scientific" approaches to research. The billions of dollars that have been spent worldwide on social research and development appear to have had little impact on the quality of educational life. Despite an increase in the technical proficiency of teachers and increasing methodological sophistication of researchers, education appears to be becoming an increasingly problematic endeavor. Teachers suffer high levels of stress and frustration, and student achievement levels remain static or decrease. Scientific, technicist approaches alone appear ineffective in dealing with the problems of our social and educational systems (Bok, 1990; Bowers & Flinders, 1990).

This state of affairs should not be surprising if we take account of the severe limitations of "expert" knowledge as we currently conceive it. Traditional scientific approaches to research have tended to focus on a limited number of variables, which fail to reflect the pervasive complexities of social life. Further, expertise in any area of study has tended to become increasingly narrow with the demands of specialization. Current pressures encourage researchers to restrict the focus of their activities, limiting their ability to develop comprehensive and effective understandings of real-life situations, while at the same time preventing them from engaging in long-term activities that have a direct impact on school or community life.

Further, the scientifically validated methodology of "stating the problem," "defining the concepts," and "formulating hypotheses" related to a "theoretical framework" results in outcomes that incorporate the researchers' own world views. The researchers' perceptions and interpretive frameworks become imposed on the research processes. Dudgeon, Oxenham, Scully, and Badman (1991), writing in the Australian context, suggest that "not only do non-Black or non-Aboriginal academics exploit Aboriginal people for data which they feel a right of access to, but more significantly, they process the data through their own cultural values." Hence, the end product is often presented in a way that Aboriginal people cannot relate to and incorporates a philosophy and values that are inappropriate to and misrepresentative of Aboriginal concerns.

Though the recent shift toward qualitative research is more open to other world views, the research act is still largely framed according to the cultural imperatives and personal agendas of researchers or those who engage them. The result is the re-institution of systems of teaching, learning, and administration that are experienced by participants in schools as oppressive or inappropriate.

Biographic note. When I first started working as a schoolteacher in a remote, traditional Aboriginal community I felt as if I had entered another world. I still remember clearly the early days of my experience as I struggled to come to grips with the knowledge that the expertise gained through my training and professional experience were inadequate in the context of a people who were so different from myself. In the first months of teaching in this situation, I became aware of the many traps and pitfalls into which

I could unintentionally fall while coping with my task of teaching the children of the community. I know now that in enacting my ordinary, taken-for-granted ways of teaching, I imposed many inappropriate and culturally demeaning experiences on the children in my charge. I see it as the blundering of a blind man in strange territory. I just could not "see" what I was doing.

Even at the community level I made many mistakes. On one unforgettable occasion I attempted to gain rapport with parents by showing films to the assembled community one evening. The angry response that erupted at the commencement of the first film, and the consequent complete evacuation of the area as shouting men called women and children away, left me somewhat bewildered and more than a little frightened. I had, in my ignorance, shown a film of a sacred ceremony not meant for the eyes of any but initiated men.

My tentative entry into the Aboriginal "camp" the next morning to apologize for my blunder would have been humorous to any spectator. I expected to be physically attacked or speared at any moment. Walking up to one of the men I explained that I wished to apologize for whatever I had done wrong the previous evening. He looked up genially from the side of his small fire and said softly, "That's all right, Mr. Stringer. We talked about it and decided that you were a white man, and you just didn't know."

IMPLICATIONS OF POSTMODERN THEORY

Because deconstruction of all facets of social life is almost inherent in the genre, postmodern literature has provided little practical guidance for the educational practitioner. With the exception of scholars such as West (1989), few postmodern writers accept the challenge to define the means by which teachers, administrators, and researchers can develop more socially constructive ways of accomplishing their professional objectives. A number of underlying ideological and evaluative themes, however, can be identified within postmodern writing. These themes provide a broad framework from which more specific guidance for the everyday activities of educational research may be derived.

Foucault (1972), for instance, describes the ongoing subjugation of subordinates and clients by those people who hold positions of power and authority. He writes of the need to liberate people from the repression and exploitation that they experience within institutions of modern society. He advocates the elimination of these systems of subjugation, which he portrays as "the fascism in our heads," by exploring and building upon the open qualities of human discourse as well as by intervening in the way knowledge is produced and constituted at the local level. He proposes that we should cultivate and enhance localized planning and decision making, resisting ways of organizing and working that are oppressive or exploitative. Foucault (1984) instructs us "to prefer what is positive and multiple, difference over uniformity, flows over unities, mobile arrangements over systems" (p. xiii). This view stands in contrast to the rigidly stylized routines that are often an implicit feature of scientific research. Derrida's (1976, 1978) writings complement the ideological position implied in Foucault's work. Derrida suggests that we find new ways of writing "texts" that minimize the power of people in positions of authority (whom he labels "culture producers") to impose their perceptions and interpretations onto the situations that they control. In an educational context, this would limit the power of experts and professionals to impose their own culturally derived world views onto school texts, reports, plans, curricula, and so forth. Derrida's work implies the need for organizational structures and processes that create greater opportunities for popular participation and, therefore, a more democratic determination of the way schools operate.

A compelling argument for a more active approach to resolving social and educational problems is provided by West (1989). His notion of "prophetic pragmatism" advocates an explicitly political mode of cultural criticism that relies on a combination of critical intelligence and social action. He advocates ways of living and working together that encourage participation in dealing with the issues that affect our day-to-day lives. His pragmatism urges experts, including scientists and philosophers, to give up their search for the foundations of truth and the quest for certainty, and to apply their scholarly tools to the current problems of ordinary people.

West's pragmatism reconceptualizes philosophy "as a form of cultural criticism that attempts to transform linguistic, social, cultural and political traditions for the purposes of increasing the scope of individual development and democratic operation" (p. 230). By implication, he advocates a rethinking of the way in which those with expertise apply their knowledge and skills. Experts, his writing suggests, should not define the social world of people, or be in control of the organizations, events, and activities that shape their lives. Rather, expertise should be made available to assist people to deal with the problems they confront. West thereby urges a practical approach to all social activity. With Dewey, he advocates fundamental economic, political, cultural, and individual transformations based on the ideals of accountable power, small-scale associations, and individual liberty. This can be attained, he implies, only through the reconstruction of basic institutions, together with the practices and pre-conceptions that are embedded within them. For West, pragmatism is practice that makes a difference.

On a political level, West advocates solidarity with "the wretched of the earth," so that by educating and being educated by struggling people, professionals and experts will be able to relate the life of the mind to their collective experience. He calls for a regeneration of the social forces of the people in the service of creative democracy. West's postmodern perspective highlights in this way the need for those engaged in research to find practical ways to modify and adapt their work, so that it becomes more directly relevant to people's lives.

A CHARACTERIZATION OF THE POSTMODERN

Let me try to summarize, on a broad canvas, some of the recurrent themes of postmodern thought. Generally, a postmodern perspective stands in opposition to

1. The abstract, theoretical, or doctrinaire
2. Grand plans and large-scale narratives
3. Enforced uniformity
4. Fixed, inflexible systems
5. Rigid institutional circumscription of what is correct
6. Failure to acknowledge "other voices" — minorities, women, workers, and so forth
7. Writing of authoritative "texts" by leaders, bureaucrats, or experts

The postmodern genre is not opposed to *all* forms of centralization, control, expertise, or structured organization, but focuses on the negative impact of the concentrations of power common in modern forms of organization. Postmodern views tend, conversely, to emphasize

1. Respect for the popular and vernacular
2. Open discourse, rather than closed or restricted discussion
3. Pluralistic, organic strategies for development of plans and procedures
4. The coexistence and interpenetration of meaning systems
5. The authenticity of "other voices"
6. Preference for what is multiple, for difference
7. Flexibility and mobility of organizational arrangements, including divisions of labor

8. Local development of texts, techniques, and practices
9. Restructuring of the authority of cultural producers

Applying this summary to educational research, conventional scientific approaches do not provide an adequate basis for inquiry. We would need to take into account the inherent social and political factors of research, and to actively engage the people who, until now, have been viewed as either subjects or consumers of research. The postmodern impulse also suggests a more active engagement of the "hidden curriculum" (Lynch, 1989) so that research activity deals directly with the social functions and outcomes of education.

In summary, my reading of the postmodern outlined above may be characterized by a set of values that provide the foundations for a socially responsive approach to educational research. Research processes should be

1. Democratic — enabling participation of people
2. Equitable — acknowledging people's equality of worth
3. Liberating — providing freedom from oppressive, debilitating conditions
4. Enhancing — enabling the expression of people's full human potential

In accordance with the intent of a liberating and enhancing approach to social activity, participant well-being is best defined locally, according to the perceptions and values of the people at hand. Community workers in the Northern Territory of Australia, for example, developed a set of "Key Concepts" that were used to evaluate the impact of their activities (Kelly & Gluck, 1985). Their aim was to foster procedures that enabled the people with whom they were working to maintain

1. Pride — feelings of self-worth
2. Dignity — feelings of autonomy, independence, and competence
3. Identity — affirmations of people's social identities
4. Control — local people's control of resources, decisions, actions, events, and activities
5. Responsibility — people's ability to be accountable for their own actions
6. Solidarity — the coherence groups of which people are part
7. Place/Space — work in places chosen by the people; in spaces where they are comfortable

These concepts provide the means to check, at the level of the group and individual, the impact of the social arrangements that define the parameters of inquiry.

Biographic note. The blunders perpetrated in the education of Aboriginal people continue to haunt me. Few, if any, of the above factors have been taken into account in providing schooling to Aboriginal children. In West Australia a European-Australian, middle class curriculum is taught by European-Australian middle class teachers, using methodologies designed for middle class European-Australian students. Texts and materials are drawn predominantly from European-Australian experience, so that in many classrooms one still has to search for an image derived from the Aboriginal experience. The message is not that Aboriginal people aren't important; it is that they don't, for all intents and purposes, even exist.

Children, sometimes very young children, have been taken from their homes and families and sent many miles away for schooling. There they have been taught in many overt and covert ways that the path to recognized personhood is to become like a "white man." Aboriginal people have been denied the opportunity, in any but tokenistic ways, to participate in the development and delivery of education to their children. The impact of schooling on the lives of Aboriginal people has, in its totality, been one of denial of the worthwhileness of Aboriginal personhood and Aboriginal culture. We are just learning how to reverse this destructive process.

Some Aboriginal people talk of the need for "two-way education"; that is, forms of schooling that enable their children to acquire skills needed for the non-Aboriginal world, but that are enhancing rather than denigrating of Aboriginality. Many independent Aboriginal schools are attempting to show how this can be done.

SOCIALLY RESPONSIVE RESEARCH

The values outlined above echo many of the ideas of the Brazilian educator, Paulo Freire (1974). Freire advocates a liberative approach to education that enables people to become conscious of the oppressive forces in their lives and to take transformative action. This perspective was developed in a context where economic and political oppression is an ongoing feature of Brazilian social life. It is also relevant, however, to those societies where mechanistic and highly controlling bureaucracies threaten to dehumanize people who live and work within their sphere of influence.

Freire's third world context makes it comparatively simple to delineate "oppressors" and "oppressed." In the first world, however, the simple oppressor/oppressed formulation is not a powerful way to characterize the social world. Modern industrialized societies comprise a complex web of interlocking classes and statuses, and a simplistic rendering of this as oppressor/oppressed provides a naive characterization of the social forces at work. More sophisticated forms of analysis are required, which clearly delineate the nature of the oppressions experienced by people and the ways in which those oppressions are built into their daily lives. The point at which people attempt to unravel the problems that affect their day-to-day social and professional activities is where educational research becomes relevant to the process of "conscientization." By the collaborative exploration of problems, researchers can assist administrators, teachers, parents, and students to develop increasingly sophisticated understandings of their situations.

Collaborative and participatory approaches to educational activity contrast markedly with the styles of management and administration common in many school systems. Schools, in their current forms, tend to function as highly centralized, autocratic institutions that provide poor preparation for responsible, democratic citizenry. Further, teachers tend to use individual competition as a prime means of motivating students, providing a poor environment for collaborative, cooperative approaches to education.

Berger, Berger, and Kellner (1973) note the fragmentation and alienation caused by pitting individuals against each other in what they describe as "merciless competitive conflict." As they suggest, institutions such as schools legitimate and perpetuate conflict through their emphasis on competitively based individual achievement. They point to the need for forms of teaching that liberate people from the influences of conflictual competition by emphasizing the security, belonging, and solidarity of collective life.

Because of the nature of their professional expertise, researchers have opportunities to assist educators and lay people to deal more holistically with educational problems, moving past the ongoing social mythology related to such limited concepts as "achievement levels" and "test scores" to develop more inclusive analyses. Through collaborative involvement in the processes of research and development, researchers have the opportunity to enact the democratic and equitable intent of a socially responsive education. The sharing of people's diverse knowledge and experience — expert, professional, and lay — enables the creation of projects and programs that have the potential to extend the range of the human resources available to schools. The central role of the researcher in this context becomes more facilitative and less directive.

Biographic note. The best school for Aboriginal children that I have observed was one developed by a group of Aboriginal people for their own children. They built a large bough-shelter for a school building, then hired a teacher who, over a period of months, helped them to plan the details of the organization and operation of their school, including all facets of the curriculum. The school was a place where Aboriginal children, all of them, were actively engaged in learning, where they attended every day, and where the experience of being Aboriginal was integrated as an important component of the classroom and school. It was in marked contrast to most Aboriginal schools, replicas of suburban "white" schools, where a suburban curriculum is taught in a suburban environment under the direction of a suburban teacher, where Aboriginal people have little part to play in the education of their children, and where Aboriginal people and Aboriginal ways have no place in the ongoing life of the classrooms.

What was it that made the school successful? Each day the integrated nature of the learning experiences of the children was enhanced by the presence of members of the Aboriginal community who acted as teachers, under the direction of the non-Aboriginal teacher. The teacher-in-charge commenced each day by planning and preparing learning activities with a small group of community teachers, none of whom had any formal training. They learned the processes involved in teaching as they worked. The curriculum and the timetable were designed by the community with the needs of their children in mind. The result could be seen in the enthusiasm and comfortableness of the children at school. (One of the few complaints of the teacher-in-charge was that the children spent *too much* time in school!)

On one occasion I wrote (Stringer, 1985):

> I have visited the school four times now, for periods up to three days, and I am always excited by the experience. To see Aboriginal children working purposefully and happily, to talk with the adults about *their* school, and to feel the Aboriginal ethos as a harmonious part of the whole setting gives me hope that maybe . . . we can fashion a form of schooling which is not alien to Aboriginal children. We have a lot to learn from this school. (p. iii)

This example highlights the creative interaction between the "expert" teacher and community members. They worked together through an extended period of investigation and planning to enable the community to undertake a complex and difficult task. The success of their enterprise indicates the extent of the possibilities for community-oriented educational activity and provides a model for participatory, action-based research and development.

Principles of Socially Responsive Research

The fundamental principle of *empowerment* provides the overarching concept for a socially responsive approach to educational research. Empowerment is derived as much from the way in which people work together on a day-to-day basis as from the workings of political institutions. The fundamental premises of empowerment are that people have

1. *Control* of their own situations, and feelings of control
2. *Decision-making* opportunities that enable them to define their priorities and determine their directions
3. *Means* to affect the events and activities that have an impact on their lives

These are, of course, statements of an ideal nature. They do not provide direct guidance for everyday research activities. They do provide, however, the basis for the development of *criteria* by which researchers can evaluate the social impact of their activities. Specific principles are best defined by people in their local situations, according to their own ways of interpreting the meanings of democracy, equality, liberation, and enhancement. The principles outlines below, delineated by research and development workers at the Centre for Aboriginal Studies at Curtin University in West Australia (Stringer, McCauley, Bedford, Kickett, & Satour, 1990), provide one example of the type of guidelines that can be formulated.

For these workers, the principles that guide practice include the following key factors: relationships, communication, coordination, participation, and inclusion. Each of these factors is seen to have an impact on the democratic, equitable, liberative, and enhancing qualities of activities. They were explicated by the Curtin group as follows:

Relationships That Are Socially Responsive

1. Promote feelings of equality for all the people involved
2. Maintain harmony between people
3. Avoid conflicts when possible, and
4. Resolve conflicts that arise
5. Accept people as they are, not as they ought to be
6. Encourage personal, cooperative relationships, rather than impersonal, competitive, or authoritarian relationships
7. Acknowledge the feelings and subjective relations of others

Communication That Is Socially Responsive

1. Regularly informs people of what is happening
2. Listens carefully to what people are saying
3. Accepts and acts upon what people say
4. Can be understood by all participants
5. Is honest, open, and sincere
6. Is socially and culturally appropriate

Coordination That Is Socially Responsive

1. Assists in the formation and development of local leadership
2. Assists people to plan activities which have a high likelihood of success
3. Evaluates progress on a formative basis
4. Coordinates the activities of all groups
5. Ensures that all people benefit from activities, projects, or services

Participation Is Facilitated By Coordination That

1. Maximizes the involvement of participants
2. Enables people to do things for themselves, rather than having it done for them
3. Provides support for people as they learn
4. Encourages plans and activities that people are able to accomplish themselves
5. Deals directly with local people rather than with their representatives or employees

Inclusion That Is Socially Responsive

1. Includes all groups relevant to the setting
2. Is comprehensive in recognizing issues — social, economic, cultural, and political rather than focusing narrowly on specific skill or subject outcomes
3. Ensures cooperation with other agencies involved in the local setting (p. 6)

These principles provide broad guidance to professional activities in any social arena. They do not prescribe particular ways of working, but act as criteria that can be used to judge the efficacy of plans and practices.

Practical Routines for Socially Responsive Research

The principles outlined above imply a change in the role and status of the educational researcher. They suggest a shift from disinterested observer to involved participant; and a shift from "expert" to co-participant whose knowledge and skills are of no more value than those of other people. The role of the researcher is conceived as one of team membership.

This change in role and status implies a corresponding change in the forms and styles of research operations. The specific expertise of the researcher is applied to the agendas of those who are subject to the research and for their benefit, rather than to the agendas related to "objectivity," "theory building," or, more mundanely, "vita building." Objectivity or rigorous research procedures are not irrelevant in these contexts but are applied in different ways, so that both the processes and the outcomes of educational research become open to, and in some cases adjudicated by, all groups associated with the research.

The routines in the next section, which were developed by Aboriginal and non-Aboriginal workers at the Centre for Aboriginal Studies at Curtin University (Kickett, McCauley, & Stringer, 1987), were designed to assist Aboriginal groups in dealing with the issues and problems that are a continuous part of their experience as a racial and cultural minority in Western Australia. Similar routines have been the basis for several research and development projects with Aboriginal groups, and they provide an example of the ways in which research processes can operate according to the principles of socially responsive research.

An important characteristic of these routines is that they are stated in terms that can be easily understood by people in the community. Although set out in linear form, they are interactive and hermeneutic; that is, different parts of the routines, or even different routines, may be enacted simultaneously in order to accomplish the objectives of the activity.

Biographic note. I was recently engaged in community action with a group of parents and students concerned with the style of education being offered by their local high school. Although just one member of the group, I was able to work with other members, through a series of meetings and discussions, to examine the particular problems being faced in this situation, to define a number of general underlying problems (a form of analysis and theorizing), and then to develop a plan for a special school program that would address the problems.

Our meetings were attended regularly by parents and students, and the plan that we developed was innovative, educationally sound, and attractive to various groups: parents, potential students, and educational authorities. My "expertise," while not engaged formally, was used as part of the resources available to the group as we worked through our analysis and planning. We were all engaged, in a real sense, in a research and development project. This type of research and development work can be engaged in as an organic process that uses a wide variety of techniques, a diverse set of routines, multiple exit points, and numerous outcomes.

A COMMUNITY-ORIENTED
RESEARCH AND DEVELOPMENT ROUTINE:
LOOK/THINK/ACT

Research, as it is traditionally carried out, has long been a mystic process to lay persons. The desire for objectivity and rigor associated with clinical and experimental procedures removes much research work from the ongoing social world of the community and encapsulates activity in a strange and impersonal world beyond the comprehension of the uninitiated. Impersonal procedures and an elusive argot confine the activities and outcomes of scientific research to a narrow audience of fellow scholars. In the educational arena few teachers and administrators read the academic journals in which most research outcomes are reported.

The following routine illustrates one way to engage community groups in research and development processes. Its simplicity makes it a powerful tool for orienting people to activities usually the province of professionals. The routine enables researchers to "get started" at the community level by providing cues for ongoing research activity and developing a context for ongoing action by the groups that participate. Called the LOOK/THINK/ACT routine by research and development workers at the Centre for Aboriginal Studies at Curtin University, this routine incorporates activity usually described by researchers as "statement of the problem," "hypotheses," "data collection," "analysis," and "implications." It can be engaged in at any level of an organization and by any group: principals, teachers, students, parents, community members, or researchers.

The LOOK/THINK/ACT routine encompasses three types of activity. Looking enables people to "build a picture" of their situation, to gather information about the situation, and to observe what is happening. Researchers may think of these activities as encompassing definition of the problem and data gathering. Thinking enables people to reflect on their situation, to analyze issues, and to delineate their concerns. Researchers usually conceive of this activity as definition, analysis, and/or theorizing. Acting means doing something about the situation and responding to the analysis. Researchers traditionally develop implications at this phase of the process.

This routine provides the bare bones of a research process. Detail is built into each of these sections as people involved in the project develop clear ideas of what they are trying to do, why they are trying to do it, and how they can go about it. The aim is to enable people to work through the process together, so that they feel ownership for the analyses and plans that are formulated. This ownership is one of the most powerful motivating forces in any social activity. It is the reason why those who facilitate the research processes should fight the temptation to interpret the situation for the group, provide preformulated analyses, or present plans or agendas that have been developed in isolation from the group processes.

Biographic note. I was once asked by an Aboriginal group to help its members re-establish their organization, which had almost ceased to function. Through the executive committee, I arranged to meet with the many associated subgroups to talk about whether they wanted the organization, what it should do, and how it should operate. This involved considerable "theorizing" about what had been going on in the lives of Aboriginal people in the area, as well as discussion of various arrangements that could help meet their concerns. This "talking" took a number of months, but once it was completed, we held a large meeting with people from all the groups in the area. Plans that had been discussed and developed in the previous months were ratified at the meeting, and the organization successfully recommenced its operations.

Research processes were incorporated into the developmental processes of the organization. A "survey" made possible the delineation of "the problem," leading to explorations of competing "hypotheses" related to the origins of the problem. The survey also made possible the collection of a broad range of "data" related to the needs of the people in the area. Information was categorized and presented to people as part of the ongoing "analysis" of the situation. My own research skills were directly available to the people in the region and enabled them to engage in a rigorous developmental process.

Look—Building the Picture

In the first phase of this routine the researcher works with relevant groups to determine the research agendas and processes and to begin gathering a body of germane information. Preliminary action might take the form of an informal survey to determine the groups who constitute the cultural setting of the research and the individuals who could or should be involved in the research process. At this stage the researcher focuses on maximizing the involvement of relevant groups and engaging these groups in an exploration of the issues around which the project is centered.

A style of research well suited to this approach is ethnographic, where researchers work with the "natives" in the setting to record and elaborate their world views. Definitions of the situation are formulated in conjunction with the groups involved, and their perceptions and interpretations become the basis for further development. Informal interviews, which take place in people's own localities, provide an initial information base and are followed by intensive participant observation that links the researcher to all relevant groups in the "community" in which the researcher is grounded. The initial data base, determined by the issues around which the project is formulated, is extended as data collection, analysis, and planning proceed. The process is designed to assist people to "build a picture" of their situation, a shared set of perceptions and understandings that become the basis for ongoing research and development work.

Biographic note. For a recent curriculum development project at the Centre for Aboriginal Studies at Curtin University, I managed the production of a training program for non-Aboriginal staff in a state welfare agency. It was designed to assist them to develop culturally appropriate ways of working with Aboriginal people. Initial survey work was carried out by Aboriginal and non-Aboriginal workers. Because survey methods based on written materials were deemed to be culturally inappropriate, the research team traveled throughout the state interviewing a broad cross-section of relevant people. These included the agency's Aboriginal workers, non-Aboriginal managers, field workers, and office staff, as well as Aboriginal clients and community members.

Using semi-structured interview techniques, research workers were able to record the issues and problems that concerned staff of the agency in their work with Aboriginal people, to recognize the problems experienced by Aboriginal people who were clients of the agency, and to record people's ideas about the content and style of training that workers should receive.

Not only did the process provide an excellent data base, but both worker and client groups responded positively to the opportunity to provide input to the development of the training program. The information became incorporated into a training program and a package of curriculum

materials that enabled Aboriginal workers in the agency to provide training programs for non-Aboriginal staff.

Think—Analyzing the Situation

Analysis begins when people reflect on their situation, when they start to
ask questions such as "What is happening here?" The emphasis in this part
of the routine is to move people past the simplistic or distorted analyses
that stem from an outmoded or dysfunctional cultural mythology, or
through the often distorted lenses of culture producers. Through dialogue
between individuals and groups in the setting, people are able to explore
other ways of seeing their world and interpreting their situation. This
process is similar to Freire's "conscientization," enhancing the capacity to
develop analyses that enable people to deal effectively with the problems
of social life.

There are many techniques that enable people to develop more effective explanatory frameworks or theories that move them past their taken-
for-granted perceptions and interpretations. The first stages of analysis
provide opportunities for people to meet informally and reflect on the
nature of their problems. At a later stage it may be appropriate for people
to work in groups to collectively extend their analysis in more structured
ways. The definition and categorization of phenomena, the mapping of
linkages between events, and the exploration of themes provide ways of
developing and extending analysis.

Biographic note. Many Australian Aboriginal people have been taught
that the reason for their impoverishment and dependence lies in their
own deficiencies. Reflection on their situation helps them to look past
explanations derived from a colonial experience. At a workshop on alcohol
abuse presented to Aboriginal community people at Curtin University, a
three-factor model of "drinking behavior" was discussed. As the workshop
progressed the model was found to be inadequate in dealing with some of
the realities of Aboriginal community life, and modifications were explored. The Aboriginal participants were delighted with this "new way of
seeing" the situation. One of them said to me, "I used to think of alcohol
like a blanket covering my community; I thought of my people as alcohol-
ics. Now [that] I can see it this way, now [that] I can see the different
things that are happening, I can see things that I can do about drinking in
my community!"

The seminar challenged both the theoretical framework initially presented in the three-factor model, and the taken-for-granted assumptions

of the Aboriginal people present. It was a process that reflected a dynamic relationship between theory building and the data provided by the real-life experience of the participants.

Act—Planning Action Processes

Basic planning processes can be applied in any situation where people wish to plan activities that will assist them in dealing with the problems and issues around which the project is centered. Planning is a starting point that gives direction to later activity. An approach used extensively by research and development workers at the Centre for Aboriginal Studies at Curtin University is outlined below.

WHAT	What are the issues and problems?
	What are we trying to accomplish?
	What do we want to happen?
HOW	How can we deal with the issues, problems?
	How can we work, step by step?
	How will we go about each step?
WHO	Who will be involved?
	Who will do each task as we work through each step?
WHEN	When will each action occur?
WHERE	Where will each action occur?
WHY	Why are we doing this?
	What are our overall goals?

More sophisticated planning procedures may be incorporated into any developmental process, but this framework provides an effective tool that may be used in the early stages of a planning activity or project.

Biographic note. The curriculum development program for state welfare workers mentioned earlier began with the analysis of survey data that focused on the training needs of the agency workers. This process was followed by planning workshops using frameworks that enabled participants to formulate appropriate training strategies, content, and materials for each category of agency work (management, field staff, office staff). The project team made a special effort during this planning process to ensure that Aboriginal perspectives were incorporated into the program and that training processes were socially and culturally appropriate to both Aboriginal trainers, who were to facilitate training sessions, and non-Aboriginal workers for whom the program had been developed.

CONCLUSION

In this chapter I have discussed the implications of postmodern theory for the practice of educational research, linking these implications with community, action-based research and development processes. These processes are suggested in response to the limits of much of the scientific, technicist approaches that have dominated the educational arena in recent decades. My intent is not to discredit the use of the scientific and technical, which continue to provide significant contributions to our search for understanding, but to extend the thinking of researchers about the nature and outcomes of their work.

This is, in a sense, a practical exercise in the sociology of knowledge, challenging researchers to actively engage the many worlds of meaning that are a concomitant part of every social, cultural, and educational setting. A commitment to confront the politics of everyday life as those systems of meaning are negotiated in the social arena, and to artfully engage in exploratory and analytical work that extends people's knowledge and understanding, appears, at first glance, to be at odds with many of the dictums of scientific research methods.

The engagement of the experienced world, however, provides an empirical grounding for research, and this should be the basis for any rigorously scientific study of the social world. In accordance with the postmodern genre of writing that I have outlined, the underlying pragmatism of research attempts to derive theoretical insights from ongoing participation in social life and to make those insights directly applicable. While broader or more objective explanatory frameworks may be derived from macro-analyses of small-scale projects, the focus for socially responsive educational research lies in the micro-analysis of events at the local level.

Biographic note. As a young student of sociology I was enticed by the possibilities of the hypothetico-deductive method. Here was the means, I thought, by which social scientists could establish the laws of human behavior, leading to a greater ability to predict and control the social world and thus a greater ability to deal with its problems.

But as the limitations of inferential statistics became increasingly evident, my expectations diminished. Much of the research in the social sciences appeared to have little effect on the particular social and educational problems that concerned me. Eventually, I ceased to believe that the objective, abstracted search for knowledge would have a significant impact on the problems I confronted in helping provide education for Aboriginal people. In recent years I have worked directly with Aboriginal people, supporting them where possible in their search for better education. The application of academic skills at the local community level has provided me with constant intellectual challenges. The sociology and philosophy of knowledge, including the nature of theorizing and the status of knowledge, are a constant part of my work. The challenge of taking information and skills, which are part of the meaning system within my professional sphere, and integrating them with the meaning systems of the Aboriginal and bureaucratic worlds, is a demanding, but rewarding, assignment.

REFERENCES

Baudrillard, J. (1983). *Simulations*. New York: Semiotext, Foreign Agent Press.

Berger, P., Berger, B., & Kellner, H. (1973). *The homeless mind*. New York: Random House.

Bok, D. (1990). *Universities and the future of America*. Durham, NC & London: Duke University Press.

Bowers, C. A., & Flinders, D. J. (1990). *Responsive teaching: An ecological approach to classroom patterns of language, culture, and thought*. New York: Teachers College Press.

Derrida, J. (1976). *Of grammatology*. Baltimore: Johns Hopkins University Press.

Derrida, J. (1978). *Writing and difference*. Chicago: University of Chicago Press.

Dudgeon, P., Oxenham, D., Scully, M., & Badman, S. (1991). *Special usages of tertiary institutions: Aboriginal participation in higher education*. Unpublished paper, Curtin University of Technology, Perth, Australia.

Foucault, M. (1972). *The archeology of knowledge*. New York: Random House.

Foucault, M. (1984). *The Foucault Reader* (P. Rabinow, Ed.). New York: Pantheon

Freire, P. (1974). *Pedagogy of the oppressed*. New York: Seabury Press.

Huyssens, A. (1984). *After the great divide: Modernism, mass culture, postmodernism*. Bloomington: Indiana University Press.

Jameson, F. (1990). *Signatures of the visible*. New York: Routledge.

Jameson, F. (1991). *Postmodernism, or, the cultural logics of late capitalism*. Durham, NC: Duke University Press.

Kelly, A., & Gluck, R. (1985). *A community development approach to work with Aboriginal communities*. Perth: Curtin University of Technology (WAIT).

Kickett, D., McCauley, D., & Stringer, E. (1987). *Community development processes: An introductory handbook*. Perth: Curtin University of Technology.

Lynch, K. (1989). *The hidden curriculum*. London: Falmer Press.

Lyotard, J-F. (1984). *The postmodern condition: A report on knowledge*. Minneapolis: University of Minnesota Press.

Stringer, E. (1985). Preface. In R. Dickinson (Ed.), *Yiyili: An Aboriginal community school*. Perth: Curtin University of Technology (WAIT).

Stringer, E., McCauley, D., Bedford, T., Kickett, D., & Satour, T. (1990). *Facilitating Aboriginal community planning processes*. Unpublished workbook, Curtin University of Technology, Perth, Australia.

Ulmer, G. (1989). *Teletheory: Grammatology in the age of video*. London: Routledge.

West, C. (1989). *The American evasion of philosophy*. Madison: University of Wisconsin Press.

10

Continuing Dilemmas of Life History Research

A Reflexive Account of Feminist Qualitative Inquiry

PETRA MUNRO

> We are all aware of the often uneasy relationship between teaching and theory. One reason is that we are not accustomed to theorizing daily life. Theory exists on some meta-level in some domain where thought and logic rule. But daily life is often so noisy we can't even hear ourselves think. The other reason is that the language of theory is rarely the language of things. The work of theory is too often a sensible emptiness.
>
> — Jo Anne Pagano (1991, p. 194)

The dichotomization of teaching and theory, as Jo Anne Pagano suggests, serves to split the world into separate and distinct domains. As a feminist, my work as a teacher educator/researcher is grounded in the belief that the separation between theory and practice distorts the reality of the research process. This separation serves to maintain traditional hierarchies that function to legitimatize certain forms of knowing over others, thereby maintaining dominant relations of power (Flax, 1989; Mascia-Lees, Sharpe, & Cohen, 1989). In reconceptualizing theory to fit my experience as a woman, I view theory as intricately woven into the daily struggle to make sense of my life and provide some thread of continuity and sense of community.

This view of theory as embedded in our daily lives was central to my choice of a research method as I began my recent field-work with women teachers.[1] In seeking research methods more consistent with my feminist goals, four major concerns were pertinent. The first was the need for a method that would allow women to discuss their lives in their own voices. The second was the need for a method that would allow me to convey the contradictory, partial, and subjective nature of a life history. Third, I wished to employ a method that was collaborative. Last, I required a methodology that would allow me to practice the self-reflexivity necessary for revealing my biases as well as the emergent and evolving nature of my understandings. My recent research, conducting six life histories with women teachers, presented me with numerous challenges and surprises, which have provided an opportunity to reflect once again on the "uneasy" relationship between theory and practice.

As I began this research I was sensitive to the feminist goals of establishing collaborative and nonexploitative research relationships, placing myself reflexively within the work to avoid objectification, and conducting research that would be transformative (Anderson, 1989; Grumet, 1990; Lather, 1986). Yet, these goals were not unproblematic. Trying to establish collaborative research relationships presented me with ethical and theoretical dilemmas for which I was unprepared. First, did my desire for collaboration mask the unequal power relations that assumed that I could impose a research relationship on my participants? Second, did my political standpoint and feminist perspective threaten to subvert the meanings my participants gave to their lives and roles as women? Was I, by limiting the categories of analysis to my feminist perspectives, undermining my goal of trying to understand the meanings women give to their experiences? Last, in trying to represent the intersubjective process in the text by including multiple voices, was I reducing the stories of these women, focusing attention on my story rather than theirs? This chapter recounts my emerging struggles with these dilemmas. But first let me describe the context in which this work took place.

INVISIBLE MENDING: THE SEARCH FOR A METHOD

I began with the feminist aim of seeking a method that would allow me to recover the marginalized voices of women teachers and the meanings they give to their experiences. Jane Marcus (1984) refers to this process of recovering women's voices as "invisible mending." My initial attraction to qualitative research methodologies had been the acknowledgment of multiple and partial truths, the intersubjective nature of the construction of knowledge, and the need for contextual and holistic descriptions (Clifford, 1986; Wolcott, 1990). Yet, my explicitly feminist viewpoint, with its focus on transformation, seemed at odds with ethnography's focus on description. In seeking a methodology that would allow for and value personal voice, be collaborative, and foster transformation, life history seemed to present the most viable alternative.

The current focus on acknowledging the subjective, multiple, and partial nature of human experience has resulted in a revival of life history methodology. What were previously criticisms of life history, its lack of representativeness and its subjective nature, are now its strength (Geiger, 1986; Plummer, 1983). Life history's primary goal is an account of one person's life in her or his own words elicited or prompted by a researcher (Langness & Frank, 1981; Plummer, 1983; Watson & Watson-Sparks, 1985). Life history studies provide an opportunity not only to explore the effects of social structures on people but to portray the ways in which people themselves create culture (Mandelbaum, 1973; Sheridan & Salaff, 1984).

For feminists seeking to recover the lost voices of women who have been denied access to public space because of "patriarchial notions of women's inherent nature and consequent social role," life history has provided one alternative methodology (Smith, 1987, p. 7). In addition to life history's usefulness for studying persons whose history has been marginalized, life histories are particularly well suited to illustrating aspects of culture not usually portrayed by other means, such as women's view of their culture (Langness & Frank, 1981). According to the Personal Narratives Group (1989), life histories are especially suitable for illuminating several aspects of gender relations, including (1) the construction of the gendered self-identity, (2) the relationship between the individual and society in the creation and perpetuation of gender norms, and (3) the dynamics of power relations between men and women. I hoped that life history's potential for illuminating the dynamic interaction between human agency and hegemonic forces would highlight the experiences of women teachers as they negotiated and resisted imposed meanings. Life history methods can also provide a research methodology for addressing concerns that research be situated contextually, challenge the norm of objectivity by acknowledging the intersubjective process of meaning making, and be collaborative and reciprocal. Finally, by providing opportunities that allow people to become "visible and to enhance reflexive consciousness" (Myerhoff, 1982, p. 101), the life history process can address feminist concerns that research be empowering and transformative.

ENTERING THE FIELD

The selection of the "life historians"[2] working with me in this project was as much arbitrary and serendipitous at the time as it now seems logical. For the sake of brevity, I shall focus on two of the six participants in the study.

In hindsight, it comes as no surprise that I first heard of Brenda while overlooking the Minnesota chain of lakes from several thousand feet in the air. On our first meeting, Brenda talked of viewing life as a landscape, viewing the world through a geographer's eyes, where use of time and space reveals much more than the spoken word. As I casually described my current interest and work to the mother of one of Brenda's students, my seatmate on a flight from Milwaukee to Portland, she insisted that I must speak with Brenda; she would be just the person I was looking for. I wondered, Could I call a perfect stranger, someone I had never met and ask her to tell me her life story? Why would someone confide in and trust a total stranger with their life story?

Clio, the second life historian with whom I am working, came to my attention by more conventional methods. A phone call to the local school district asking for the names of retired women social studies teachers resulted in her name. I was surprised at her immediate willingness to meet with me to learn about the project. Even more surprising was her willingness, after only one hour together, to sign the Protection of Human Subjects consent form, in which she agreed to do a minimum of five interviews; allow me to do supplementary interviews with family, friends, and colleagues; and share personal documents. What were her motivations? I wondered.

At my initial meeting with the life historians, I explained the nature of the project and my hope that we would work collaboratively together. By being honest about my expectations and eliciting theirs, I hoped that the life historians would be full participants in the research process. In addition to stating my research aims, I explained that they would receive copies of all transcribed interviews and that the final narratives would be given to them for feedback.

Throughout the following months I met with Clio weekly for several hours in her home, interviewed several former colleagues, and participated in several of her social events. Because Brenda lived 120 miles away, I met with her every other week for three to four hours, and visited her for extended periods in which I observed her in her school setting and interviewed her colleagues, administrators, and students. Both life historians were generous with personal documents, sharing pictures, favorite books, letters, and their own writings and publications.

Often it was they who took the initiative in directing the research process. Their initiative in suggesting and arranging supplementary interviews often made me wonder, though, just who was "in control" of the research relationship. Brenda arranged for me to interview her principal on my first visit to her school. Both participants suggested names of others whom I should interview in order to gain a better picture of who they were. Despite my goal of collaboration, I thought to myself, "Wasn't it I who really was supposed to be in control?" I began to question not only how collaborative our relationship was, but also my true intentions in pursuing collaboration. I began to reconsider the assumptions and nature of the collaborative relationship as I faced this first dilemma regarding the role of power in the collaborative process.

COLLABORATION: WHAT'S POWER GOT TO DO WITH IT?

Feminists have been particularly sensitive to seeking alternatives to the traditional, hierarchical research relationship, which they see as potentially exploitative and as a reification of patriarchial power relations (Christman, 1988; Lather, 1986; Stacey, 1988). Ethnographic research, due to its focus on understanding the insider's or emic meaning, has shifted the traditional focus of power from the researcher to the researched. Agar's (1980) notion of the informant as "one up" inverts the traditional hierarchy by creating the subject as expert. However, the dualisms and dichotomy of the research relationship are still maintained. The alienation between the researcher and researched resulting from this subject/object polarity is what I sought to avoid (Gitlin, 1990).

Like others engaged in collaborative research, I was hoping to establish an egalitarian, reciprocal relationship that acknowledged the mutual and two-way nature of the research (Duelli-Klein, 1983; Golde, 1970; Miller, 1990; Reinharz, 1979; Robertson, 1983). The informant is neither a passive, objectified function of data nor the insider on which the researcher is dependent for insight. Both the researcher and researched are active participants in the research relationship, and knowledge is viewed as socially and intersubjectively constructed.

Imposing Collaboration? Defining the Nature of the Relationship

One way in which I hoped to acknowledge the collaborative nature of the research relationship was by having each of the life historians keep a personal journal of her reactions to our ongoing work together. In addition to engaging them in the research through reflective writing, I hoped the journals would provide me with an understanding of the intersubjective nature of the research process. Despite what I thought were my well-intentioned goals, both participants rejected this suggestion, saying I could ask them questions, but they did not wish to write independently.

Thus, my first attempt at establishing a "collaborative" relationship was flatly rejected. I sensed that my request was perceived as a demand that did not conform to my participants' conceptualization of the research process. My heightened sensitivity to avoiding an exploitative research relationship had not taken into account the fact that my participants had their own reasons and agendas for participating in the study. In essence, my assumption of the need for a collaborative relationship underscored my perception of them as disempowered, thereby disregarding their power to determine the nature of the relationship.

My focus on collaboration had not taken into account that the life historians would develop their own framing of our relationship. When I arrived at Clio's home for our first interview she was in the process of preparing coffee and warming freshly baked bread. She commented, "I thought about using my good china, but then decided that this was work and settled on using the everyday dishes." Brenda, answering the phone during one of our interviews, replied that she was working and would have to get back to the caller later. For these women, we were engaged not in chatter between friends, but in serious work. These incidents highlighted for me the multiple meanings that the participants created for understanding their role in the research process. What I thought would be enjoyable talk, they conceived of as work. I was now faced with understanding the implications of their positioning themselves in a working relationship. Did they see themselves as co-workers, employer and employee, or colleagues? Perhaps more important, how did they define work? What did work mean to them? What was the importance of their categorizing our relationship as work? What implications did this have in reconceptualizing the roles and responsibilities of both the researcher and researched? These questions made clear the negotiated and constructed nature of the research relationship.

In establishing a collaborative relationship I believed I would also share my story. I engaged in life history research because of its reciprocal nature involving mutual storytelling (Connelly & Clandinin, 1990). Connelly and Clandinin emphasize the importance of the mutual construction of the research relationship by advising the researcher to be "aware of constructing a relationship in which both voices are heard" (p. 4). In addition to the paradox of the researcher "constructing" a mutual relationship, collaboration becomes particularly problematic when a life historian is not interested in hearing the researcher's story. Often when I spoke to Brenda, telling her about myself, she seemed disinterested and looked confused as to why I should talk so much when I was there to hear her story. Was I imposing my story on her? Was it to be the case that I as researcher became objectified in my role as passive listener? In attempting to construct a collaborative relationship, whose needs were really being served?

I struggled to define the nature of our relationship. My own understanding of collaboration implied that the nature of the relationship should be that of friends. This conflicted with their perception of our relationship as work. The businesslike nature of our relationships seemed at odds with my goal of collaboration. My evolving understanding of Brenda's and Clio's framing of our relationship as work led me to be cautious in being too friendly. If this was a truly collaborative relationship, I felt the need to recognize and respect their desire to maintain a working relationship.

I wondered whether my search for collaboration had turned into what Marilyn Strathern (1987) calls "a metaphor for an ideal ethical situation in which neither voice is submerged by the Other" (p. 290). Was collaboration a delusion in which I could mask my discomfort with the hierarchical nature of the research relationship by submerging our differences? Or, was the ultimate goal of the research process merely a selfish one designed to gain understanding of myself by detour of the others? Strathern (1987) reminds us that feminists traditionally are suspicious of the ethnographer's desire for collaboration, a fear of being appropriated and spoken for. In my case, the "other" was myself, and the fear that I would in some way misrepresent or take advantage of them seemed to persist.

My efforts to establish collaboration seemed in vain. Was it to be as McRobbie (1982) and Stacey (1988) have suggested, that no matter how hard we try to establish an egalitarian relationship, the research relationship is inherently unequal and potentially exploitative, that despite our attempts to establish friendships, the perceived status and power differential between the researcher and researched will always influence the research relationship? These questions became particularly problematic as I attempted to situate myself in the research and acknowledge the intersubjective nature of the research process.

Collaboration and Subjectivity: Getting "Too" Close?

Researchers engaged in ethnography or participant observation have long revealed the dualistic and contradictory nature of the researcher/researched relationship by discussing the emotional as well as intellectual complexities of working in the field (Bowen, 1964; Golde, 1970; Powdermaker, 1966; Shostak, 1981). Ethnographers engaged in close and long-term relationships with "informants" have stressed the delicate nature of the field relationship, which demands openness and trust, even while it demands distance in order to retain analytical competency (Everhart, 1977). The researcher is warned not to become too close to the "subject" lest he or she lose the objectivity necessary for analysis.

Feminists engaged in ethnographic work have pointed out the exploitative and unrealistic nature of pretending to be the "objective" bystander (Abu-Lughod, 1990; Roman & Apple, 1990; Stacey, 1988). The rejection of a grand narrative, in light of the fact that realities are historically and culturally situated, has resulted in feminists pursuing subjectivity in order to, as Abu-Lughod (1990) puts it, "reclaim objectivity to mean precisely the situated view" (p. 15). In trying to be truly collaborative, I believed this meant not only acknowledging the subjective nature of the life historians' experiences, but also revealing my own situated position.

There seemed to be a tension between the need to place myself in the research process and the potential of revealing too much, thus predisposing the participants to my analytical categories. Although I knew, in theory, that notions of objectivity were false, I was afraid of imposing my analytical perspective by getting "too" close. My goal was to understand how *they* perceived their lives as teachers. In some ways revealing too much about myself seemed in conflict with my goal of using a life history methodology that would allow the life historian to speak for herself. I faced the contradiction of wanting an open and honest relationship, and one that would allow me to maintain the distance I felt I needed.

The tension between wanting to be open and honest, yet not predispose the life historians to my biases, was problematic even before I began the research process. I was cautioned that my strong feminist position might "blind" me, causing me to see only what I wanted to see. I often wondered if others conducting research were warned that they would focus too much on class if they were Marxists, or too much on culture if they were ethnographers. Why was my predisposition any more dangerous? In contrast, I felt that openly acknowledging my subjectivity would allow me to tap the intersubjective process by "attuning me to where self and subject are intertwined" (Peshkin, 1988, p. 20).

Women writing about other women (Bateson, 1989; Chevigny, 1984; Heilbrun, 1988) have described the process of understanding another woman's life as one of empathy, identification, and ultimately separation with their informants. I sensed that without the process of identification, difference could not be illuminated. The identification or connection, the subjective experience I sought, seemed central to understanding them and was necessary to write their life stories. These connections were, however, partly dependent on my willingness to reveal my own story. Again, I wondered how much I should share.

I struggled. During the first interview and explanation of the project, I was careful not to reveal too much. I was cautious not to identify myself as a feminist, for fear that this might raise red flags or signal what I hoped to hear. In the interviews I held back comments about my own experiences and tried to maintain neutral facial expressions so as not to lead them on or dispose them in any significant way. I wanted the themes to emerge from their stories. What role, if any, did they see gender playing in their lives as teachers? What meanings did they give to their lives as teachers? Would these stories emerge naturally if I told them too much? Like Kathy Anderson (Anderson, Armitage, Jack, & Wittner, 1990), I questioned if it was truly the life historian's understanding of her experience that I was seeking, or if I was structuring the interview so that the subject would tell the story that conformed to my orientation. Throughout the interviews it was difficult to listen without trying to make sense of the women's stories and place them within my theoretical framework. I often worried that this tendency was interfering with my ability to listen carefully to what the life historians were actually saying.

This was complicated by the fact that after the first interviews, I tentatively identified three major themes. In the interviews that followed I felt my questions were guided by my need to gain a clearer understanding of these themes rather than allowing the participants to talk in a more open-ended manner. At the start of our fourth interview Brenda mentioned that she wanted to talk about her travels, a significant part of her story, which she felt she hadn't discussed. I, on the other hand, was anxious to hear more about what she had called her "allies" and the role they played in her life as a female teacher. She deferred to my request, yet I wondered afterward how collaborative our interview had been.

In wanting to truly honor the voices of these women teachers, I faced another dilemma as I began supplementary interviews with their former students, colleagues, and administrators. My original intention was to conduct these interviews in an effort to enhance the subjective and contextual picture of the women with whom I was working. The life historians freely recommended persons they believed would help me and would be open to being interviewed. As I started these supplementary interviews, I began to question my own motives. When I asked Brenda's principal to tell me the story of how Brenda became division chair, I actually wanted to hear the other side of the story in order to identify incongruencies that might help me see the role gender played in Brenda's school life. I was also curious how the principal's description of Brenda would differ from her own or mine, hoping to gain more insight into Brenda's own frame of reference.

These supplementary interviews were—and continue to be—very helpful in illuminating the subjective nature of our experiences, yet I wonder what role they have in a collaborative research relationship. I wonder if they undermine the purpose of feminist narrative inquiry, which seeks to validate women's voices and experiences as truth. Sheridan and Salaff (1984) maintain that

> Contradictory statements and actions are not necessarily false fronts that should be eliminated. On the contrary, sensitive recordings of inconsistencies in what people say or do may show how perceptions of objective reality actually reflect different levels of more complex realities. (p. 17)

This notion of expanding subjectivity through increasing the reflexive process by holding "reality" up to multiple mirrors certainly provides an opportunity to reflect the infinite and complex understandings of reality (Ruby, 1982). However, I worry deeply about the potential loss of women's voices in this array of infinite possibilities. Does the pursuit of subjectivity lead us into the abyss of relativity? More important, can the collaboration of women and the findings of our research be acknowledged when all voices are equally valid?

Seeking subjectivity through collaboration continues to raise provoking questions. Although I have not found a resolution to my continuing efforts to make sense of the research relationship, I am more cautious about naming the process collaborative or even suggesting that the research process can ever truly be collaborative. I say this especially in light of the fact that the research relationship in the field is only one aspect of the collaborative process. Genuine reciprocity entails not only sensitivity to the research relationship, but also an account of the research process and relationship in the final text. The problem of representation, of both the stories and the intersubjective process, presented me with my final dilemma.

Writing the Text: "Where's My Life in All of This?"

In trying to achieve a collaborative research relationship, the process and product of the research cannot be separated. Trying to extend collaboration into the writing of the text is problematic when the analysis and write-up remain the exclusive concern of the researcher. According to Judith Stacey (1988), "the lives, loves, and tragedies that field work informants share with a researcher are ultimately data, grist for the ethnographic mill, a mill that has a truly grinding power" (p. 23).

Leslie Roman (1989) points out that the ethnographer is written into the text, but rarely appears as a social subject in relation to those that she or he researches. An accounting of the relationship, its dynamics, and its role in achieving understanding is traditionally left out due to the subjective nature of the research relationship. Feminists (Anderson, Armitage, Jack, & Wittner, 1990; Harding, 1989; Mies, 1983) have warned against the dangers of de-materializing research accounts by stripping them of the economic, cultural, and political conditions under which fieldwork has been conducted.

In seeking to establish a collaborative text, I was concerned with not only placing myself in the text, but questioning what role the life historians should play in the analysis and writing up of the text. As I have just suggested, it is in the final product, or text, in which collaboration has proved most difficult (Crapanzano, 1980; Langness & Frank, 1981; Visweswaran, 1988). In attempting to construct a truly feminist, collaborative text, I conceived of three essential elements: (1) my own self-reflexive account of the story, (2) the intersubjective creation of the story, and (3) the "actual" stories of the life historians. How to present these in a manner that did justice to each, while not reducing to a secondary position the story of the participants themselves, presents a continuing dilemma. How do I balance the stories of the life historians, my reflexive account, and their recollections of the research process without relegating their stories to a lesser position?

Susan Geiger (1990) suggests that at one end of the spectrum of textual representation lies erasure of the participant through anonymous generalizations from her story that objectify her as just another "text." At the other end lies total identification or attempted merger in an effort to erase not the person, but the reality of differences. In order to avoid either of these extremes, I hoped to represent the voices of the life historians in the text by incorporating their feedback on the transcripts, engaging them in a discussion of the salient themes, and, ultimately, having them comment on the final narrative so as to include their reactions to it in a written form.

At this point, the reaction of the life historians to my including them in the interpretative process has been their acknowledgment that it is a subjective process and that therefore their own interpretations are no more valid than mine. Brenda commented at our last session, after discussing what I felt were the emergent themes, that she saw parallels between the research process and the classroom. Just as she expected students to create their own meaning and take what they needed from the classroom experience, she trusted that I would do the same.

In being left alone with the task of constructing their life histories, I am acutely aware of not wanting to succumb to "vanity ethnography" (Van Maanen, 1988). I am also self-conscious about experimenting with the text in a way that might seem disrespectful to or alienate the participants. I wonder, for example, how they would feel if I presented them with an integrated text that interwove the multiple voices throughout the narrative. Would they see this as diminishing their stories? If I used innovative postmodern textual representations, such as cartoons, poems, or pictures, interspersed throughout the text as a means of representing the complexity of our stories, would they find this a fair representation of their lives? In choosing to represent these narratives in alternative forms, am I elevating my need to make a political and theoretical statement, or am I trying to do justice to the stories of women teachers?

NO CONCLUSION

The dilemmas discussed here present no easy solutions, if, in fact, there are solutions at all. The questions of representation, self-reflexivity, and subjectivity in the collaborative process are ongoing questions. Will degree of reflexivity or subjectivity, or mode of representation provide "better" criteria for establishing a feminist method? What about the goal of feminist research to be emancipatory or empowering? What criteria will be established to assess this? Again, I believe we are asking the wrong questions if we seek only to impose one theory for another because we are still trapped within an essentialist notion of truth.

My quest for understanding the role of theory has not led me to new feminist definitions or methods but has led me to a deeper understanding of ways of knowing and how these are deeply embedded in the relational acts of the research process. My relationships in the field not only provide my primary source of data, but, as Marcus (1982) suggests, in the process of self-reflection they become the epistemological base from which interpretations and claims originate. My understanding of the multiple ways we create, negotiate, and make sense of the power relations in our lives has been enlarged. I only hope that my feminist position continues to situate me in and alert me to these crucial issues. For it is only from this position that I can even attempt to achieve the collaboration that I seek.

NOTES

1. This research is part of a larger study that I conducted for my dissertation (Munro, 1991). This research was funded in part by the Center for the Study of Women in Society at the University of Oregon. I would like to acknowledge Janice Jipson, David Flinders, Harry Wolcott, and the Women's Study and Research Group at the University of Oregon for their honest and insightful feedback central to the development of this chapter.

2. The term "life historians" is suggested by Marjorie Mbilinyi (1989) as an alternative to the objectifying labels "informant" or "subject."

REFERENCES

Abu-Lughod, L. (1990). Can there be feminist ethnography? *Women and Performance: A Journal of Feminist Theory, 5*(1), 7–27.

Agar, M. H. (1980). *The professional stranger: An informal introduction to ethnography.* New York: Academic Press.

Anderson, G. (1989). Critical ethnography in education: Origins, current status and new directions. *Review of Educational Research, 59*(3), 249–270.

Anderson, K., Armitage, S., Jack, D., & Wittner, J. (1990). Beginning where we are: Feminist methodology in oral history. In J. Nielson (Ed.), *Feminist research methods* (pp. 94–112). Boulder, CO: Westview Press.

Bateson, M. C. (1989). *Composing a life.* New York: The Atlantic Monthly Press.

Bowen, E. S. (1964). *Return to laughter.* New York: Doubleday.

Chevigny, B. (1984). Daughters writing: Toward a theory of women's biography. In C. Ascher, L. DeSalvo, & S. Ruddick (Eds.), *Between women* (pp. 357–381). Boston: Beacon Press.

Christman, J. (1988). Working the field as female friend. *Anthropology & Education Quarterly, 19*(2), 70–85.

Clifford, J. (1986). Introduction: Partial truths. In J. Clifford & G. E. Marcus (Eds.), *Writing culture: The poetics and politics of ethnography* (pp. 1–26). Berkeley: University of California Press.

Connelly, F. M., & Clandinin, D. J. (1990). Stories of experience and narrative inquiry. *Educational Researcher, 19*(4), 2–14.

Crapanzano, V. (1980). *Tuhami: Portrait of a Moroccan.* Chicago: University of Chicago Press.

Duelli-Klein, R. (1983). How to do what we want to do: Thoughts about feminist methodology. In G. Bowles & R. Duelli-Klein (Eds.), *Theories of women's studies* (pp. 105–116). London: Routledge.

Everhart, R. (1977). Between stranger and friend: Some consequences of "long term" field work in schools. *American Educational Research Journal, 14*, 1–15.

Flax, J. (1989). Postmodernism and gender relations in feminist theory. In M. R. Malson, J. F. O'Barr, S. Westphal-Wihl, & M. Wyer (Eds.), *Feminist theory in practice and process* (pp. 51–74). Chicago: University of Chicago Press.

Geiger, S. (1986). Women's life histories: Methods and content. *Signs, 11*(2), 334–351.

Geiger, S. (1990). What's so feminist about women's oral history? *Journal of Women's History, 2*(1), 169–182.

Gitlin, A. D. (1990). Educative research, voice and school change. *Harvard Educational Review, 60*(4), 443–466.

Golde, P. (1970). *Women in the field: Anthropological experiences.* Chicago: Aldine.

Grumet, M. (1990). On daffodils that come before the swallow dares. In E. W. Eisner & A. Peshkin (Eds.), *Qualitative inquiry in education: The continuing debate* (pp. 101–120). New York: Teachers College Press.

Harding, S. (1989). Is there a feminist method? In N. Tuana (Ed.), *Feminism & science* (pp. 17–32). Bloomington: Indiana University Press.

Heilbrun, C. G. (1988). *Writing a woman's life*. New York: Norton.

Langness, L. L., & Frank, G. (1981). *Lives: Anthropological approach to biography*. Novato, CA: Chandler & Sharp.

Lather, P. (1986). Research as praxis. *Harvard Educational Review, 56*(3), 257–277.

Mandelbaum, D. G. (1973). The study of life history: Gandhi. *Current Anthropology, 14*(3), 177–206.

Marcus, G. E. (1982). Rhetoric and the ethnographic genre in anthropological research. In J. Ruby (Ed.), *A crack in the mirror: Reflexive perspectives in anthropology* (pp. 163–171). Philadelphia: University of Pennsylvania Press.

Marcus, J. (1984). Invisible mending. In C. Ascher, L. DeSalvo, & S. Ruddick (Eds.), *Between women* (pp. 381–397). Boston: Beacon Press.

Mascia-Lees, F. E., Sharpe, P., & Cohen, C. (1989). The postmodernist turn in anthropology: Cautions from a feminist perspective. *Signs, 15*(1), 7–34.

Mbilinyi, M. (1989). I'd have been a man. In Personal Narratives Group (Eds.), *Interpreting women's lives* (pp. 204–207). Bloomington: Indiana University Press.

McRobbie, A. (1982). The politics of feminist research: Between text, talk and action. *Feminist Review*, pp. 46–57.

Mies, M. (1983). Towards a methodology for feminist research. In G. Bowles & R. Duelli-Klein (Eds.), *Theories of women's studies* (pp. 117–125). London: Routledge.

Miller, J. (1990). *Creating spaces and finding voices: Teachers collaborating for empowerment*. Albany: State University of New York Press.

Munro, P. (1991). *A life of work: Stories women teachers tell*. Unpublished doctoral dissertation, University of Oregon, Eugene.

Myerhoff, B. (1982). Life history among the elderly. In J. Ruby (Ed.), *A crack in the mirror: Reflexive perspectives in anthropology* (pp. 99–117). Philadelphia: University of Pennsylvania Press.

Pagano, J. (1991). Moral fictions: The dilemma of theory and practice. In C. Witherell & N. Noddings (Eds.), *Stories lives tell* (pp. 193–206). New York: Teachers College Press.

Personal Narratives Group. (1989). *Interpreting women's lives: feminist theory and personal narratives*. Bloomington: Indiana University Press.

Peshkin, A. (1988). In search of subjectivity — one's own. *Educational Researcher, 17*(7), 17–21.

Plummer, K. (1983). *Documents of life: An introduction to the problems and literature of a humanistic method*. London: Allen & Unwin.

Powdermaker, H. (1966). *Stranger and friend: The way of an anthropologist*. New York: Norton.

Reinharz, S. (1979). *On becoming a social scientist: From survey research and participant observation to experiential analysis*. San Francisco: Jossey-Bass.

Robertson, C. (1983). In pursuit of life histories: The problem of bias. *Frontiers, 7*(2), 63–69.

Roman, L. G. (1989, April). *Double exposure: The politics of feminist materialist ethnography*. Paper presented at the annual meeting of the American Educational Research Association, San Francisco.

Roman, L. G., & Apple, M. W. (1990). Is naturalism a move away from positivism?: Materialist and feminist approaches to subjectivity in ethnographic research. In E. W. Eisner & A. Peshkin (Eds.), *Qualitative inquiry in education: The continuing debate* (pp. 38–74). New York: Teachers College Press.

Ruby, J. (Ed.). (1982). *A crack in the mirror: Reflexive perspectives in anthropology*. Philadelphia: University of Pennsylvania Press.

Sheridan, M., & Salaff, J. W. (1984). *Lives: Chinese working women*. Bloomington: Indiana University Press.

Shostak, M. (1981). *Nisa*. New York: Vintage Books.

Smith, S. (1987). *A poetics of women's autobiography*. Bloomington: Indiana University Press.

Stacey, J. (1988). Can there be a feminist ethnography? *Women's Studies International Forum, 11*(1), 21–27.

Strathern, M. (1987). An awkward relationship: The case of feminism and anthropology. *Signs, 12*(2), 276–292.

Van Maanen, J. (1988). *Tales of the field*. Chicago: University of Chicago Press.

Visweswaran, K. (1988). Defining feminist ethnography. *Inscriptions*, (3/4), 27–44.

Watson, L., & Watson-Sparks, F. (1985). *Interpreting life histories: An anthropological inquiry*. New Brunswick, NJ: Rutgers University Press.

Wolcott, H. (1990). On seeking—and rejecting—validity in qualitative research. In E. W. Eisner & A. Peshkin (Eds.), *Qualitative inquiry in education: The continuing debate* (pp. 121–152). New York: Teachers College Press.

THEORY IN PERSPECTIVE

Part III serves to refocus the topic of theory once again, this time by situating theory relative to contemporary understandings of qualitative thought. Some of these understandings are made accessible by attending to the hermeneutic traditions of inquiry, others can be gained from the rhetorical analysis of qualitative research, while still further insights are offered by a critical assessment of the field itself. The following chapters take up each of these perspectives in turn.

First, in Chapter 11, John Smith argues that qualitative researchers are concerned generally with interpretation, and specifically with the interpretation of meanings. This special focus draws their inquiry within the sphere of hermeneutics, a tradition first developed to guide the interpretation of written texts and later extended to a broader range of interpretive processes. Hermeneutics offers not one but multiple perspectives, which Smith illustrates by contrasting three distinct versions of hermeneutic inquiry: validation, critical, and philosophical. Validation hermeneutics assumes that meaning can be objectively assessed and that the aim of inquiry is to do so. Critical hermeneutics strives to interpret meanings free of ideological distortion, allowing researchers to compare how things are with how they could possibly become once we have empowered ourselves to see the historical and cultural determinants of meaning. Philosophical hermeneutics assumes that meaning is a product of dialogical encounters between interpreters and the subjects of interpretation. Here inquiry is viewed as ordinary conversation, as a social process for getting to know others as well as ourselves at a deeper level of understanding than would otherwise be possible.

In many ways, Smith's chapter reiterates issues and themes found in the previous accounts of theory at work. His aim, beyond this, is to raise issues to a level at which they are informed by a broader discourse, thus helping us understand why different qualitative researchers might well disagree or pursue different lines of reasoning to arrive at their own particular styles and methods of research. Generally speaking, validation, critical, and philosophical hermeneutics set forth three significantly different conceptions of inquiry.

Chapter 12 also deals with conceptions of inquiry, but from yet another perspective. Its author, Henry St. Maurice, develops an approach to research informed by the ancient arts and modern scholarship of rhetoric. He looks specifically to "the rhetoric of inquiry," a specialization that has contributed to the current revival and renewed interest in rhetorical studies. The rhetoric of inquiry draws on a variety of academic fields, including dramatics, speech communication, writing, media studies, and political science. Its focus is on the construction of scholarly arguments and the persuasive functions of theory.

Rhetorical studies have not traditionally been common in education, at least in part because scientific norms have long urged researchers to adopt the style and realism of natural history. Indeed, rhetoric is often maligned in the atmosphere of this ideally dispassionate search for truth. Nevertheless, St. Maurice not only brings into focus the rhetorical foundations of social inquiry, but also illustrates how basic concepts such as invention, disposition, and elocution can be used to make explicit otherwise taken-for-granted developments in qualitative thought. St. Maurice is careful to note that while rhetorical analysis is in itself something of an art, it offers a twofold promise: first as a means for increasing our awareness of the voice and agency that stand behind theory, and second as a reminder that, to quote St. Maurice, "methodological discussions could be more like conversations than monologues." The latter argument is particularly apropos in this volume because one of our main purposes has been to provide a forum for reflective, candid discussions of research.

In the final chapter, Howard Becker readily acknowledges the necessity of theory, concluding that researchers would not even know where to begin without at least an implicit theory of knowledge from which to work. Becker also recognizes the importance of theory, particularly now that qualitative researchers are less sure than they once were of being on the right track. But beyond this, Becker urges us to take a more self-reflective stance than we typically do with respect to theoretical and methodological concerns. Stepping back from our preoccupation with epistemological debates, we can view these debates as an ongoing part of the social organization of research. Here we might ask, for example, when do these epistemological concerns become most troublesome? And although our theories may well be riddled with obvious flaws, when are they still good enough to generate informative research?

From Becker's perspective, what makes our methods and theories "good enough" has as much to do with organizational factors as it does with philosophical argument. Theory and methods are good enough depending on our purposes, audiences, the consensus and conventions of our research community, the stage of the research, how much time and money we plan to invest, as well as other worldly matters. Educational researchers who often draw on multiple disciplines and address multiple audiences are especially open to criticism for not meeting the different standards and demands of different groups. These difficulties come with the job. Yet, Becker is not arguing that we simply leave epistemological concerns for the philosophers of science to worry about. His point, rather, is that their worries need not paralyze research for being less than perfect.

11

Hermeneutics and Qualitative Inquiry

JOHN K. SMITH

Human beings do and say things for reasons. The cluster of "theories" one holds at various levels about human nature, the nature of society, the nature of a particular social setting or context within which an expression occurs, and so on are crucial to the interpretations one offers of these reasons. The "theoretical" background that one brings to the interpretation of the expressions of others shapes not only one's understanding of the intentions and motivations that stand behind these expressions, but also one's understanding of the intentions and motivations that stand behind one's own expressions. In short, to understand others requires that one interpret their expressions in terms of an already existing web of background meanings or "theories." And, by the same token of course, to understand oneself, as one engages in the process of understanding others, requires that one interpret one's own expressions in terms of an already existing web of background meanings or "theories."

Researchers, being human, also do and say things for reasons. The "theories" researchers hold at various levels about human nature, the nature of society and of particular social settings, and so on, along with the images they have of themselves as researchers, are crucial to the interpretations they offer of these reasons. The "theoretical" background inquirers bring to the interpretation of expressions shapes their understandings of the intentions and motivations behind the expressions of others as well as their own. For researchers to understand others, and themselves in the process, requires that they interpret expressions in light of an already existing web of background meanings or "theories."

Based on these relatively uncontroversial premises, the central claim advanced in this chapter can be stated quite directly: As qualitative inquirers attempt to understand who they are and what they do as inquirers, they must come to terms with hermeneutics—especially with the challenge hermeneutics presents to inquiry. By deepening their understanding of understanding itself, qualitative inquirers may well find interesting answers, but not, of course, definitive or final ones, to questions concerning the nature of qualitative inquiry and, in particular, concerning the kinds of claims that can be made for the results of this form of inquiry. Put simply, because hermeneutics is a theory of understanding, it is also, not surprisingly, a theory of self-understanding.

However, a complication immediately arises that makes the lives of those who undertake qualitative inquiry both more complex and more interesting. This complication originates in the fact that hermeneutics is far from a univocal school of thought. There are at least three different versions of hermeneutics — different understandings of what it means to interpret and understand — relevant to qualitative inquiry. Each version leads to a different perspective on the nature of interpretation and, most important, different understandings as to the kinds of claims inquirers can make for their interpretations.

To disentangle these complications, it is necessary to begin with a brief discussion of the focus of qualitative inquiry. This discussion will be followed by an examination of the three different versions of hermeneutics and their respective implications for our understanding of qualitative inquiry and for understanding ourselves as qualitative inquirers.

THE FOCUS OF SOCIAL AND EDUCATIONAL INQUIRY

With the end of traditional forms of empiricism and, in particular, the demise of logical positivism/empiricism and the behaviorism it supported, it is apparent that the interpretation of meaning is the central focus of social and educational inquiry. While of course it is still possible to limit inquiry to a description of physical movement in time and space, qualitative inquirers in particular must argue that the extent to which this is done is the extent to which inquiry is inadequate to its subject matter, that is, the meanings, intentions, motivations, and reasons that stand behind the expressions and actions of human beings.

There are two basic concepts that center or define the focus of social and educational inquiry — human action and social action. Human actions are those bodily movements and verbal and written expressions of people that are undertaken for reasons. The distinction here can be illustrated by the well-known example of a movement that just happens (usually for physical reasons), such as the blinking of an eye, and an expression that is the result of reasons and motives, such as winking at someone. Moreover, human action must be considered as action that is freely taken in the sense that a person could have refrained from doing what she did or could have done otherwise.

The concept of *social* must be attached to this idea of human action because the particular meaning(s) ascribed to an expression, by the person, by others, and of course by researchers, is (are) strongly conditioned by the accumulated understandings people have, in general and in particular, of social expressions, interactions, and relationships. That is, the understandings one has of the reasons and motives of another cannot be understood apart from the background knowledge or web of social meanings — what one might call theory — of the interpreter. Simon (1982) concisely summarizes what these two concepts mean for an understanding of the focus of social and educational inquiry.

> What is distinctive about . . . human action . . . is that it is meaningful; actions have subjective and intersubjective meanings that must be grasped before anyone can begin to understand why they occurred. The meaning of an action, furthermore, is not necessarily given by the agent's intentions alone, but also depends on a system of social relations that determine the conditions of ascription of responsibility. A science of action will therefore have to be a science of social meaning. (p. 24)

The task of the inquirer is the interpretation of all manner of human expressions not only in terms of the motives, intentions, and purposes of the people involved, but also in terms of the inquirer's own motives, intentions, and purposes. And, of course, this is a process of interpretation that must take place within a social and historical context.

Thus, if inquiry is to be truly adequate to its subject matter, that is, human social life, it must undertake the interpretation of the reasons, motives, and intentions that people have for their expressions. Anything less than this leads to a very "thin" form of inquiry. As Simon (1982) notes:

> We have to rely on behavioral data to suggest, support, and discredit possible interpretations of actions and imputations of reasons, but since acting is not simply behaving and reasons do not explain in the way natural causes do, interpretations of action can only be guided by the study of behavior, and never established by it. One can, after all, totally misconstrue an activity without contravening any of the statistical evidence. (p. 76)

However, to place meaning at the center of qualitative inquiry immediately raises the crucial question of where does meaning "reside." There are at least three possible responses to this question. The first is that the meaning of an expression resides with the author of that expression. If this is the case, then the ideal that guides interpreters, both inquirers and lay people alike, is the accurate depiction of the reasons and intentions that stand behind the expressions of others.

The second locates the actual meaning of an expression within, or in light of, a set of objective historical conditions. The claim is that it is possible for authors to be mistaken about what they actually meant because they are the victims of ideological distortion and false consciousness. Interpreters, presumably because they have been able to understand the historical causes of this false consciousness, can "correct" meaning or point out that what they thought they meant was not really what they meant. The final possibility argues that the meaning of an expression does not have an "independent existence" or stand prior to encounter of author and interpreter. Meaning resides neither with an author nor within a set of objective historical conditions. Rather, meaning is brought into being, and is constantly shaped and reshaped, as a result of the continuing dialogical encounter between and among people—inquirers included.

The implications of these different responses for inquiry and inquirers clearly go well beyond these brief and simple statements of position. In order to examine these implications it is necessary to turn to what was referred to above as "the challenge hermeneutics presents to inquiry."

THE CHALLENGE OF HERMENEUTICS

The challenge of hermeneutics has been expressed as follows: How is it possible, *or is it even possible at all*, "to render accounts of subjectively intended meaning objective in the face of the fact that they are mediated by the interpreter's own subjectivity" (Bleicher, 1980, p. 1). This challenge leads straight to the issue of the kind of relationship that exists between one subjective being and another subjective being as the former attempts to interpret the interpretations of the latter—or as they each attempt to interpret the interpretations of the other. When put this way, it is clear that those issues immediately arise with respect to what qualitative researchers do when they undertake the interpretation of meaning and what status can be given to their interpretations.

The importance of this view requires one further comment. It is clear that the interpretation of meaning must take place within a context. In the paradigmatic case of the interpretation of written texts, this means that to understand an individual part of a text requires that one understand the whole text; yet, it is equally the case that to understand the whole text requires that one understand the individual parts. Interpretation requires a movement back and forth between parts and whole. In the case of the interpretation of intentional, meaningful human expressions, historical expressions included, the same situation applies. The interpretation of meaning can only be pursued with a constant movement back and forth between the particular expression and the web of meanings within which that expression is embedded. In that this process allows for no natural or nonarbitrary starting or ending points, it is best thought of in terms of a circle—a condition most often referred to as the *hermeneutic circle*.

This circular requirement on the process of interpretation poses some very interesting and thorny problems. Undoubtedly the most difficult of these problems refers to the challenge of hermeneutics in that it focuses on the extent to which the interpreter is a part of the circle or context within which the interpretation must be realized. That is, everybody is somebody or has a place in the world and can only attempt to interpret the expressions of others from that particular place in the world. Everybody has certain or particular interests, values, and purposes that are brought to the interpretation of the expressions of others. As is well recognized, there can be no theory-free observation or theory-free interpretation. But, having accepted this point, one must then ask about how far to go with this no theory-free idea or about how much the inquirer is a part of the circle. The kind of answer one gives to this question makes a great deal of difference to one's understanding of qualitative inquiry.

ORIGIN AND DEVELOPMENT OF HERMENEUTICS

More than anywhere else, it is to hermeneutic theory that one can turn for insight into these issues. Although hermeneutics is far from a unitary school of thought, most people who discuss this perspective share the general concern

> that what is distinctive about human understanding is that it is always in terms of some evolving linguistic framework that has been worked out over time in terms of some historically conditioned set of concerns and practices. In short, hermeneutical thinkers argue that language and history are always both conditions and limits of understanding. (Wachterhauser, 1986, pp. 5–6)

The origin of the modern concept of hermeneutics can be found in the seventeenth century with reference to biblical commentary (exegesis) and the need to set forth appropriate rules for this commentary (hermeneutics). This approach to biblical interpretation came to include, as early as the time of the Enlightenment, not only a grammatical analysis, but also an analysis of the historical context of any particular biblical account. Therefore, only a short step was necessary to broaden the concept of hermeneutics to the level of a general methodology for the interpretation of all written texts.

Over the course of the nineteenth century a shift of major consequences took place in the development of hermeneutics. As various people, Schleiermacher (1819/1985) in particular, began to reflect on the nature of understanding itself, hermeneutics was reconceptualized not only as a tool to solve the problems of textual interpretation (philological hermeneutics), but also as a source of reflection on the nature and problem of interpretive understanding itself (general hermeneutics). Schleiermacher "defined [hermeneutics] as the study of understanding itself" (Palmer, 1969, p. 40) and, in doing so, he planted the seeds of two ideas that have remained important to contemporary hermeneutics.

First, the problem of understanding moved beyond the level of the analysis of textual expressions to address the more encompassing issue of how it was possible for one member of a culture or historical time period to understand a member of another culture or historical time period. Second, Schleiermacher's (1985) idea of understanding as a "divinatory" process, or a process of re-experiencing, meant that the meaning of an expression resided with the author. The hermeneutical task was seen as that of putting oneself in the place of the author in the sense that one would be able thereby to reconstruct the thinking of the author.

By the mid- to late 1800s hermeneutics was moving away from its status as a methodology of philology toward becoming a philosophy of meaning for all human expressions, written or otherwise. Bauman (1978) summarizes this transition as follows: "The philosophical reflection on the activity and results of hermeneutics moved beyond the mere critique of texts and began to ask difficult questions about the nature and the objective of historical knowledge as such; indeed of social knowledge in general" (p. 8).

In the last part of the nineteenth century hermeneutics was again reshaped with the work of Dilthey (1926/1985). Dilthey attempted to establish hermeneutics as the methodology of the cultural or moral sciences (*Geisteswissenschaften*) and, in doing so, he offered a direct challenge to the claim that the method and methodology of the natural sciences must be the basis for the study of "things human." He argued that since the facts and phenomena of the natural world are impersonal — that is, they have no inner experiences — it is possible to explain those facts in terms of historical and universal principles. The facts and phenomena of social life, to the contrary, because they involve the inner experiences or inner life of human beings, cannot be treated in an impersonal, ahistorical manner. As Howard (1982) notes with reference to Dilthey's position:

> What is characteristic of our experience of cultural phenomena is precisely our sense that these cannot be relegated to a "non-self" category, that they exist, rather, as "for-us" kinds of phenomena, and that the attempt to relegate them to the category of non-human systems . . . empties them of the character that makes them special. (p. 15)

There are two related aspects of Dilthey's (1985) attempt to establish hermeneutics as the methodology of the cultural sciences that must be emphasized. First, the influence of Schleiermacher led Dilthey to think of understanding in psychologistic terms — as an event of re-experiencing in which one discovers another in oneself or as an event of reconstructing within oneself the inner life of another. This meant that the referent point for judging whether an interpretation is correct or incorrect must ultimately reside in the other.

Second, Dilthey built a tension into hermeneutics that has lasted until this day (see, for example, Bleicher, 1980; Hughes, 1958; Palmer, 1969). Dilthey considered himself a "stubborn empiricist" in that he desired an approach to the study of human expressions that could realize the same certainty of knowledge as he presumed was available in the natural sciences. To achieve this goal, he was led to regard the expressions of human historical and social life as "givens" that could be accurately depicted or understood through hermeneutical analysis. However, to make good on his desire for this type of objectivity, he had to hold that an interpreter is able to stand outside of her own history as she interprets the meanings of others. This possibility ran afoul of his other point about the historically contextual nature of all interpretation. There was a problem here, an internal contradiction in effect, that he was unable to resolve. This is a version of the same problem, mentioned earlier under the label of the challenge of hermeneutics, that has remained a central preoccupation of hermeneutic thinkers.

RESPONSES TO THE CHALLENGE OF HERMENEUTICS

Among the various contemporary versions of hermeneutics, there are at least three that are of particular interest to qualitative researchers — *validation*, *critical*, and *philosophical* hermeneutics. It is in regard to these versions that some of the most important and lively debates have taken place among leading hermeneutical thinkers such as Habermas (1986), Gadamer (1986), Hirsch (1967), Betti (1980), Apel (1980), and Ricoeur (1986). Each response has different implications for our understanding of what qualitative inquirers are doing when they do qualitative inquiry and for the status of the interpretations offered as a result of their inquiries. Each of the three versions will be briefly described.

Validation Hermeneutics

Validation (or objectivist) hermeneutics has been most prominently elaborated by Hirsch (1967, 1976) and Betti (1980). In both cases the dominant theme around which their arguments are constructed is that of what can be called the independence or autonomy of that which is interpreted. For Betti this point is expressed as follows:

> Meaning-full forms have to be regarded as autonomous with their own logic of development, their intended connections, and in their necessity, coherence, and conclusiveness; they should be judged in relation to the standards immanent in the original intention, that is, which the created forms should correspond to from the point of view of the author and his formative impulse in the course of the creative process; it follows that they must not be judged in terms of their suitability for any other external purpose that may seem relevant to the interpreter. (p. 58)

Hirsch (1976), in a slightly different way, captures this independence/ autonomy idea with his distinction between meaning and significance. The former refers to what an author actually meant or means by a written passage or an expression, whereas the latter refers to the significance of that passage or expression for the interpreter. As he notes,

> The term "meaning" refers to the whole verbal meaning of a text, and "significance" to textual meaning in relation to a large context, i.e., another mind, another era, a wider subject matter, an alien system of values, and so on. In other words, "significance" is textual meaning as related to some context, indeed any context, beyond itself. (pp. 2–3)

Meaning is thereby assigned the status of a determinate entity that can be accurately depicted, at least in principle, whereas significance can vary in that it responds to the different interests and purposes of different interpreters. This distinction grants meaning an independent existence, and makes it the necessary external referent point against which to assess whether an interpretation is accurate or inaccurate, correct or incorrect. From the perspective of validation hermeneutics the task facing the qualitative inquirer is to "get it right."

Hirsch (1976) assembles a complex argument, with numerous strands, in defense of this separation of meaning and significance and his claim for the sanctity of author meaning. There are, however, three lines of reasoning that are sufficient to summarize his position. The first line can be labeled the "argument of necessity." He says that inquiry is pointless and the concept of knowledge makes no sense in the absence of an independently existing entity to inquire about and have knowledge of. For him, "without the stable determinacy of meaning there can be no knowledge in interpretation, nor any knowledge in the many humanistic disciplines based on textual interpretation" (p. 1). Qualitative inquiry is included, of course, in the category of humanistic disciplines.

His second argument is derived from what he considers common sense or an intuitive sense of ourselves as human beings. Every human being is able to adopt, and does so routinely, a dual perspective in discourse with others and with reference to textual materials. As Hirsch (1976) puts this, "It is within the capacity of every individual to imagine himself other than he is, to realize in himself another human or cultural possibility" (p. 47). The interpretation of the expressions of others both can and most often does take place on two levels—that of assessing what an author actually means by her expression and that of the significance of that expression for the interpreter. Hirsch calls this the "empirical actuality of [the] double perspective [that is] universal in verbal discourse" (p. 49).

Finally, Hirsch (1976) invokes an ethical argument in support of the meaning–significance distinction. He begins this argument with the premise that since no one is so totally trapped in time and place that the freedom to choose aims and meanings is eliminated, choice is always possible and, of course, choice is always a matter of values and ethical responsibilities. He states that *"unless there is an overriding value in disregarding an author's intention (i.e., original meaning), we who interpret as a vocation should not disregard it"* (p. 90; emphasis in original). The exceptions here would include those cases when it is ethically preferable to lie rather than tell the truth, when it is important to conceal true meaning in the case of young children, and so on. Beyond this, however, Hirsch says that inquirers, like everyone else, must respect the "basic moral imperative of speech, which is to respect an author's intentions" (pp. 91–92).

Given these lines of reasoning, which establish, at least for many people, the distinction between meaning and significance, the question arises as to how qualitative inquirers are to undertake the process of determining meaning. Hirsch says that one can turn to Popper's idea of falsification (see Hirsch, 1967, pp. 165–207). An inquirer begins with a hypothesis (or hypotheses) about meaning and then searches for evidence that will call the hypothesis into doubt. If such falsifying evidence is uncovered, the inquirer must revise the interpretation. Throughout this process of constantly testing one's interpretation of meaning, "the direction is still toward increased probability of truth, since the very instability imposed by unfavorable evidence reduces confidence in previously accepted hypotheses and to that extent reduces the probability of error" (pp. 151–152).

Although in making this case for falsification, Hirsch (1967) is talking about a method of interpretation, he is not arguing for an established methodology of interpretation. The process of interpretation cannot be reduced to a rule-bounded or mechanical process. However, this absence of rules does not mean that "anything goes" because the attempt to accurately interpret an author's meaning is constrained by constant testing, criticism, and so on in the name of the search for truth.

Critical Hermeneutics

Critical hermeneutics differs markedly from validation hermeneutics and from philosophical hermeneutics. Critical hermeneuticists are deeply suspicious of the former because it fails to properly account for the possibility of historically formed ideological distortion and false consciousness. That is, validation hermeneutics does not adequately account for the possibility that an inquirer can understand the meaning of an author's expression better than the author him- or herself understands the meaning of that expression. The point is that authors can be mistaken about the meaning of their own expression because they are the victims, unknowingly of course, of false consciousness and ideological distortion.

The task facing critical hermeneuticists is to provoke practical engagement — empowerment and emancipation — in the light of historical truth. This is a truth that can be understood in terms of the vision of a society free from ideological distortion and distorted communication. As Bleicher (1980) puts it, for critical hermeneutics

> the meaning embedded in objectivications of human activity is understood objectively and then confronted with the "author's" self-understanding of the intentions underlying them. By synthesizing explanatory and interpretive procedures it is hoped that it may be possible to demonstrate to social actors why they thought what they thought, why it may have been wrong, and how the mistake could be corrected. (p. 144)

Over the years, Habermas (1971, 1975, 1979), as much as anyone else, has sought to justify a critical hermeneutical stance. Initially this justification was undertaken in terms of the model of Freudian psychoanalysis. Criticisms of this model led him to shift focus and see critical hermeneutical self-reflection in terms of a theory of legitimation and what can be called a "counterfactually projected reconstruction." The latter means that power relationships in society can be understood by comparing "normative structures existing at a given time [in a society] with the hypothetical state of a system of norms formed, *ceteris paribus*, discursively" (1975, p. 113).

This position is deeply entangled with Habermas's arguments about the "ideal speech situation" in that the task of the inquirer is to assess what people would have meant by their expressions if they had been undertaken under the conditions of free and open communication. As Thompson (1981) notes, the point is to analyze "how societal members would have interpreted their needs and established their norms if they had accomplished these tasks under the conditions of an ideal speech situation" (p. 170). Thus, the task is to compare, at the level of a thought experiment, how things are in a society with how they might possibly be.

One major aspect of this comparative process focuses on the idea of "generalizable interests." The idea in this case is that hermeneutical critique must be framed by the specification for all involved, especially the inquirer, of those interests that they think are "generalizable," by an interpretation of their needs in regard to these interests, and with an understanding of the norms that are justified by the condition of free and open communication. This projection of possibilities, in that it is, and never can be more than, a thought experiment, cannot be directly confirmed. However, indirect confirmation is entirely possible because we are capable of assessing a variety of empirical indicators, including, especially, historical ones, that focus on how things actually are versus how they might be. These indicators might include an examination of the disjuncture between how laws are applied and how they should be applied, an understanding of how certain voices and interests are excluded from the political process, and so on.

The determination of meaning in light of objective historical conditions imposes certain conditions on the inquirer — ones that go beyond the validation hermeneuticist's attempt to falsify hypotheses. In the case of the inquirer influenced by critical hermeneutics, the task is not only to depict how people interpret their situations, but also to elaborate the social and historical determinants that may have limited or distorted their interpretations. For Comstock (1982) there are at least four elements involved in this process. First, the inquirer must present, particularly by drawing upon other studies,

> empirical findings and analytic theories in ways that clearly show the historicity and constructness of social conditions. Conditions must be shown, not to be the consequences of immutable laws, but to be structures and processes constructed by elites with specific interests and intentions. (p. 382)

The next element involves an elaboration of the "dialectical tension between the historically created conditions of actions and the actor's understanding of these conditions" (Comstock, 1982, p. 383). This move requires the researcher to link the meanings and understandings of people "to the social processes and structures that create and maintain them" (p. 383). It is at this point that the inquirer establishes the needed elements for an examination of the understandings of people in light of objective historical conditions.

Third, there is the need for critique. Because the conditions of false consciousness and domination often prevent people from truly understanding their own situations and intentions, it is the task of the inquirer to critique the "dominating ideology which prevents the participants from recognizing the possibilities immanent in the present" (Comstock, 1982, p. 384). In other words, the inquirer must demonstrate to people, through an historical account and an analysis of present social conditions, how the interpretations they give to their own situation and that of others are the result of ideological distortion—what they think is the case is not really the case.

Finally, inquiry must result in transformation or in emancipation and empowerment. Those influenced by critical hermeneutics are interested not only in a depiction of motivations and intentions, but also in greater self-understanding on the part of people. That is, the inquirer must reorient and energize people to take action. This is not merely a side issue because, as Comstock (1982) notes, "dialogic education is integral to every research program which treats subjects as active agents. . . . [The point is] not simply to enlighten but also to inform and initiate political action" (p. 386).

Philosophical Hermeneutics

The philosophical version of hermeneutics differs markedly from the previous two versions and, in doing so, offers different implications for qualitative inquiry and inquirers. In this case, hermeneutics is not about the accurate depiction of meaning or about the assessment of meaning in light of objective historical conditions. Rather, hermeneutics has deep ontological importance because it treats understanding as our "primordial mode of being in the world" (Gadamer, 1975, p. 130).

Possibly the major underlying theme in the development of this version of hermeneutics is a critique of the ideas that knowledge is a matter of accurate representation and that we can somehow extract ourselves from our own historical traditions to criticize those traditions from this "outside" standpoint. These ideas are illusions because, as Palmer (1969) notes in his discussion of Gadamer, "finite, historical man always sees and understands from his standpoint in time and place; he cannot . . . stand above the relativity of history and procure 'objectively valid knowledge'" (p. 178).

Given this point, what kind of hermeneutics is philosophical hermeneutics? Gadamer (1975) initiates his discussion with an analysis of our relationship to works of art. He says that if one approaches art from the standpoint of a spectator, then art can illuminate nothing of consequence for us. Our interaction with art is reduced to the level of emotive reaction or the expression of aesthetic pleasure. For him, to the contrary, the meaning of a work of art can be realized only if there is an interactive relationship between the work and the interpreter in the sense that just as the interpreter asks questions of the work of art, the work of art asks questions of the interpreter. To "observe" a work of art, with the intent of understanding, means that the interpreter must participate in that work because it is only the act of understanding itself that brings meaning into being.

This claim that art is presented only through the interpreter can be broadened to cover all attempts at understanding. Understanding is not a matter of accurately depicting a meaning that exists prior to and independent of the study of what is being transmitted. To the contrary, "understanding must be conceived as a part of the process of the coming into being of meaning, in which the significance of all statements — those of art and those of everything else that has been transmitted — is formed and made complete" (Gadamer, 1975, p. 146).

One of the most important aspects of Gadamer's (1975) defense of this idea that meaning is not out there awaiting discovery, but is brought into being through the act of understanding, is his defense of the related concepts of prejudice (i.e., prejudgment) and effective historical consciousness. In the former instance, he argues against the Enlightenment "prejudices against prejudices" (p. 240). The Enlightenment philosophers, in their desire to banish all authority for knowledge claims except those based on the authority of scientific reason, attempted to establish the possibility of presuppositionless interpretation and the possibility of knowledge without preconceptions. Gadamer says that this attempt was seriously in error because "the historicity of our existence entails that prejudices, in the literal sense of the word, constitute the initial directness of our whole ability to experience" (p. 9). It is only in the presence of our prejudices that we are open to our own experiences and allow these experiences to make a claim on us.

In that the source of those prejudices that constitute our being is our past — our traditions — this leads to the related concept of effective historical consciousness. For Gadamer (1975), we are always part of a tradition

long before tradition is a part of us. The task of effective historical consciousness is thus to bring our tradition to the level of explicit realization
because "true historical understanding must take account of its own histor-
icality" (p. 267). And, if this is so, then it is clear that "a proper hermeneutics would have to demonstrate the affectivity of history within understanding itself" (p. 267).

Does this mean then that we are all trapped by our prejudices and
entombed within our own particular historical traditions? This is not the
case for at least two reasons. First, we must always be open to risking and
testing our prejudices in our dialogical encounters with others. Second,
traditions are "living" or are always in the process of being reshaped
through reinterpretation. Contrary to the reification of tradition that
Gadamer (1975) ascribes to the Enlightenment, he counters that "tradition
is constantly an element of freedom and of history itself. Even the most
genuine and solid tradition does not persist by nature because of the iner-
tia of what once existed. It needs to be affirmed, embraced, cultivated"
(p. 250).

The encounter with an historical text or with the expressions of others
is a dialogical encounter in which the interpreter questions the text and
the text questions the interpreter. This is an "open" encounter that cannot
be distilled into a series of how-to-do-it rules. Rather, all one can do is to
illuminate the concept of effective historical consciousness in terms of the
concept of the fusion of horizons. For Gadamer (1975) a "horizon is the
range of vision that includes everything that can be seen from a particular
vantage point" (p. 269) — the vantage point being, of course, our prejudices. Yet, it is important to note that our horizon is not closed or shut off
from the horizons of others because no one is ever completely confined
and constrained by his present prejudices. Horizons change: "Thus the
horizon of the past, out of which all human life lives and which exists in
the form of tradition, is always in motion" (p. 271).

When one encounters another, it is not a matter of abandoning one's
own standpoint and grasping that of the other. On the contrary, a dialogical encounter of questions and answers is a fusion of horizons.

> The horizon of meaning within which a text or historical act stands is ques-
> tioningly approached from within one's own horizon; and one does not leave
> his own horizon behind when he interprets, but broadens it so as to fuse it
> with that of the act or text. Nor is this a matter of finding the intentions of
> the actor in history or in the writer of the text. The dialectic of question and
> answer works out a fusion of horizons. (Palmer, 1969, p. 201)

In short, philosophical hermeneutics is not about a method for objectively valid understanding, but is rather about understanding itself. This

version "is concerned not so much with understanding more correctly (and thus with providing norms for valid interpretation) as with understanding more deeply, more truly" (Palmer, 1969, p. 215).

If inquirers influenced by validation hermeneutics are to focus on the attempt to falsify hypotheses in the search for an accurate rendering of meaning, and those under the sway of critical hermeneutics are to focus on making transparent the conditions of false consciousness that have distorted meaning in the name of emancipation and empowerment, what is the situation for inquirers who adopt this philosophical perspective on hermeneutics? In this case, inquiry is very much like, or continuous with, routine conversation in that it is first and foremost a practical and moral activity, not an epistemological or technical activity.

The most immediate consequence of viewing inquiry in practical/ moral terms is that there is no particular or special procedures the inquirer must undertake in order to realize an interpretation. Certainly, it is always possible for an inquirer to employ various techniques, such as triangulation and member checks, as he attempts to understand another. But these activities are not at all mandatory. Sometimes they will seem the reasonable thing to do; sometimes not. Inquirers must make these judgments — and, of course, justify as best as possible why they chose to do one thing as opposed to another — as they go along in their attempt to understand the meanings and intentions that stand behind the expressions of the people with whom they are dealing in any particular setting. Just as is the case with our day-to-day attempts to understand others, there is no pre-established process for the interpretation of meaning and intentions. One does what seems reasonable given the situation at any given time and place.

Thus, inquiry is very much a practical task, and understanding is very much a practical accomplishment. Moreover, it is always an ethical and moral task (see Chapter 1, this volume). In that at their core human beings are ethical and moral beings, understanding is at its core ethical and moral.

CONCLUSION—HERMENEUTICS AND QUALITATIVE INQUIRY

Even if not articulately held, it is clear that inquirers have some sort of image or "theory" about themselves as inquirers. This is a "theory" that strongly conditions the inquirers' understanding of the nature of inquiry and the status that is granted the interpretations of the meanings and intentions that result from inquiry. As it turns out, however, the above review of different versions of hermeneutics demonstrates that there is not a univocal position on these questions. Depending on the version of her-

meneutics accepted, inquirers think differently about themselves and
about the results of their work.

For those inquirers influenced by validation hermeneutics, it is both
possible and proper to think of inquiry as the search for the accurate
depiction of what someone means by her expressions. The regulative ideal
that guides inquiry is objectivity or the accurate depiction of authorial
meaning. Moreover, there is a method that guides this search for truth —
that of Popperian falsification. Although no one is bold enough in this era
of postempiricism to talk in terms of certitude of an interpretation, it is
clear that some interpretations can be considered more accurate or objective than others. Thus, the claim can be made that an interpretation
accurately depicts what someone really meant by an expression. This is a
claim of truth that must be assented to by all concerned in the absence of
data that undermine that interpretation.

For those inquirers influenced by critical hermeneutics, the depiction
of the meaning of an expression is relatively unproblematic. What is more
problematic is the assessment of the meaning of that expression in light of
objective historical conditions. It is entirely possible, if not likely, that an
inquirer can understand what a person actually meant better than the
person himself can understand what he meant. Inquiry is about clarifying
the true conditions under which distorted understanding may have occurred — a clarification that must lead to practical action or to emancipation and empowerment of those whose understandings have been distorted.

For those inquirers influenced by philosophical hermeneutics, inquiry
is much like routine conversation. The inquirer engages in dialogue with
another in the attempt to arrive at a mutual understanding of the meanings and intentions that stand behind each other's expressions. In this case,
the ideas of an objective interpretation in the sense of accurately depicting
the meanings of another and of correcting the meanings of another in
light of an objective interpretation of ideological distortion are illusions.
The meanings of expressions are brought into being through the encounter
of interpreter and interpreted, and these meanings are constantly shaped
and reshaped as we go along. As such, no particular interpretation has
any greater epistemic privilege or standing than any other interpretation.
People may disagree over alternative interpretations, but this is a disagreement that cannot be resolved through reference to an external referent
point. The circle of interpretation can be broadened and deepened, but it
is a circle from which escape is not possible.

Thus, we have three different images of the qualitative inquirer — as
one who is able to accurately or objectively interpret the interpretations
of others; as one whose knowledge of objective historical conditions is able

to demonstrate to others how and why what they think they meant is not what they really meant; and as one whose interpretations are another contribution to an ongoing process of the interpretation and reinterpretation of meaning.

Is one understanding of qualitative inquiry and qualitative inquirers better than the others? Although the advocates of each version of hermeneutics obviously think so, this is not the time or the place to address this question. What can be concluded at this point, however, is that the kind of understanding one has of understanding makes a great deal of difference to the understanding one has of qualitative inquiry.

REFERENCES

Apel, K-O. (1980). *Towards a transformation of philosophy*. (G. Adey & D. Frisby, Trans.). London: Routledge.

Bauman, Z. (1978). *Hermeneutics and social science*. London: Century Hutchinson.

Betti, E. (1980). Hermeneutics as the general methodology of the *Geisteswissenschaften*. In J. Bleicher (Ed.), *Contemporary hermeneutics* (pp. 51–94). London: Routledge.

Bleicher, J. (1980). *Contemporary hermeneutics*. London: Routledge.

Comstock, D. (1982). A method for critical research. In E. Bredo & W. Feinberg (Eds.), *Knowledge and values in social and educational research* (pp. 370–390). Philadelphia: Temple University Press.

Dilthey, W. (1985). Awareness, reality: Time and the understanding of other persons and their life expressions. In K. Mueller-Vollmer (Ed.), *The hermeneutics reader* (pp. 148–164). New York: Continuum. (Original work published 1926)

Gadamer, H-G. (1975). *Truth and method*. (G. Bardon & J. Cumming, Trans. & Eds.). New York: Seabury Press.

Gadamer, H-G. (1986). On the scope and function of hermeneutical reflection. In B. Wachterhauser (Ed.), *Hermeneutics and modern philosophy* (pp. 277–299). Albany: State University of New York Press.

Habermas, J. (1971). *Knowledge and human interests*. (J. Shapiro, Trans.). Boston: Beacon Press.

Habermas, J. (1975). *Legitimation crisis*. (T. McCarthy, Trans.). Boston: Beacon Press.

Habermas, J. (1979). *Communication and the evolution of society*. (T. McCarthy, Trans.). Boston: Beacon Press.

Habermas, J. (1986). A review of Gadamer's *Truth and method*. In B. Wachterhauser (Ed.), *Hermeneutics and modern philosophy* (pp. 243–276). Albany: State University of New York Press.

Hirsch, E. (1967). *Validity in interpretation*. New Haven, CT: Yale University Press.

Hirsch, E. (1976). *The aims of interpretation*. Chicago: University of Chicago Press.

Howard, R. (1982). *Three faces of hermeneutics*. Berkeley: University of California Press.

Hughes, H. (1958). *Consciousness and society*. New York: Knopf.

Palmer, R. (1969). *Hermeneutics*. Evanston, IL: Northwestern University Press.

Ricoeur, P. (1986). Hermeneutics and the critique of ideology. In B. Wachterhauser (Ed.), *Hermeneutics and modern philosophy* (pp. 300–339). Albany: State University of New York Press.

Schleiermacher, F. (1985). General hermeneutics and grammatical and technical interpretation. In K. Mueller-Vollmer (Ed.), *The hermeneutics reader* (pp. 72–97). New York: Continuum. (Original work published 1819)

Simon, M. (1982). *Understanding human action*. Albany: State University of New York Press.

Thompson, J. (1981). *Critical hermeneutics*. Cambridge: Cambridge University Press.

Wachterhauser, B. (1986). Introduction. In B. Wachterhauser (Ed.), *Hermeneutics and modern philosophy* (pp. 5–61). Albany: State University of New York Press.

12

The Rhetorical Return

The Rhetoric of Qualitative Inquiry

HENRY ST. MAURICE

*Out of the quarrel with others we make rhetoric; out of the quarrel
with ourselves, poetry.*

— *W. B. Yeats (1953)*

A poem by Wallace Stevens entitled "An Ordinary Evening in New Haven" (1949/1959) is a rumination about the ways that reality is perceived; in Stevens's words, it is

> . . . part of the never-ending meditation,
> Part of the question that is a giant himself;
> Of what is this house composed if not of the sun,
> These houses, these difficult objects, dilapidate
> Appearances of what appearances,
> Words, lines, not meanings, not communications (p. 146)[1]

Later in the poem, Stevens describes two approaches to reality, contrasting ways of knowing that he calls Alpha and Omega: "the infant A standing on infant legs," and "twisted, stooping polymathic Z." He says that

> both alike appoint themselves the choice
> Custodians of the glory of the scene,
> The immaculate interpreters of life. (pp. 146–147)

---

[1]The author acknowledges the application of this poem to the rhetoric of inquiry by John Nelson (1987, pp. 407–434).

He then adds that both approaches to reality are ways of seeking

> The poem of pure reality, untouched
> By trope or deviation, straight to the word,
> Straight to the transfixing object, to the object
> At the exactest point at which it is itself. (p. 147)

In this chapter, I discuss the ways that dreams about "poems of pure reality" affect educational researchers, especially those using qualitative methods of studying learning, teaching, and schooling. I will raise "gigantic" questions about how knowledge is constituted and approach them through the ancient arts and modern scholarship of rhetoric. Traditionally, rhetoric has been the study of the "tropes or deviations" used in fashioning words into communications. For more than 20 centuries, rhetorical studies were among the liberal arts maintained as foundations of Western education and culture. In our century, modern science has become a pre-eminent way of knowing about reality, supplanting traditional humanistic studies with the rigorous pursuit of empirical representations that supposedly go "straight to the transfixing object" of study.

During the past few decades, however, rhetorical studies have been undergoing a revival as many scholars and researchers ask how representations are constructed and whether there can be any "immaculate" representations. These questions are pertinent to all varieties of disciplined inquiry, and especially to researchers studying the complex environments of schools through qualitative research methods. For these pursuits, the rich traditions and current vigor of rhetorical studies, particularly that branch called "rhetoric of inquiry," offer fruitful approaches to theories and concepts.

THE RHETORIC OF INQUIRY

The field of rhetoric is ancient and complex; most cultures have rhetorical traditions that antedate written language. Aristotle defined rhetoric as "an ability in each particular case, to see the available means of persuasion" (p. 36). In the West, classical, medieval, and renaissance rhetoricians developed detailed technical manuals for public and private persuasion, most notably the legal or political address, based on such prototypes as Ciceronian orations. Accruing centuries of rhetorical theory and practice, recent versions of rhetoric are concerned with any process by which, as Edwin Black (1981) says, "through the medium of language, a private attitude becomes a public faith" (p. 177).

Disciplined research is such a process: Theories, methods, data, and findings are mediations or, in Stevens's phrase, "appearances of appearances." The fundamental components of disciplined inquiry are linguistic artifacts devised and assembled for communicative purposes. Most contemporary philosophers of science have discarded positivistic conceptions that any such language can strictly and reliably produce empirically verifiable propositions, but it is less commonly recognized that studies of rhetoric can be used to analyze disciplined inquiry. Although rhetorical studies are usually based in academic disciplines of dramatics, speech communications, writing and media studies, with branches in legal studies and political science (Bitzer & Black, 1971; Fish, 1989; Lanham, 1988; Scardamalia & Bereiter, 1986; Shapiro, 1988), many rhetoricians take as their subject the discourse of disciplined research, or "rhetorics of inquiry" (Nelson, Megill, & McCloskey, 1987; Simons, 1989). Rhetoricians of inquiry study general topics relevant to educational research, focusing on the construction of scholarly argument (see Bazerman, 1988; Davis & Hersh, 1987) or examining discourses in specific disciplines such as anthropology, sociology, philosophy, or psychology—fields that comprise the most frequent approaches to educational inquiry (see Billig, 1987; Brown, 1987; Eagleton, 1983; Geertz, 1988; Leary, 1987; McKeon, 1987; Simons, 1990).

Rhetorical studies are not prominent in most works of educational research (for notable exceptions, see Cremin, 1988; Firestone, 1987; Floden, 1985). Instead, a narrow and dismissive conception of "mere rhetoric" prevails, either as a handy synonym for bombast or as a way of discriminating degrees of propositional validity (Gaonkar, 1990). For example, in the third edition of *Handbook of Research on Teaching*, Thomas Romberg and Thomas Carpenter (1986) say that, in some studies of mathematics teaching,

> one is trying to penetrate the rhetoric of educational discourse in order to discern a deeper meaning of the events being studied. The term *rhetoric* is used in a nonpejorative sense, to connote commonly accepted ways of describing school events, and refers to those uses of the rhetoric of education that tend to attribute common practices and shared beliefs to schools and teachers. (p. 866)

Rhetoric is here said to consist of everyday discourse that researchers set out to analyze. While not excessively derogatory, neither is this an even-handed sense of the term: It omits researchers' own discourse and the rhetoric of their "deeper" meanings.

In contrast, rhetoric of inquiry is aimed at giving a fair share of attention to *verba*, a researcher's means of discussion, as well as *res*, the matter under discussion. Both terms are equivalent if not covalent; as Clifford Geertz (1988) says,

> the separation of what someone says from how they say it—content from form, substance from rhetoric, *l'écrit* from *l'écriture*—is as mischievous in anthropology as it is in poetry, painting, or political oratory. (p. 27)

Under the rubric of "rhetoric of inquiry" are a broad range of approaches to disciplined research. There are as many forms of rhetoric as there are histories, philosophies, and technologies of communications. It may be generally said nevertheless that in rhetorics of inquiry researchers' theories and methods are examined as constructions deliberately assembled from definite elements for specific purposes and shaped by particular circumstances. Studying the rhetoric of inquiry can be especially useful for educational researchers who identify their theories and methods as "qualitative" or "interpretive," because these methodologies seem to share with rhetoric a central focus on the construction of meanings.

THE RHETORIC OF QUALITATIVE INQUIRY

In Stevens's poem, the alpha and omega figures take different approaches, but each insists that its purposes "keep coming back and coming back / To the real." Although so-called "qualitative" approaches are not easily categorized, they seem, in contrast to so-called quantitative approaches, to share conceptions of reality defined in terms of irregularities; as Frederick Erickson (1986) says, in interpretive approaches to research "surface similarities mask an underlying diversity. In any given situation, one cannot assume that the behaviors of two individuals, physical acts with similar form, have the same meaning to the two individuals" (p. 126). Qualitative inquiry entails assumptions that reality is either inherently ambiguous, under continuous reconstruction, or both.

How then does a researcher following this approach presume to represent such protean realities? Is a qualitative "poem of pure reality" possible? Qualitative researchers have frequently defended the authenticity of ethnographic portraits in terms of "grounded theories" that are said to emerge in the processes of investigation (Glaser & Strauss, 1967) or in terms of extensive "thick descriptions." Further, the unique perspectives of participant observers are said to obtain two kinds of knowledge, called "etic" and "emic," about social and cultural institutions and transactions (Kirk & Miller, 1986; Spindler & Spindler, 1982). Approached as rhetoric, these hallmarks of qualitative research can be analyzed as communicative strategems that are successfully persuasive despite, or perhaps because of, denials of overtly persuasive intentions.

Qualitative researchers who would deny or demur their use of persuasive communications do so at the risk of self-contradiction, for the circular reason that interpretive studies are in themselves subjects for interpretation. Sociocultural realities are mediated twice: in the first place by systems of symbols under study, which are then altered by the specialized symbol-systems that researchers use in theorizing, recording, analyzing, and reporting. Amidst so many ambiguities, researchers' disclaimers and self-effacement cannot exempt their theories, data, and reports from partiality, in both senses of the term: incompleteness and parochiality. Bound to tell the truth but unable to tell it all, an ethnographer faces uncompromising choices over what to say and what to leave unsaid; Vincent Crapanzano (1985) calls this quandary "Hermes' dilemma."

> The ethnographer must make use of all the persuasive devices at his [sic] disposal to convince his readers of the truth of his message, but, as though these strategies were cunning tricks, he gives them scant recognition. His texts assume a truth that speaks for itself—a whole truth that needs no rhetorical support. His words are transparent. He does not share Hermes' confidence. When Hermes took the post of messenger of the gods, he promised Zeus not to lie. He did not promise to tell the whole truth. Zeus understood. The ethnographer has not. (pp. 52–53)

As many current qualitative researchers assert, large hypotheses and fruitful methods are no assurances that sociocultural reality can be completely represented in their works.

Many researchers also agree that partial representations are also parochial ones. In spurning positivistic assumptions of "transparent" data and findings, qualitative researchers have come to directly address their own interests, values, and idiosyncrasies. As Stephen Tyler (1987) says:

> The urge to conform to the canons of scientific rhetoric has made the easy realism of natural history the dominant mode of ethnographic prose, but it has been an illusory realism, promoting, on the one hand, the absurdity of "describing" nonentities like "culture" or "society" as if they were fully observable, though somewhat ungainly, bugs, and on the other, the equally ridiculous behaviorist pretense of "describing" repetitive patterns of action in isolation from the discourse that actors use in constituting and situating their action, and all in simple-minded surety that the observers' grounding discourse was itself an objective form sufficient to the task of describing acts. (p. 207)

Hermes' dilemma, then, requires ethnographers not only to face choices in making their messages partial but also to say how their partisan choices were made.

Among researchers who call for self-reflective approaches to inquiry, there is general agreement that, as long as theories and methods are constructed within specific contexts, then the conduct of disciplined inquiry entails explicit commentaries on researchers' own thoughts, values, and circumstances. In other words, inquiry involves explicit discussions of means and matter among its subjects and objects. This premise is a continuation of a sophistic tradition that, in the words of rhetorical historian Michael Leff (1987),

> collapses the modernist dichotomy between theory and practice. In this view, theorizing . . . is a product of the way that we encounter and filter the phenomena of the world, and it is enmeshed in the texture of our ordinary experience. In short, the construction of theory is itself a form of practice and is not categorically distinct from other forms of activity. (p. 24)

Approached through this "modern sophistic," inquiries about reality are always firmly attached to that reality.

Appeals for critical and self-reflective approaches to research are especially notable among groups that have not traditionally participated in making research policies and theories, but instead have had policies and theories made about them (Anderson, 1989; Fabian, 1990; Lather, 1986). Addressing this point, Edward Said (1989) says:

> Look at the many pages of very brilliantly sophisticated argument in the works of the meta-theoretical scholars, . . . and you will begin perhaps suddenly to note how someone, an authoritative, explorative, elegant, learned voice, speaks and analyzes, amasses evidence, theorizes, speculates about everything — except itself. (p. 212)

Questions about the voice of the researcher in qualitative inquiry are being raised within its parent disciplines of anthropology, sociology, and psychology by scholars who have taken a linguistic turn through ancient studies of grammar, logic, and rhetoric as well as through modern disciplines of linguistics, philosophy, history, and literature. Although these issues are too wide-ranging to summarize here, they reverberate in Said's (1989) query about the various poems of reality put forth by contemporary human scientists: "Who speaks? For what and for whom?" (p. 212)

At the conjunction of the speaker's voice and the audience's attention, rhetoric takes shape. In the following section, a few brief examples of rhetorical analysis will be offered to show how the rhetoric of inquiry can add to the shades of interpretation that qualitative researchers seek, if not to tell the whole truth, to at least tell their partial truths more persuasively.

RHETORICAL ANALYSIS EXEMPLIFIED

There are many tools for analyzing a rhetor's words and an audience's expectations. In the West, one of the oldest and most generally accepted schema is the Ciceronian set of five rhetorical stages, as follows: the *invention* of argumentative premises, the *disposition* of argumentative terms, the *memorization* of topics and terms, the *elocution* of topics and terms in selected words and phrases, and the formal *delivery* of an argument (Black, 1981; McKeon, 1987; Vickers, 1988). Despite its apparent rigidity, Cicero's matrix has been altered and adapted by generations of rhetoricians for sophisticated studies of argumentative architecture. In an extended example pertinent to educational research within quantitative traditions, David Leary (1987) has shown how advocates of new methods of psychology at the turn of the twentieth century constructed their arguments in the classical format with which most scholars were then familiar.

In the sections that follow, I will present short examples of the rhetoric of qualitative educational research that embody three Ciceronian stages: invention, disposition, and elocution. These stages are chosen to exemplify analytical frames that I believe are appropriate for contemporary qualitative research discourses, which appear mostly as texts rather than speeches. Far from definitive, these analyses are offered here as brief samples of complex approaches to disciplined research and critique.

Invention

The first part of the Ciceronian pentad involves the invention of topics, or points of departure for reasoned inquiry. In this context, topics are defined according to the spatial metaphor at their root: The Greek word *topos* literally means "place" (Aristotle, 1991, p. 46). The rhetorical meaning of "topic" is evident in the physical terms commonly offered to describe it; for example, Leff (1983) suggests "resource," or "seat," of argument, adding, "Normally [explanation of the term] takes the form of an allegory, where, to cite the classic example, the rhetor is a hunter, the argument his quarry, and the topic a locale in which the argument may be found" (p. 23). Instances of this allegory include such designations for topics of argument as "knowledge-base" or "standpoint."

In most qualitative research, the starting point of the inquiry is frequently an individual, either an informant or a participant observer; also frequent as a point of departure is a locale, such as a classroom, school, neighborhood, or community. Such topics involve implicit claims that the subject is a singular instance with wide implications, despite customary disclaimers limiting the validity and generalizability of research based on a particular person or place.

One ethnographer might claim as a topic the importance of social class among school children, by emphasizing conflicts of values and disparities of resources in schools. In the same settings and with the same informants, another ethnographer could instead portray the subtleties of language development among differing social groups, interpreting specific events as instances of sociolinguistic processes. Both researchers may defend their choices of topics in terms of theoretical or methodological validity, but each chosen strategy must be judged according to two standards: first, internal coherence: is the topic clearly stated? next, external consistency: does the topic fit the conclusions? Through tests of coherence and consistency applied by sponsors, colleagues, or disciples, successful topics are found persuasive.

An effective topic often can be a simple term that leads toward very singular and very general meanings, such as the brilliant way that Lincoln took up "dedication" in his "Gettysburg Address." For an example pertinent to qualitative educational research, consider the way that Linda McNeil (1986) took the topic "control" as the organizing strategy for a detailed ethnography of curriculum implementation in a single high school, connecting that data to national and international issues.

Disposition

Once a specific subject or strategy has been selected, the researcher must give it credible disposition or, in other words, portray the subject sufficiently. As Erickson (1986) points out, narrative vignettes have didactic, analytical, and evidentiary functions.

> The . . . task of the narrator is rhetorical, by providing adequate evidence that the author has made a vivid analysis of what the happenings meant from the point of view of the actors in the event. The particular description . . . both explains to the reader the author's analytic constructs by instantiation and convinces the reader that such an event could and did happen that way. (p. 150)

In successful qualitative research, credible topics are presented in convincing narratives. In drawing a similar distinction between narrative and argument in the discourse of social science, Jerome Bruner (1986) also associates validity and rhetorical force, saying, "The arts of rhetoric include the use of dramatic instantiation as a means of clinching an argument whose basis is principally logical" (p. 12). Disposition is the art of selecting instances that convincingly portray theories, data, and findings to an audience.

Elocution

Once topics are chosen and instance selected, means of expression are crafted. The elocution, or words and phrases, of qualitative research are far from transparent, but rather provide rich ore for rhetorical studies. An especially versatile instrument of analysis was first proposed by Kenneth Burke (1945/1969), a pioneer of symbolic interactionist approaches to sociology and a broadly influential rhetorical theorist (Geertz, 1988; Gusfield, 1989; Simons & Melia, 1989). Elements of communicative action, or in Burke's (1945) terminology "motives," can be categorized in a "dramatist pentad" as follows:

> In a rounded statement about motives, you must have some word that names the *act* (names what took place in thought and deed), and another that names the *scene* (the background of the act, the situation in which it occurred); also you must indicate what person or kind of person (*agent*) performed the act, what means or instruments he used (*agency*), and the *purpose*. (p. xv)

Burke's pentad provides a framework for analyzing the elocution of research discourses, particularly those in which the author's voice and self-reflection are featured. Take, for instance, Harry Wolcott's (1988) qualitative study, "Adequate Schools and Inadequate Education." Wolcott first sets the scene for dramatic actions, a series of encounters with "Brad," a young man who has surreptitiously taken shelter on his property. Although the study's agent is clearly Brad, the agencies of the narrator's relationship with Brad both as an employer and as interlocutor are described in animating detail. As with any drama, there are tensions and resolutions, mainly having to do with Brad's finding shelter and employment, but the central purpose of the study is Brad's disrupted schooling career.

By Burkean standards, Wolcott's ethnography succeeds in articulating the motives of both characters, in a fully rounded pentad of motives, including collaboration as well as conflict. Wolcott, in short, having chosen a topic and disposing it in a narrative, describes the complex tangle of motives that bring researcher and subject together. As Burke (1950/1969) recommends,

> The *Rhetoric* deals with the possibilities of classification in its *partisan* as-
> pects; it considers the ways in which individuals are at odds with one another,
> or become identified with groups more or less at odds with one another.
> . . . Identification is affirmed with earnestness precisely because there is divi-
> sion. . . . If men were not apart from one another, there would be no need
> for the rhetorician to proclaim their unity. (p. 22)

Wolcott's report portrays a process in which he both identifies with Brad and stands apart from him. The interrelations among the actors, their purposes, and their settings can be said to be the dramatic flesh on the logical bones of the topic. This vividness enhances both the authenticity of the author's voice and the report's credibility. More important, by contrasting the themes of identification and division, the ethnographer's rhetoric opens questions about links between his own interests and those of his subject, so that both the politics of schooling and the politics of qualitative research are at issue.

Incidentally, both the title of Wolcott's article and a key sentence of its conclusion employ a specific rhetorical technique that has been codified and analyzed by rhetoricians for thousands of years: the polyptoton, repeating a word in a different form (Vickers, 1988, p. 497). Wolcott (1988) concludes his study as follows: "After so carefully making provision for Brad's schooling, society now leaves his continuing education to chance, and we are indeed taking our chances" (p. 245). Here as throughout, the author's voice is fully in evidence and the reflections are unquestionably his own. The cadence in which the words "adequate" and "chance" are repeated, however, is a technique of proven force, which would have been known to Isocrates, Cicero, or Ramus in their respective places, languages, and times.

Summary

In these abbreviated samples of rhetorical analysis, three Ciceronian stages of the rhetoric of qualitative research have been discussed. Rhetoric, however, is not reducible to formulas governing the invention of topics, their narrative disposition, or the eloquence with which they are presented. The rhetoric of qualitative inquiry involves more than making convincing cases, cogent vignettes, or striking phrases. Couched in each qualitative study are arguments for theoretical and methodological validity, as well as for political and philosophical viability. In raising the author's voice and stating intentions more explicitly than has been customary in modern human sciences for over a century, qualitative researchers discard the role of neutral spectator to take outspoken sides in contentious debates. Raising these voices brings obligations; as Geertz (1988) concluded, "now that such matters are coming to be discussed in the open, rather than covered over with a professional mystique, the burden of authorship seems suddenly heavier" (p. 138).

IMPLICATIONS FOR EDUCATIONAL RESEARCH

Are the credibility of the ethnographic text or the validity of the ethnographer's work diminished by self-consciousness about the ways that words are used in ethnographic writing? That, of course, depends on particular audiences and their predispositions to believe researchers' accounts. It is not the purpose of rhetoric of inquiry to determine whether a research report is credible, but rather to ask what makes it credible in certain circumstances. According to this approach to the rhetoric of qualitative inquiry, the author's voice is an important part of the research program's theoretical validity and methodological effectiveness. Furthermore, there are political implications in the presence of the author's voice as well as in its absence.

A rhetoric of inquiry does not provide bases for general judgments but rather shows ways to question how bases are built and maintained. By turning discourse upon itself, contemporary rhetoricians cannot prescribe successful communications, only describe them in their settings. Emphasizing this point, Donald McCloskey (1988) states:

> A rhetorical analysis has this limit: that it can wisely and well tell how a speech has gone in the past, but cannot be expected to provide the world's greatest secret for the future. It can show how Cicero in *Pro Archia* exploited tricolon, how Descartes exploited rhetoric to attack rhetoric itself, or how Jane Austen in *Northanger Abbey* exploited an irony that was always intended, covert, finite, and stable. But rhetoric cannot be finished and formulaic, or else anyone could be a Cicero, Descartes, or Austen. The chimera of a once-finished formula for language must be left to Fregean philosophy or to magic. (p. 403)

There are evidently no formulas for poems of pure reality in rhetorics of inquiry. In order to produce works that are self-reflexive and persuasive, those who would conduct qualitative educational research as a form of *praxis* must continuously reconstruct their questions about themselves, their languages, their theories, their methods, and their situations.

Educational researchers have recently been engaged in extensive discussions of the merits of qualitative theories and methods versus those of quantitative ones (Eisner & Peshkin, 1990; Lincoln & Guba, 1987; Mishler, 1990; Phillips, 1987; Sherman & Webb, 1988; Smith & Heshusius, 1986). Since rhetoricians have studied processes of deliberation for thousands of years, greater awareness of rhetoric can be of use in examining these issues. Among other benefits to be realized from the study of rhetoric by educational researchers, I will mention two: contextual detail and collegial debate.

First, by using rhetoric to focus on interactions among specific advocates and their audiences, researchers could give more detailed scrutiny to the disciplinary contexts of methodological discussions. It is all too frequent that questions about theory and research are cast in narrow historical perspective; for instance, contemporary accounts do not usually mention that educational research in the past three decades has been affected by agendas set by centralized bureaucracies favoring particular kinds of data and findings. The impact of such political interests on educational research goes unmentioned in most discussions of quantitative and qualitative methodologies (cf., Cherryholmes, 1988; Popkewitz, 1984). Rhetoric, comprising arts of civic discourse, is well-stocked with means of analyzing the political purposes and consequences of theories and research programs. Although there are some examples of detailed rhetorical analyses of educational theory and research (e.g., Firestone, 1987; Floden, 1985; Reid, 1987), possibilities for fresh work are nonetheless abundant.

Next, another benefit to be obtained through increased study of the rhetoric of inquiry in educational research would be readier acceptance of wider debate. Among researchers with common or diverse disciplinary backgrounds, methodological discussions could be more like conversations than monologues. As Brian Vickers (1988) points out,

> Rhetoric is, after all, committed to there being at least two sides to every question, and being able to speak for either. This can be presented as a trivial accomplishment, but it can also be seen as a profound recognition that truth itself is not single and immutable, and that no one school of thought has a monopoly over it. . . . Rhetoric is by its very nature committed to freedom of thought and freedom of speech. (p. 210)

Educational researchers who bring awareness of the rhetorics of inquiry to bear upon conflicts over theories and methods could grant that the very existence of ongoing debate testifies to a breadth of possibilities in their field of study, rather than a harbinger of wars to be won by convincing victories or pluralistic truces (e.g., Gage, 1989; Howe, 1988). Rhetorics of inquiry, as arts of communication grounded in specific social circumstances, are neither means to methodological unity or to pluralism (also called "compatibilism"), but rather are ways of debating different disciplinary approaches in terms of their contexts and consequences.

Because both quantitative and qualitative methods stem from common roots in modern philosophies of science, many theorists claim that debates over theories and methods can be suspended in the name of pluralism. Pluralism, however, is more easily advocated than achieved. Deep conflicts have occurred among educational researchers over reassessments of theoretical assumptions. Qualitative researchers have been accused of relativistic conceptions of knowledge and truth, and in rejoinder have countered with insinuations that their accusers' theories are flawed by positivist reductionism. Among these debates over pluralism, eclecticism, or postmodernism, disciplined research has lately come to resemble a Babel of countless dialects.

The ancient arts and modern scholarship of rhetoric can offer ways to navigate amidst these conflicts by turning attention to specific discursive strategies employed in various forms of disciplined inquiry. Rhetorics of inquiry focus on points of intersection among approaches to research, where researchers seek to explain their motives, methods, and findings to various audiences. These focal points are unstable, because discourses are shaped by ideas that are partial and interests that are partisan, each attached to particular situations. A rhetoric of inquiry is not a way of rising above those ideas and interests to a distant viewpoint beyond them, but rather offers ways of joining and shaping the conversations in which they are articulated.

CONCLUSION

Human actions are always guided by rules that define what is possible, but sets of rules are themselves always under debate, and alternative sets eventually emerge. All rules and all games, including language games, therefore do not prevent conflict so much as institutionalize dialogues about it. As Burke (1950/1969) says, rhetoric

> must lead through the scramble, the Wrangle of the Market Place, the flurries and flare-ups of the Human Barnyard, the Give and Take, the wavering line of counterpressure, the logomachy, the onus of ownership, the Wars of Nerves, the War. . . . Rhetoric is concerned with the state of Babel after the Fall. (p. 23)

For all their complexity, theories and methods that human beings use to study nature, themselves, and their social arrangements are never complete. The poem of pure reality is always out of reach, but real poets do their work within real worlds and their poems do have real effects. Stevens (1949/1959) concludes his poem by telling how "wandering mariners," having once seen a new land, could no longer see their home in the same way.

> . . . an alteration
> Of words that was a change of nature . . .
> Their countrymen were changed and each constant
> thing. (p. 152)

Like a poet, an ethnographer seeks to alter words and so challenge the boundaries of familiarity.

In brief, qualitative educational research can be analyzed using approaches that poets and rhetoricians have used for centuries. If qualitative research involves researchers' conscious voicing of their beliefs about phenomena, then researchers must pay as careful attention to the mechanics of their communication as to their husbandry of phenomena. Especially in works aimed at interpreting educational transactions, processes of communications are both means and matter. For this reason, educational researchers pursuing qualitative approaches will find pertinent theories and methods in the much-maligned arts of rhetoric. Far from arid or obsolete, rhetoric lives and flourishes.

REFERENCES

Anderson, G. (1989). Critical ethnography in education: Origins, current status, and new directions. *Review of Educational Research, 59*(3), 249–270.

Aristotle. (1991). *On rhetoric: A theory of civic discourse* (G. Kennedy, Ed. & Trans.). New York: Oxford University Press.

Bazerman, C. (1988). *Shaping written knowledge: The genre and activity of the experimental article in science.* Madison: University of Wisconsin Press.

Billig, M. (1987). *Arguing and thinking: A rhetorical approach to social psychology.* New York: Cambridge University Press.

Bitzer, L., & Black, E. (Eds.). (1971). *The prospect of rhetoric.* Englewood Cliffs, NJ: Prentice-Hall.

Black, E. (1981). *Rhetorical criticism: A study in method* (2d ed.). Madison: University of Wisconsin Press.

Brown, R. (1987). *Society as text: Essays on rhetoric, reason and reality.* Chicago: University of Chicago Press.

Bruner, J. (1986). *Actual minds, possible worlds.* Cambridge, MA: Harvard University Press.

Burke, K. (1969). *A grammar of motives.* Berkeley: University of California Press. (Original work published 1945)

Burke, K. (1969). *A rhetoric of motives.* Berkeley: University of California Press. (Original work published 1950)

Cherryholmes, C. H. (1988). *Power and criticism: Post-structural investigations in education.* New York: Teachers College Press.

Crapanzano, V. (1985). Hermes' dilemma: The masking of subversion in ethnographic description. In J. Clifford & G. Marcus (Eds.), *Writing culture* (pp. 52–53). Berkeley: University of California Press.

Cremin, L. (1988). *American education: The metropolitan experience.* New York: Harper & Row.

Davis, P., & Hersh, R. (1987). *Rhetoric and mathematics.* In J. Nelson, A. Megill, & D. McCloskey (Eds.), *The rhetoric of the human sciences* (pp. 53–68). Madison: University of Wisconsin Press.

Eagleton, T. (1983). *Literary theory: An introduction.* Minneapolis: University of Minnesota Press.

Eisner, E. W., & Peshkin, A. (Eds.). (1990). *Qualitative inquiry in education: The continuing debate.* New York: Teachers College Press.

Erickson, F. (1986). Qualitative methods in research on teaching. In M. Wittrock (Ed.), *Handbook of research on teaching* (3rd ed.; pp. 119–161). New York: Macmillan.

Fabian, J. (1990). Presence and representation: The other and anthropological writing. *Critical Inquiry, 16*(4), 753–772.

Firestone, W. (1987). Meaning in method: The rhetoric of quantitative and qualitative research. *Educational Researcher, 16*(7), 16–21.

Fish, S. (1989). *Doing what comes naturally: Change, rhetoric and the practice of theory in literary and legal studies.* Raleigh, NC: Duke University Press.

Floden, R. (1985). The role of rhetoric in changing teachers' beliefs. *Teaching and Teacher Education, 1*(1), 19–32.

Gage, N. (1989). The paradigm wars and their aftermath. *Teachers College Record, 91*(2), 135–150.

Gaonkar, D. (1990). Rhetoric and its double: Reflections on the rhetorical turn in the human sciences. In H. Simons (Ed.), *The rhetorical turn: Invention and persuasion in the conduct of inquiry* (pp. 341–366). Chicago: University of Chicago Press.

Geertz, C. (1988). *Works and lives.* Stanford, CA: Stanford University Press.

Glaser, B., & Strauss, A. (1967). *The discovery of grounded theory: Strategies for qualitative research.* Chicago: Aldine Press.

Gusfield, J. (Ed.). (1989). *Kenneth Burke on symbols and society.* Chicago: University of Chicago Press.

Howe, K. R. (1988). Against the quantitative–qualitative incompatibility thesis, or: Dogmas die hard. *Educational Researcher, 17*(8), 10–16.

Kirk, J., & Miller, M. (1986). *Reliability and validity in qualitative research.* Beverly Hills, CA: Sage.

Lanham, R. (1988). The "Q" question. *South Atlantic Quarterly, 87*(4), 654–700.

Lather, P. (1986). Research as praxis. *Harvard Educational Review, 56*(3), 257–277.

Leary, D. (1987). Telling likely stories: The rhetoric of the new psychology, 1880–1920. *Journal of the History of the Behavioral Sciences, 23,* 315–331.

Leff, M. (1983). The topics of argumentative invention in Latin rhetorical theory from Cicero to Boethius. *Rhetorica, 1*(1), 23–44.

Leff, M. (1987). Modern sophistic and the unity of rhetoric. In J. Nelson et al. (Eds.), *Rhetoric of the human sciences* (pp. 19–37). Madison: University of Wisconsin Press.

Lincoln, Y., & Guba, E. (1987). *Naturalistic inquiry.* Beverly Hills, CA: Sage.

McCloskey, D. (1988). The limits of expertise: If you're so smart, why ain't you rich? *American Scholar, 57*(3), 393–406.

McKeon, R. (1987). *Rhetoric: Essays in invention and discovery* (M. Backman, Ed.). Woodbridge, CT: Ox Bow Press.

McNeil, L. (1986). *Contradictions of control: School structure and school knowledge.* New York: RKP.

Mishler, E. (1990). Validation in inquiry-oriented research: The role of exemplars in narrative studies. *Harvard Educational Review, 60*(4), 415–442.

Nelson, J. (1987). Seven rhetorics of inquiry: A provocation. In J. Nelson, A. Megill, & D. McCloskey (Eds.), *Rhetoric of the human sciences: Language and argument in scholarship and public affairs* (pp. 407–434). Madison: University of Wisconsin Press.

Nelson, J., Megill, A., & McCloskey, D. (Eds.). (1987). *Rhetoric of the human sciences: Language and argument in scholarship and public affairs.* Madison: University of Wisconsin Press.

Perelman, Ch., & Olbrechts-Tyteca, L. (1969). *The new rhetoric: A treatise on argumentation.* Notre Dame, IN: Notre Dame University Press.

Phillips, D. C. (1987). *Philosophy, science, and social inquiry: Contemporary methodological controversies in social science.* New York: Pergamon Press.

Popkewitz, T. S. (1984). *Paradigm & ideology in educational research: The social functions of the intellectual.* Philadelphia: Falmer Press.

Reid, W. (1987). Institutions and practices: Professional education reports and the language of reform. *Educational Researcher, 16*(8), 10–15.

Romberg, T., & Carpenter, T. (1986). Research on teaching mathematics. In M. Wittrock (Ed.), *Handbook of research on teaching* (3rd ed.; pp. 850–873). New York: Macmillan.

Said, E. (1989). Representing the colonized: Anthropology's interlocutors. *Critical Inquiry, 15*(2), 205–225.

Scardamalia, M., & Bereiter, C. (1986). Research on written composition. In M. Wittrock (Ed.), *Handbook of research on teaching* (3rd ed.; pp. 778–803). New York: Macmillan.

Shapiro, M. (1988). *The politics of representation: Writing practices in biography, photography, and policy analysis.* Madison: University of Wisconsin Press.

Sherman, R., & Webb, R. (Eds.). (1988). *Qualitative research in education: Unity in variety.* London & Philadelphia: Falmer Press.

Simons, H. (Ed.). (1989). *Rhetoric in the human sciences.* London: Sage.

Simons, H. (Ed.). (1990). *The rhetorical turn: Invention and persuasion in the conduct of inquiry.* Chicago: University of Chicago Press.

Simons, H., & Melia, T. (Eds.). (1989). *The legacy of Kenneth Burke.* Madison: University of Wisconsin Press.

Smith, J., & Heshusius, L. (1986). Closing down the conversation: The end of the quantitative–qualitative debate among educational inquirers. *Educational Researcher, 15*(1), 4–12.

Spindler, G., & Spindler, L. (1982). *Doing the ethnography of schooling.* New York: Holt, Rinehart & Winston.

Stevens, W. (1959). An ordinary evening in New Haven. In S. Morse (Ed.), *Selected poems.* New York: Vintage. (Original work published 1949)

Tyler, S. (1987). *The unspeakable: Discourse, dialogue, and rhetoric in the postmodern world.* Madison: University of Wisconsin Press.

Vickers, B. (1988). *In defence of rhetoric.* New York: Oxford University Press.

Wolcott, H. (1988). Adequate schools and inadequate education: The life history of a sneaky kid. In R. Jaeger (Ed.), *Complementary methods of educational research* (pp. 221–250). Washington, DC: American Educational Research Association.

Yeats, W. (1953). *Autobiography: Consisting of Reveries over childhood and youth, The trembling of the veil, and Dramatis personae.* New York: Macmillan. (Original work published 1919–1939)

13

Theory

The Necessary Evil

HOWARD S. BECKER

EPISTEMOLOGICAL WORRIES

Qualitative researchers in education have begun to question the epistemological premises of their work. Or, at least, someone in the arena is questioning those premises, and the questioning worries the researchers who actually do the work of studying schools, students, and education close up. Attacks on qualitative research used to come exclusively from the methodological right, from the proponents of positivism and statistical and experimental rigor. But now the attack comes from the cultural studies left as well, from the proponents of the "new ethnography," who argue that there is no such thing as "objective knowledge" and that qualitative research is no more than an insidious disguise for the old enemy of positivism and pseudo-objectivity.

The attack can conveniently, if somewhat misleadingly, be labeled as "theoretical." Convenient because it is not a question of empirical findings; misleading because the theory involved is not substantive. These worries, which used to take the form of a concern with the theoretical bases of our substantive findings, now focus on the theory of knowledge that underlies the whole enterprise. What bothers qualitative researchers in education, I think, is that they are no longer sure, as they once were, that they are doing things the "right way." They worry that the work they do may be built on sand, despite all their care and precautions, all their attempts to answer the multitude of criticisms that greet their efforts, and all their attempts to still the qualms that arise from within—that the whole thing will count for nothing in the end. Not only that our work will not be accepted as scientific, but also that that model of scientific work we aspired to is now discovered to be philosophically unsound and in need of serious rethinking. Who are we kidding with all this science talk? Why don't we admit that what we do is just another kind of story, no better or worse than any other fiction?

How shall we understand all this? Are these realistic worries? Are we building on sand? Is what we do just another story?

Theory or Social Organization?

We can take these debates at face value, worry over their content, and try to answer all the questions asked of us. That's the conventional way to deal with such problems. The literature discussing qualitative research in education parallels similar discussions in sociology and, especially, anthropology. These discussions center on the relative merits of qualitative and quantitative research, on the problems or virtues of positivism, on the importance (or danger) of subjectivity, and so on.

These are, of course, serious problems in the philosophy of social science. It is not clear how any of us, qualitative or quantitative, can justify what we produce as certified or warranted or credible knowledge. Whatever safeguards we take, whatever new tricks we try, questions can be, and are, raised. Qualitative research—we might better say research that is designed in the doing; that therefore is not systematic in any impersonal way; that leaves room for, indeed insists on, individual judgment; that takes account of historical, situated detail, and context and all that— research of that kind is faulted for being exactly all of those things and therefore not able to produce "scientific," objective, reliable knowledge that will support prediction and control. Research that tries to be systematic and impersonal, arithmetic and precise, and thereby scientific, is faulted for leaving out too much that needs to be included, for failing to take account of crucial aspects of human behavior and social life, for being unable to advance our understanding, for promising much more in the way of prediction and control than it ever delivers.

Epistemological issues, for all the arguing, are never settled, and I think it fruitless to try to settle them, at least in the way the typical debate looks to. If we haven't settled them definitively in two thousand years, more or less, we probably aren't ever going to settle them. These are simply the commonplaces, in the rhetorical sense, of scientific talk in the social sciences, the framework in which debate goes on. So be it.

Also, so what? Because I don't mean those remarks fatalistically. I don't counsel resignation, acceptance of an inescapable tragic fate. No. There's nothing tragic about it. It's clearly possible, on the evidence we have all around us, to find out things about social life in ways that are more or less good enough, at least for the people we are working with now. It's happened often enough in the past, and there's no reason to think it can't continue to happen.

This is exactly the import of Thomas Kuhn's (1962) analysis of science, as I understand it. Whenever scientists can agree on what the questions are, what a reasonable answer to them would look like, and what ways of getting such answers are acceptable — then you have a period of scientific advance. At the price, Kuhn is careful to point out, of leaving out most of what needs to be included in order to give an adequate picture of whatever we are studying, at the price of leaving uninspected and untested a great deal that might properly be subjected to investigation, that in fact desperately needs investigation.

That's alright. Because, though everything can be questioned, we needn't question it all at once. We can stand on some shaky epistemological ground Over Here for as long as it takes to get an idea about what can be seen from this vantage point. Then we can move Over There, to the place we had been treating as problematic while we took Over Here for granted and, taking Over There for granted, make Over Here problematic for a while. It's John Dewey's point: Reality is what we choose not to question at the moment. There's also Lily Tomlin's point, as it comes out of the mouth of Trudy the Bag Lady, no mean philosopher herself: "After all, what is reality anyway? Nothin' but a collective hunch." And she adds, "Reality is the leading cause of stress amongst those in touch with it" (quoted in Wagner, 1986, p. 18).

Any working scientist must have a position on such questions, implicit or explicit (and the better shape the science is in, the more the positions are implicit), just in order to get on with the work. Any working researcher's positions on these questions are likely — the chief fear of the philosophically minded — to be inconsistent, just because they have to be taken ad hoc, to deal with immediate problems of getting the work done. Not only is inconsistency unavoidable, it is the basis of everyday scientific practice.

For instance, I am devoted to qualitative work and think that the criticisms made of "simpleminded counting" are often quite correct. But I also rely, whenever I can, on data from the U.S. and other censuses. I'd be crazy not to. Any sensible analysis of social life will want to take into account the age distribution of the population studied, even though we know that people routinely misstate their ages. Why else are there so many more people who are 25 than there are 24 and 26 year olds? When we write and talk about schools and education, we routinely take into account the relative size of various ethnic and racial groups as reported in the census, even though we know that those numbers simply report what people choose to put down as their race, which may have no relation at all to either biological or social fact. We use those numbers even though we know they are riddled with errors that demographers themselves have exposed.

Similarly, the hardest-nosed positivists, if anyone will admit to being such any more, routinely take into account all sorts of knowledge acquired with the help of "soft" methods, without which they couldn't make sense of their data. They might not admit it, but the interpretations they make of "hard findings" rely on their own understanding of the less easily measured, though still easily observed, aspects of social life.

In short, we all, qualitative and quantitative workers alike, have to use methods we disapprove of, philosophically, just to get on with it and take account of what must be taken account of to make sense of the world.

The Necessary Evil

So we all have to be epistemological theorists, know it or not, because we couldn't work at all if we didn't have at least an implicit theory of knowledge; we wouldn't know what to do first. In that sense, theory is necessary.

But the question raised about the justification for what we do, which is what these theories are, cannot be definitively answered. That's an empirical generalization, based on the simple observation that we are still discussing the matter. To spend a lot of time on unanswerable questions is a waste of time (see Lieberson, 1982) and quite paralyzing. If you have convinced yourself that what you are doing can't be justified reasonably, it's hard to get up the energy necessary to do it. It seems better to continue discussing the problem in hope of finding the answer that satisfies you and the people who are aggravating you about the warrant for your conditions.

In that sense, the pursuit of epistemological and similar questions in the philosophy of social science is evil. If you're accustomed to this dilemma, it isn't a great trouble — you make a choice and go about your business. But some researchers — most especially graduate students — are especially vulnerable to the questioning doubts that paralyze thought and will and work. For them the evil is serious. To repeat, we still have to do the theoretical work, but we needn't think we are being especially virtuous when we do. Theory is a dangerous, greedy animal, and we need to be alert to keep it in its cage.

SOCIAL ORGANIZATIONS

From a different vantage point, we can see debates over method and its justification as the kind of thing that happens in the world of social science, as a recurring social phenomenon to be investigated rather than a serious epistemological problem — in other words, to paraphrase ethno-methodologist Harold Garfinkel, as a topic rather than an aggravation. And we can ask sociological questions about debates like this: When, in the life of a discipline, or of a researcher (as my remarks about graduate students suggested) or of a piece of research, do these questions become troubling? Who is likely to be exercised about them? How do such unresolved and unreasonable debates feed into the social organization of the discipline?

The Relativistic Specter

To ask such questions immediately raises the specter of a paradoxical situation in which I presume, on the basis of a social science analysis that is itself philosophically unjustified, to give you the social science lowdown on a critique of what I am at the moment doing. It's a kind of debunking, not unlike psychoanalytically inclined writers who respond to criticism with an analysis of the unconscious motives of their critics. That is just the problem that is giving some contemporary sociologists of science fits, because they understand perfectly well that their analysis of the workings of science is in some sense a critique of science. If the critique is correct, then it applies to the analysis that produced the critique. You can see where that leads.

An alternative position is to accept the reflexivity this involves, indeed to embrace it, and then use our knowledge of the social organization of science to solve the problems so raised. In other words, if it's an organizational problem, the solution has to be organizational. You don't solve organizational problems by clarifying terms or arguments. Organizations are not philosophies, and people don't base their actions on philosophical analyses. Not even scientists do that.

Science Worlds, Chains of Association

What does it mean to speak of the social organization of an intellectual or scientific discipline? We can speak here of scientific worlds in analogy to the analyses that have been made of art worlds (see Becker, 1982). These analyses focus on a work of art — a film, a painting, a concert, a book of poetry — and ask: Who are all the people who had to cooperate so that that work could come out the way it did? This is not to say that there is any particular way the work has to come out, only that if you want your movie to have orchestral music in the background, you will have to have someone compose the music and musicians play it; you can easily, of course, have no music, but then it will be a different film from one whose action is accompanied by a score.

An art world is made up of all the people who routinely cooperate in that way to produce the kind of works they usually produce: the composers, conductors, and performers who produce concert music; the playwrights, actors, directors, designers, and businesspeople who produce theater works; the writers, designers, editors, and businesspeople who produce novels; the long list of everyone from director and actors to grips and accountants and caterers and transportation captains who work together to make Hollywood films; and so on.

The cooperation that makes up an art world and produces its characteristic works depends on the use of conventions, standardized ways of doing things everyone knows and depends on. Examples are musical scales, forms like the sonnet or the three movement sonata, the Hollywood feature film, the pas de deux — a list that can be so standardized. When everyone in an art world recognizes and uses the same conventions, collaboration proceeds easily, economically, somewhat at the expense of originality and variety. If we all agree to use the twelve-tone scale of Western music, we know that players and listeners alike will know and be able to deal with our music, but we give up the opportunity to use scales constructed differently.

That's an art world. A science world, by analogy, consists of all those people who cooperate to produce the characteristic activities and products of that science. This means more than the people who make up the scientific community to which Kuhn called our attention. It includes, for instance, the people who provide the materials with which the science works: the experimental animals, the purified chemicals and water to experiment on them with, the carefully controlled spaces to do it all in For social science it typically means, importantly, the people who provide us with data by gathering statistics, doing interviews, being interviewed, letting us observe them, collecting and giving us access to documents. Just as with art works, the kinds of cooperation that are available, and the terms on which they are available, necessarily affect the kind of science that can be done. A contemporary example is the conflict over the use of laboratory animals in biological research.

One of the distinctive characteristics of science worlds (as opposed, e.g., to art worlds) is the emphasis on proof and persuasion, on being able to convince other people by commonly accepted "rational" methods to accept what you say even though they'd rather not. Bruno Latour (1987) has made this the cornerstone of his analysis in "science in action." He speaks of scientists trying to get more and more people to accept their statements, enrolling "allies" with whom opponents of their statements will also have to contend. Footnotes and appeals to the literature serve to line up allies with whom people who disagree with you will also have to disagree. In Latour's analysis, people agree with each other not because there is a basic scientific logic that decides disputes, and certainly not because Nature or Reality adjudicates the dispute, but because one side or the other has won a "trial of strength," on whatever basis such trials are decided in that community. In a series of provocative dicta, Latour says things like (I am paraphrasing), "It is not that scientists agree when the facts require them to, but rather that when they agree, what they agree on become the facts."

A beginning on this kind of (what we might call) organizational epistemology is to note that every way of doing research and arriving at results is good enough, good enough for someone situated at some point in the research process (see Becker, 1986). If it weren't good enough for someone, no one would be doing it. Whom it has to be good enough for and when it has to be that good are empirical questions that depend on the social organization in which that bit of knowledge arises.

The most general finding here is that, though every scientific method has easily observed technical flaws and is based on not very well hidden philosophical fallacies, they are all used routinely, without much fear or worry, within some research community. The results they produce are good enough for the community of scientific peers that uses them. The flaws will be recognized and discounted for; the fallacies will be acknowledged and ignored. Everyone knows all about it, knows that everyone else knows all about it, and they have all agreed not to bother each other about it. So the census, with all the flaws I alluded to, is plenty good enough for the rough differentiations social scientists usually want to make. But that's because the social scientists who use census data have the collective hunch that these data are good enough for the purposes they will put them to, not because the flaws don't exist. Few enough people we would ordinarily think of as white say they are black, and few enough people we would ordinarily think of as black say they are white, to change any conclusions we base on these numbers, and we don't think the difference between 24 and 25 large enough to invalidate the conclusions we base on age statistics.

An interesting corollary of this is that what methods and data are acceptable depends on the stage of the scientific process at which they are used and presented, and the purpose they are used for. At an early stage of the scientific process, for instance, we are mainly playing, exploring ideas for the further ideas or explorations they might lead us to. We don't much care whether the results are valid or not, or whether the conclusions are true. What we really care about is that the discussion proceed, that we find something interesting to talk about. This stage may take place over a cup of coffee, in a seminar, in casual conversation with a colleague. I remember a seminar with Everett Hughes, in which a student interrupted one of his discursive explorations on a "fact" he had heard somewhere to say that later research had shown the fact wasn't true. Without breaking stride, Hughes asked what the new fact was, and continued to explore its possibilities.

In fact, it is often seen as an intellectual mistake to dismiss ideas at this stage of work just because they might not be true. The worst thing that can happen to a research community, in some sense, is to run out of researchable problems. Yuval Yonay (in preparation) has pointed out that researchers will often accept all sorts of anomalies if the general position containing them opens up a lot of new researchable questions, whose exploration can produce publishable papers and the feeling of progress.

At a somewhat later stage in the research process, we are mainly interested in getting an idea worth the time and effort we are going to put into it. At this point, not just any idea will do. We want some assurance that the idea we choose will bear the weight we are going to put on it, that it is not so unsupported in fact that taking it as a starting point will not leave us stranded, that taking it seriously will produce a result. Some look in the literature to see what others have done and how it worked out. Before we go to the trouble of writing a research proposal or setting up a project—a more sizeable investment than one makes in a casual conversation—we want to know that we are building on a solid foundation. We subject what we find in earlier reports to careful scrutiny, and bring more rigorous methodological standards to bear, because we don't want to waste our time. If there's something wrong with this way of working, we want to know it now. Putting down a larger bet, we want better odds.

We could pursue this analysis through a variety of steps. What kind of rigor do we demand before we accept a journal article for publication or a paper for the annual meeting of the tribe? (Here we might note the role of practical considerations. While everyone insists that only the highest standards are employed in choosing papers for these purposes, it is also well-known that scientific associations meeting in hotels commit themselves to fill a certain number of rooms with paying customers; otherwise they will be charged for the meeting rooms, the Presidential Suite, and so on. The best way to ensure that a sufficient number attend the meeting is to accept their papers for the program and require that everyone on the program register for the meeting. The people who organize these programs usually receive a nicely worded double message: maintain standards and maximize participation. It's not clear that these are compatible.)

A final stage has to do with what work receives the highest honor, which does not take the form of a prize but rather of imitation. What research becomes paradigmatic in the Kuhnian sense, providing exemplars of the work that a particular scientific community has standardized on, has taken as exemplifying the problems, methods, and styles of reasoning that everyone will work on? Oddly enough, at this stage we aren't really very critical, precisely because a whole community has accepted this work as paradigmatic. All the mechanisms of scientific training and community formation that Kuhn (1962) describes combine to convince people that what everyone already believes is what they better believe too. Obviously it doesn't always work that way but, of necessity, it does work that way every time a scientific community adopts a paradigmatic way of working.

SPECIALIZATION
(PHILOSOPHICAL AND METHODOLOGICAL WORRY AS A PROFESSION)

When intellectual specialties reach a size sufficient to support specialization (this is one of those demographic facts I spoke of earlier), they often (and in the social sciences almost invariably) develop specialties in theory and methodology and philosophy of science (as it applies to their particular discipline). The specialists in these topics do some work that members of the discipline think is necessary to the entire enterprise but that has become too complex and specialized for everyone to do for themselves.

The social sciences have probably (this is speculative intellectual history and could be checked out in the appropriate monographs) developed specialized methodologists and philosophers of science because they have come under attack, in ways that hurt, from people who think that the enterprise is not philosophically (especially, "scientifically") defensible. The attacks have frequently come from the natural sciences and have had serious practical consequences in the struggle for academic recognition and advantages (faculty positions, research funds, etc.), so they have been seen as requiring answers. The job therefore must be done and, to be done right, must be done by people who can hold their own in that kind of argument, people who know the latest stuff and the most professional styles of argument.

One consequence of turning this part of our business over to specialists is that the specialists have interests that don't fully coincide with ours. They play to different audiences. Philosophers of science, even if they come from our own ranks, have as at least part of their audience the world of professional philosophy, at least that part of it that concerns itself with their topic. What makes them useful to us is also what makes them difficult. They know all the tricks of philosophers of science in large part because they have become philosophers and are part of that world. In consequence, they are sensitive to the opinions of other philosophers of science, philosophers who do not have one foot in one of the social sciences, even when those people's opinions push them in directions that are not relevant to the concerns of working scientists.

Philosophers and theorists of knowledge, concerned to meet the standards of the philosophical discourse they are involved in, frequently follow their logic to conclusions that make the day-to-day work of science impractical or impossible. They seem to conclude that social science, as we now do it, can't be done. I'm reminded of Donald Campbell, who used to say that these people are very convincing, but, if they're right, then what have we been doing all these years? That is, to say that it can't be done is only to say that it can't be done in a way that meets some set of standards that is not extant in the research community in which the work is actually being done.

The same thing is true when we consider the specialists who deal with technical questions, claiming to derive the warrant for their strictures from philosophical premises. Science is, remember, a cooperative enterprise in which all the cooperators have something to say about what is done. That includes, to bring this down to some earthy and necessary considerations, the people who pay for what is done and the people who are the objects (or subjects, since what term we use to describe these people is contested) of our study.

A simple example: Some years ago a distinguished sociological methodologist reasoned that the newly invented technique of path analysis could be used to deal with measurement error in survey research. It was quite easy and straightforward: All you had to do was have the same interviewers interview the same respondents on three separate occasions using the same interview guide. Easy enough, except that neither interviewers or respondents would cooperate. The interviewers felt like fools asking the same people the same questions over and over again and, when they got their nerve up to do it, the respondents wouldn't answer: "You asked that twice already. Are you stupid? Or what?" The philosophical theory and its technical application were clear; the social logic was off.

Great advances in social science often depend on increases in funding. For years, most of what was known about fertility came from detailed analyses of the data of the Indianapolis Study, in its time the most detailed body of materials available on married couples' choices about how many children to have and when to have them. A major step forward occurred when increased funding made it possible to use national samples to study the decisions of couples to have children. It had never, of course, been methodologically defensible to use Indianapolis as a surrogate for the entire United States, but what choice was there? So it was used. Once a "more adequate" sample became available, the ante was upped, to the point that when I asked a leading demographer what he would do if he could no longer finance national surveys of fertility, he could not consider the question seriously; you just had to have them and that was that. In the same way, Bronislaw Malinowski's enforced four-year stay (as an interned enemy alien) in the Trobriand Islands set a new methodological standard for how long and in what degree of intimacy anthropologists had to be in contact with "their people."

In other words, general statements of what must be done to be scientifically adequate rely, usually without acknowledgment, on practical matters and, in this, they follow rather than lead everyday practice.

Audiences (and especially the people whose lives and activities we study) react to what we say in variable ways, and researchers worry about that. Some of our philosophical and epistemological and theoretical concerns have to do with justifying what we do to such "external" audiences.

Educational research is particularly vulnerable to problems of justification. Everything educational researchers do has some consequence for people in the education business. Do we find that one method of teaching is superior to others? The people who are committed to the others—not just "philosophically" but also by virtue of not knowing how to do the new thing or having built their reputations on the way they now do it—will want to find reasons why these results are not valid.

I don't mean that research is just mercenary. It's more complicated than that. If you have a reason to look for trouble, you're more likely to look. Every method having flaws, if you look, you'll find. As I remarked earlier, every way of doing business is good enough—for someone at some time for some purpose. Conversely, no way is good for all purposes and all people at all times. So it is always possible to criticize how things are done if you are a different person at a different time with a different purpose.

FINALLY

To come full circle, the reasons and the people and the times for research are organizational facts, not philosophical constructs. Epistemology and philosophy of science are problems insofar as we cohabit with the people who make those topics their business and are thus sensitive to their opinions, questions, and complaints. Educational researchers, poised uneasily as they are between the institutions of (mostly) public education, the scientific and scholarly communities of the university world, and the people who give money in Washington, who aren't sure which of those constituencies they ought to take seriously, have the unenviable task of inventing a practice that will answer to all of them more or less adequately. The difficulties are compounded by the splintering of the academic component of the mix into a variety of disputatious factions, which is mostly what I have been discussing. No amount of careful reasoning or thoughtful analysis will make the difficulties go away. They are grounded in different standards and demands based in different worlds. In particular, as long as theory consists of a one-way communication from specialists who live in the world of philosophical discourse, empirical researchers will not be able to satisfy them. In my own view, we (the empirical researchers, among whom I still count myself) should listen carefully to those messages, see what we can use, and be polite about the rest of it. After all, as Joe E. Brown remarked in the last scene of *Some Like It Hot*, when he discovered that the woman he wanted to marry was a man after all, "Nobody's Perfect!"

REFERENCES

Becker, H. S. (1982). *Art worlds*. Berkeley: University of California Press.

Becker, H. S. (1986). Telling about society. In H. S. Becker (Ed.), *Doing things together* (pp. 121–135). Evanston, IL: Northwestern University Press.

Kuhn, T. (1962). *The structure of scientific revolutions*. Chicago: University of Chicago Press.

Latour, B. (1987). *Science in action*. Cambridge, MA: Harvard University Press.

Lieberson, S. (1982). *Making it count*. Berkeley: University of California Press.

Wagner, J. (1986). *The search for signs of intelligent life in the universe*. New York: Harper & Row.

Yonay, Y. *When black boxes clash: The struggle over the soul of economics, 1918–1945*. (in preparation). Unpublished doctoral dissertation, Northwestern University, Evanston, IL.

About the Editors and the Contributors

David J. Flinders is an Assistant Professor at Trinity University. He has co-authored (with C. A. Bowers) *Responsive Teaching: An Ecological Approach to Classroom Patterns of Language, Culture, and Thought* (1990) and *Culturally Responsive Teaching and Supervision: A Handbook for Staff Development* (1991). Dr. Flinders practices educational criticism as a form of qualitative research. He received his Ph.D. from Stanford University.

Geoffrey E. Mills is an Associate Professor of Education at Southern Oregon State College where he teaches courses on curriculum, educational research, and education in anthropological perspective. Dr. Mills' current research interests include teacher education reform and school-based collaborative decision making. He received his Ph.D. from the University of Oregon.

Howard S. Becker received all his degrees from the University of Chicago, including a Ph.D. in sociology in 1951. He worked in several research organizations before becoming Professor of Sociology at Northwestern University in 1965. In 1991, he became Professor of Sociology at the University of Washington (Seattle). He has been visiting Professor at the University of Manchester and the Museu Nacional (Rio de Janeiro). He received the Commonwealth Award in Sociology and a Guggenheim Fellowship and has written several major books: *Student Culture in Medical School* (with Blanche Geer, Everett C. Hughes, and Anselm L. Strauss); *Outsiders: Studies in the Sociology of Deviance; Art Worlds;* and *Writing for Social Scientists.*

Jennifer C. Greene is an Associate Professor in the Department of Human Service Studies at Cornell University. She has major responsibility for the qualitative methods courses taught within her department's program in program evaluation. Dr. Greene's current research interests include participatory approaches to program evaluation, mixed-method designs, and quality criteria in qualitative social inquiry.

Joyce L. Henstrand received her Ph.D. from the Department of Educational Policy and Management at the University of Oregon. She currently holds an administrative position at Aloha High School in Beaverton, Oregon, and taught secondary school English for 17 years. Her professional interests include teacher culture in high schools, school reform, and ethnographic research methods.

Sandra Mathison is an Assistant Professor of Education and Director of the Evaluation Consortium at the State University of New York, Albany. She teaches program/curriculum evaluation and qualitative research methods. Her publications include various evaluation reports, two edited volumes on program evaluation, and journal articles.

Petra Munro received her Ph.D. from the University of Oregon and is currently an Assistant Professor in the Department of Curriculum and Instruction at Louisiana State University. Her teaching and research interests include curriculum theory, feminist theory, and qualitative research. She conducts life history research with women social studies teachers. Her recent publications include "Supervision: What's Imposition Got to Do With It?" in the *Journal of Curriculum and Supervision*.

Henry St. Maurice is an Assistant Professor and Director of Field Experience at the University of Wisconsin–Stevens Point. He has published articles on rhetoric and inquiry in *Educational Studies* and *The Journal of Curriculum Studies*, and has co-authored a chapter (with Thomas S. Popkewitz) on theory and methods in *The Handbook of Research on Social Studies Teaching and Learning*. He received his Ph.D. from the University of Wisconsin–Madison.

Thomas A. Schwandt is Associate Professor in the School of Education at Indiana University. Dr. Schwandt teaches courses in interpretive-qualitative methodology, program evaluation, and social science philosophy. He has published in both the fields of evaluation and research methodology. His current research focuses on the role of moral discourse in shaping conceptions and practices of inquiry. He received his Ph.D. from Indiana University in 1984.

John K. Smith is Professor of Education at the University of Northern Iowa. He is the author of numerous articles and a book, *The Nature of Social Inquiry and Educational Inquiry: Empiricism vs. Interpretation*, devoted to examining alternative paradigms and their implications for research practice.

Louis M. Smith received a Ph.D. in Psychology from the University of Minnesota in 1955. Along the way he worked in the Psycho-Educational Clinic at the University and as a school psychologist for the St. Paul (Minnesota) Public Schools. He has been in the Education Department at Washington University for almost four decades, with interests shifting gradually from traditional educational psychology, to qualitative, ethnographic, case studies of classrooms, schools, and school districts. He now focuses on "life writing" (biography and autobiography) as modes of inquiry. He has written widely, including a half dozen books with various colleagues.

Ernest T. Stringer is currently a Senior Lecturer (Professor) in the Centre for Aboriginal Studies at Curtin University of Technology in Perth, Western Australia. Dr. Stringer has worked with Australian Aboriginals as a teacher, curriculum developer, and researcher. Following the completion of his doctoral work at the University of Illinois in 1980, Dr. Stringer returned to Australia to continue his work with isolated Aboriginal communities throughout the country and has published widely in the area of Aboriginal education.

Stephen J. Thornton is Associate Professor of Social Studies and Education at Teachers College, Columbia University. His research concerns how teachers and students make sense of social studies classroom life. Dr. Thornton is the former Chair of the College and University Faculty Assembly of the National Council for the Social Studies and is currently the President of the Research in Social Studies SIG of the American Educational Research Association. His writing has appeared in numerous journals and books. Dr. Thornton received his doctoral degree from Stanford University.

Index